Women, Press, and Politics During the Irish Revival

Irish Studies
James MacKillop, *Series Editor*

Other titles in Irish Studies

Anglo-Irish Autobiography: Class, Gender, and the Forms of Narrative
Elizabeth Grubgeld

Gender and History in Yeats's Love Poetry
Elizabeth Butler Cullingford

The Gonne-Yeats Letters, 1893–1938
Anna MacBride White and A. Norman Jeffares, eds.

An Irish Literature Reader: Poetry, Prose, Drama, 2d ed.
Maureen O'Rourke Murphy and James MacKillop

Irish Orientalism: A Literary and Intellectual History
Joseph Lennon

Irish Women Writers Speak Out: Voices from the Field
Caitriona Moloney and Helen Thompson

My Self, My Muse: Irish Women Poets Reflect on Life and Art
Patricia Boyle Haberstroh, ed.

Navigations: Collected Irish Essays, 1976–2006
Richard Kearney

Two Irelands: Literary Feminisms North and South
Rebecca Pelan

Women Creating Women: Contemporary Irish Women Poets
Patricia Boyle Haberstroh

Women, Press, and Politics During the Irish Revival

◆ ◆ ◆

KAREN STEELE

Syracuse University Press

First Edition 2007
07 08 09 10 11 12 6 5 4 3 2 1

The paper used in this publication meets the minimum requirements of American National Standard for Information Sciences—Permanence of Paper for Printed Library Materials, ANSI Z39.48–1984∞™

For a listing of books published and distributed by Syracuse University Press, visit our Web site at SyracuseUniversityPress.syr.edu.

A shorter version of chapter 1 was published as "Editing Out Factionalism," in *Victorian Periodicals Review* (2002): 113–32; chapter 2 includes passages from two earlier pieces: "Raising Her Voice for Justice," in *New Hibernia Review* (Summer 1999): 85–104; and "Reading Maud Gonne: Gendered Poetics in the Advanced Nationalist Press," in *Prose Studies* 25, no. 2 (August 2002): 102–21. For the latter journal's Web site, see http://www.tandf.co.uk; chapter 3 is a revised version of an article first appearing in *Women's Studies* 29 (Summer 2000): 423–71. Copyright 2000 from "Constance Markievicz's Allegorical Garden" by Karen Steele. Reproduced by permission of Taylor & Francis Group, LLC., http://www.taylorandfrancis.com.

For permission to quote from unpublished materials from the Francis Sheehy Skeffington Papers and other collections and to reproduce selected images from the collections of the National Library of Ireland, grateful acknowledgment is made to the Council of Trustees of the National Library of Ireland. The material is the property of the Board of the National Library of Ireland and has been reproduced with their permission. Also, permission was granted to reproduce excerpts of materials (BMH WS 258) from the Military Archives of Ireland in Dublin. Finally, the lines from "Diving into the Wreck" are used with permission. Copyright © 2002 by Adrienne Rich. Copyright © 1973 by W. W. Norton & Company, Inc., from *The Fact of a Doorframe: Selected Poems, 1950–2001* by Adrienne Rich. Used by permission of the author and W. W. Norton & Company, Inc.

Library of Congress Cataloging-in-Publication Data
Steele, Karen Margaret, 1965–
Women, press, and politics during the Irish revival / Karen Steele.—1st ed.
p. cm.
Includes bibliographical references and index.
ISBN-13: 978–0–8156–3117–0 (cloth : alk. paper) ISBN-10: 0–8156–3117–0 (cloth : alk. paper)
ISBN-13: 978–0–8156–3141–5 (pbk. : alk. paper) ISBN-10: 0–8156–3141–3 (pbk. : alk. paper)
1. Nationalism and feminism—Ireland—History—20th century. 2. Ireland—Politics and government—20th century. 3. Nationalism—Ireland—History—20th century. 4. Women in politics—Ireland—History—20th century. 5. Irish newspapers—History—20th century. 6. Press and politics—Ireland—History—20th century. I. Title.
DA959.S74 2007
941.5082'1—dc22
2006101393

Manufactured in the United States of America

For Pat, Jimmy, and Sean
Mo chroí

Karen Steele is associate professor of English and director of women's studies at Texas Christian University, Fort Worth, Texas. She is also the editor of *Maud Gonne's Irish Nationalist Writings*.

Contents

Illustrations

Abbreviations

The following abbreviations have been adopted for frequently occurring citations.

ITGWU	Irish Transport and General Workers' Union
IWFL	Irish Women's Franchise League
IWWU	Irish Women Workers' Union
IWSF	Irish Women's Suffrage Federation
WSPU	Women's Social and Political Union
WWCS	Women Workers' Co-operative Society

Acknowledgments

When a book has benefited from a long gestation, the author feels particularly deep gratitude to its many supporters, commentators, critics, and cheerleaders along the way. Elizabeth Butler Cullingford and Barbara Harlow influenced this project in more ways than I can acknowledge here. My heartfelt thanks go to Margot Backus, Katie Conrad, Michael de Nie, Anne Helmreich, Sharon Harris, Linda Hughes, Margaret Kelleher, Eileen O'Halloran, Louise Ryan, Theresa Strouth Gaul, Maryann Valiulis, and Margaret Ward, who have offered suggestions or read drafts of this book at many different stages along the way, and to my hard-working, rewarding graduate students, especially Margaret Lowry, Purna Banerjee, Lindsy Lawrence, Shelley Christie, Anirundra Thapa, Sarah Yoder, David Ferman, and Jared Griffith, for our lively discussions about cultural studies, periodicals research, and Irish literature.

I have been fortunate to work alongside the committed feminist scholars of Texas Christian University, whose work has helped feminist scholarship flourish on campus, and whose efforts have helped improve the material conditions of female faculty. Special thanks to my stalwart Women's Studies colleagues Claudia Camp, Jean Giles-Sims, Joanne Green, Rhonda Keen-Payne, Bonnie Melhart, and Marcy Paul.

Texas Christian University generously funded multiple research trips related to this project. I wish to thank, in particular, Associate Provost Larry Adams for appointing me a semester's term at the TCU London Centre in the fall of 2001, Associate Provost Bonnie Melhart for supporting my research and teaching in Ireland and the British Isles, and both Claire Hutton and Warwick Gould for facilitating a University of London fellowship and for hosting a stimulating semester of talks in Irish Studies during my semester's time in London.

I owe adoring, unremitting gratitude to my two most faithful, discerning readers, Bonnie Blackwell and Bonnie Frederick, who read and commented on nearly every word that follows. If music is the food of love, then surely your incisive critiques have been my sustenance these many years. *Go raibh mile maith agat.*

Women, Press, and Politics During the Irish Revival

Introduction

> Regard yourselves as Irish, believe in yourselves as Irish. . . . Arm yourselves with weapons to fight your nation's cause. Arm your souls with noble and free ideas. Arm your minds with the histories and memories of your country and her martyrs, her language, and a knowledge of her arts, and her industries. And if in your day the call should come for your body to arm, do not shirk that either.[1]

In her rousing address to the Students' National Literary Society in 1909, Constance Markievicz implored these "rising young women of Ireland" to view autonomy as the spirit of the age. Instructing her sisterhood to view themselves as part of a nascent, if only imagined, nation, Markievicz emphasized that expressions of Irish nationality would necessarily take a wide variety of forms. Like many writers and activists of the Irish revival, she regarded the preparations for Ireland's liberty as both an intellectual and a military enterprise, one that depended equally on independent and on collective action. Markievicz's anaphoric cadences insistently return to the ideal of radical, militant femininity: "armed" womanhood. Most suggestively, for Markievicz and the majority of the women studied in this book, the well-stocked arsenal of revolution contained many diverse elements that women, specifically, could shoulder on the way to battle: Gaelic study, literary artistry, socialist organizing, feminist speech making, in addition to more familiar military tools, such as revolvers, rifles, and rounds of ammunition. Such a brash, inclusive philosophy of nationalism might profitably serve as the mantra of women writers in the advanced nationalist press.

Women, Press, and Politics examines the written legacy of Markievicz's "rising young women" by studying journalism, notably the advanced nationalist press circulating in the two decades preceding the Easter Rising of 1916. For virtually as long as there have been English-speaking champions of Irish liberty, there have been nationalist newspapers, such as the *Freeman's Journal* (established 1763), providing its readership with a political education in Irish patriotism. In the years of rebellion, notably, the United Irishmen Uprising of 1798 or the Young Ireland Rising of 1848, advanced nationalist newspapers sprang up like desert flowers after a rain. Short-lived papers such as the *Northern Star* (1792–97) and the *Irish People* (1863–65) advanced the cause of Irish independence through patriotic poetry, meeting notices, and editorials, which were largely written by the leadership of revolutionary bodies. Their writers consistently aimed both to educate readers and to recruit Irish men and women to fight for their homeland's political freedom.[2]

Although we know that poets and politicians, cultural commentators and party activists of the early twentieth century read and wrote for the advanced nationalist press, literary accounts of Ireland's great cultural renaissance, the literary revival, have largely ignored the political challenges and the aesthetic innovations that writers, especially women writers, promoted on its pages. As a feminist genealogy of nationalism, *Women, Press, and Politics* aims to remedy this oversight by exploring the literary and historical impact of women writing for the most influential body of nationalist journalism during the Irish revival, the advanced nationalist press, so called because of its extreme articulation of Irish nationalism. In contrast to the two dominant nationalist dailies, the *Freeman's Journal* and the *Irish Independent,* both of which advocated a constitutional nationalist policy of achieving Home Rule through the British Parliament in London, advanced nationalist journals focused on transforming Ireland through cultural and revolutionary means instead. The majority of the editors and contributors to the advanced nationalist press promoted the ideas and movements associated with the Irish-Ireland movement, a broad assemblage of organizations dedicated to reviving Ireland's Gaelic culture and language and to creating the conditions for Ireland's political and economic independence from Great Britain.[3]

Whereas, in earlier epochs, revolutionary newspapers emerged for a handful of years only to lie dormant for decades, in the 1890s, successive revolutionary newspapers came into their own, with later papers taking up where earlier ones left off. In the waning years of the nineteenth century, the Gaelic League, the agricultural cooperative movement, the 1798 Centenary Committee, the Irish Republican Brotherhood (IRB), and the Celtic Literary Society were but a few of the Irish-Ireland organizations that founded new advanced nationalist journals. Later, Daughters of Ireland (Inghinidhe na hÉireann), the Irish Transport and General Workers' Union, and the Irish Women's Franchise League also established weekly or monthly journals that followed suit. The key commonality of most advanced nationalist journals was editorial advocacy for Irish political autonomy that went beyond the Home Rule aims of constitutionalists or parliamentarians.[4] Advanced nationalists thus comprise a wide spectrum of Irish patriots, from militants such as Irish Republican Brotherhood member Tom Clarke and Red Branch Knights (Na Fianna) leader Constance Markievicz, to socialists such as Jim and Delia Larkin, to feminists such as Hanna and Francis Sheehy Skeffington.

Advanced nationalist journals, unlike the major Dublin dailies, were largely amateur operations, with many of their editors also serving as reporters, copywriters, and compositors. Very few of these hard-working individuals received a steady living wage for their absorbing labors; in some cases, there was barely enough income to keep the newspaper in print. Not surprisingly, then, each of these journals promoted highly particularized notions of nationalist activism: some were closely affiliated with a specific political, social, or cultural organization; others simply highlighted the preoccupations of their editors. The *Shan Van Vocht* (Poor Old Woman; 1896–99), emerging in the years prior to the centenary of the United Irishmen Uprising, focused on centenary activities that recalled the ideas, methods, and example of this earlier republican movement. The Gaelic League's newspaper, *An Claidheamh Soluis* (The Sword of Light;

1899–1922), promoted the use of Gaelic and championed a revival in Gaelic culture; though initially printed in English, it soon adopted a bilingual format and, in its later years, was almost exclusively a Gaelic-language journal. The *Workers' Republic* (intermittently published from 1898 to 1903) and, later, the *Irish Worker* (1911–14) served as textual advocates for the Irish working class, though each paper's primary objective was to expose "scandalous working conditions," thereby inspiring readers to join a trade union.

Because advanced nationalist journals and organizations took so many different forms, Irish women found numerous ways to be involved. Despite the pervasive constraints of a socially conservative society—for example, few political clubs and organizations in the 1890s were open to female members—women found the press a particularly receptive venue for various forms of nationalist expression. Indeed, newspapers were among the first textual sites where Irish women attempted to trace their long-standing literary and political participation as patriots.[5] In her speech to the "young women of Ireland," for example, Constance Markievicz was but one of the many female writers of the advanced nationalist press who labored to make visible the long history of Ireland's female "fighting ancestors," from Maeve, Fheas, and Macha to the women warriors of 1798, the female patriot poets in the *Nation*, and Markievicz's peers in Sinn Féin (Ourselves), the Gaelic League, Inghinidhe na hÉireann (Daughters of Ireland), Cumann na mBan (Irishwomen's Council), the Irish Women's Franchise League, and the Irish Women Workers' Union.

Women, Press, and Politics reconsiders women's writings in the Irish national tradition, focusing in particular on leading feminine voices in the cultural and political movements that helped launch the Easter Rising of 1916. The enduring literary achievements of some of the writers it addresses, well-known figures of the revival such as Maud Gonne (1866–1953) and Augusta Gregory (1852–1932), have been largely overlooked by scholars distracted by these women's relationships to influential men. Other writers treated in the chapters to follow, such as Hanna Sheehy Skeffington (1877–1946), Constance Markievicz (1868–1927), Louie Bennett (1870–1956), and Delia Larkin (1878–1949), have been elsewhere studied primarily in terms of their leadership in political movements—suffrage, republicanism, peace advocacy, trade unionism. None has been considered in terms of her cultural contributions to the revival. Alice Milligan (1866–1953), author of one of the first Celtic plays for the Irish National Theatre and, with her partner Anna Johnston (1866–1902), a pioneer of advanced nationalist journalism, is almost completely forgotten today.[6] By examining the innovative work of these writers from the perspective of women's artistry and women's political investments, we can best appreciate the expansive range of their cultural productions—poetry, drama, fiction, journalism—and the influence these had on other nationalists, who went on to shape Irish politics and culture in the decades to come.

Through her work editing and writing copy for the *Shan Van Vocht*, Alice Milligan charted a course for later women to follow as cultural nationalists. Maud Gonne founded the first explicitly female nationalist organization, Inghinidhe na hÉireann (Daughters of Ireland), after spending years writing for Irish separatists in the *United Irishman.* Constance Markievicz sought to normalize female militancy as the leader of the Na Fianna and as a columnist for *Bean na hÉireann* (Woman of Ireland). Delia Larkin established Dublin's first trade union for women and wrote a weekly column in the *Irish Worker* that combined suffrage advocacy, socialism, and Irish patriotism. Augusta Gregory set up Ireland's premier national theater; she also penned enduring plays and anonymous journalism that demonstrated her alliances with republicans, women, and workers. Hanna Sheehy Skeffington cofounded the militant Irish Women's Franchise League; when her organization launched its own newspaper, the *Irish Citizen,* she wrote numerous letters to the editor to publicize her ongoing skepticism about the gender politics of the Irish republican movement, of which she was a part. Louie Bennett established the Irish Women's Reform League to provide an organization with a broader platform of women's rights than simply suffrage. Like Sheehy Skeffington, she was a frequent contributor to the *Irish Citizen,* and shared editorial duties with Hanna Sheehy Skeffington after the murder of Francis Sheehy Skeffington in 1916. In the newspaper's final year, Bennett assumed editorial and financial responsibility for the paper; through her involvement with the Irish Women Workers' Union (IWWU), she refashioned the suffrage monthly into a trade union journal designed for women workers.

In tracking the literary and rhetorical achievements of these women writers, *Women, Press, and Politics* focuses on journals that were edited by or receptive to women's participation in the nationalist movement: the *Shan Van Vocht* (1896–99), the *United Irishman* (1899–1906), *Bean na hÉireann* (1908–11), the *Irish Worker* (1911–14), and the *Irish Citizen* (1912–20). Here women expressed a broad range of opinions about nationalism and its impact on women's public and private lives. They used the Irish press as a medium of exchange, sometimes exclusively among women but more often among all politically committed members of the nationalist, feminist, and labor movements. The following chapters trace the diverse strategies that women writers of the advanced nationalist press employed in grappling with the three major political movements of the day—Irish independence, woman's suffrage, and trade unionism—with varying degrees of success. As Anne Mellor and Margaret Beetham have documented in their studies of British women's political and popular writings in the nineteenth century, the public, dialogic nature of the press often afforded women radical potential for challenging oppressive and repressive models of feminine behavior, national character, and class identity.[7]

Poetics of the Advanced Nationalist Press

Irish women writers—like their male counterparts—sometimes passively absorbed political and cultural ideas about femininity and Irishness. As the opening epigraph attests, however, they also produced and promulgated quite distinctive, independent notions of Ireland's political and cultural future during an era when debates about the identity of the still-imagined nation were most intense. Many cultural commentators of the Irish revival have neglected women's sustained contributions to this cultural renaissance, in part, because they have largely overlooked the literary riches in the advanced nationalist press. At first glance, this critical oversight seems surprising because the 1890s in Ireland marked the beginning not only of a literary renaissance but also of the golden age of newspaper reading, which, in the words of Marie-Louise Legg, offered Irish citizens at the turn of the century "an important passport to entry into the modern world."[8]

Yet, as Lucy McDiarmid and Maria DiBattista have argued, the Irish revival coincided with "the incipient formation and rapid crystallization of separate, if ever overlapping, cultural spheres."[9] Precisely when women began to fill the pages of the advanced nationalist press with their poetry and prose, contemporary critics such as Matthew Arnold and Sir John Pope-Hennessy began to dismiss the literary merit of journalism because of its worrisome bent toward democracy. Yet Arnold's dismissal "belied the involvement of almost all Victorian writers with the periodical press, as contributors, editors and/or proprietors."[10] Recent studies of the Irish revival have taught us how canonical writers such as Yeats, Joyce, and Synge substantially depended on journals to publicize and broaden the appeal of their work. In relocating Yeats's poetry in its original bibliographical and sociohistorical environment, for example, Yug Mohit Chaudhry demonstrates that the revival cannot be properly understood without the vital context of late-nineteenth- and early-twentieth-century periodical culture.[11] *Women, Press, and Politics* joins this ongoing discovery of how high and low culture, poetry and populist responses, art and politics were mutually embedded in the advanced nationalist press of early-twentieth-century Ireland. Whereas recent critiques have traced the influence of literary journals in Irish modernism, *Women, Press, and Politics* considers nationalist dailies, weeklies, and monthlies based in Ireland, instead.

To recognize the significance of a popular cultural form such as radical or seditious newspapers, we must first undo the lessons of an influential Victorian who shaped twentieth-century notions of literature. In his oft-quoted jeremiad about the democratizing forces erupting at the end of the nineteenth century, Matthew Arnold articulated a mournful lament about cultural decay, one that in Arnold's mind has been prompted by the "new" style and substance of the popular press:

> But we have to consider the new voters, the democracy, as people are fond of calling them. They have many merits, but among them is not that of being, in general, reasonable persons who think fairly and seriously. We have had opportunities of observing a New Journalism which a clever and energetic man has lately invented. It has much to recommend it; it is full of ability, novelty, variety, sensation, sympathy, generous instincts; its one great fault is that it is featherbrained.[12]

Arnold's commentary inaugurated the practice of separating high and low culture, dividing the rarefied pursuits of literary artists from the crass pursuits of the journalistic rabble.[13] It is less often remarked that his coining "New Journalism" emerged out of a larger parliamentary debate about Irish independence, "a thing full of mischief and danger," in Arnold's view.[14] Embedded in his derisive description of New Journalism were Arnold's anxieties about two key challenges to British identity at the apogee of empire—femininity and Irishness—which were hopelessly entangled in Arnold's mind.[15] As his comments make clear, Arnold admired the modernity and lyricism of this New Journalism, yet he deplored what he saw as its irrational, subversive aim of interpreting and communicating the will of the people. Not coincidentally, the very qualities he delights in and decries about New Journalism are the same that he singles out for praise and reprehension in his study of Celtic literature.

Matthew Arnold's ideas about New Journalism invite the study of gender and nationalism in Irish journals because he so succinctly and presciently diagnoses the challenges to patriarchal, imperial, and British authority at the end of Victoria's reign. His insistence that the enduring art of belles lettres must be separated from the ephemera of crass journalism, his faith in the sound rationality of the Anglo-Saxon over the whimsical Celt, and his bedrock belief in the manly dominion of the upper classes over the helpless, servile masses represent the apotheosis of cultural elitism and political influence. Yet his pronouncements also reveal his anxiety about the end of Victorian High Empire and the beginning of decolonization. Thus, to no small degree, Arnold may have coined "New

Journalism" to mask his disdain for the ideas and ideologies this journalism represented.

Women, Press, and Politics examines the populist-oriented journalism of the Irish revival for how it engages two signal battles—over women's rights and over workers' rights—in the emergent Irish nation. Unlike earlier historical studies of the advanced nationalist press and recent studies of high literary journals,[16] its literary approach embraces both the art of revolutionary rhetoric and gendered innovations to literary revival forms; it does so by addressing journals that more fluidly participate in both the cultural and the political debates of early-twentieth-century Ireland. In reviewing the persuasive appeals of literary critics such as Milligan and Gregory, of nationalists such as Gonne, of socialists such as Markievicz and Larkin, and of feminists such as Sheehy Skeffington and Bennett, it explores how each writer seeks to achieve consent on debates surrounding women's participation in the future of the Irish state. At the same time, it examines the gender critique implicit in literary revisions to the revival in the pages of the advanced nationalist press, from Milligan's romances across the borders in the *Shan Van Vocht* to Gonne's feminist improvements to *Cathleen ni Houlihan*.

Guided by historians who turn to the press for testimony about and understanding of the past, and trained as a literary critic to practice contextualized close readings of the poetics of the Irish revival, I read advanced nationalist journals as texts that reflect a dynamic exchange between the cultural and ideological movements that produced and were shaped by them. Following cultural criticism on the Victorian press, I analyze Irish journals for their rhetorical and literary complexity.[17] *Women, Press, and Politics* accounts for the literary effects and generic innovations of fiction, poetry, and drama published in the advanced nationalist press. At the same time, it attends to the poetics of low art, from editorials to advertisements, as well as to the persuasive and expressive resources of news features and letters to the editors.

Although many of advanced nationalist newspapers encouraged yearly subscription, for example, each paper depended on occasional readers who could choose, issue by issue, which to purchase and read. Because the advanced nationalist press often functioned as a textual meeting place for activists throughout the thirty-two counties and beyond, it was also uncommonly devoted to the notion of readers becoming writers, through letters to the editor, guest columns, and notices, as well as amateur lyrics in homage to organizations and individuals of advanced nationalism.

Women, Press, and Politics argues that Irish advanced nationalist journals such as *Shan Van Vocht, United Irishman, Bean na hÉireann, Irish Worker*, and *Irish Citizen* represent a literary form marked by generic and formal conventions and containing a distinct history. Margaret Beetham distinguishes journals—women's journals, in particular—chiefly by their "radical heterogeneity" and "fractured rather than rigidly coherent form."[18] Certainly, this is the case with the advanced nationalist press, which combined news reportage regarding nationalism, feminism, and trade unionism with historical retrospectives, editorials, reports, correspondences, international notes, meeting notices, poems, fiction, plays, theater reviews, and literary criticism. Yet, despite this variety in its newspapers and magazines, the advanced nationalist press had many of the characteristics of literary genres. Like serial fiction, in its weekly or monthly editions, it developed key characters from the past, such as Wolfe Tone and Speranza, and introduced new figures, such as James Connolly and Maud Gonne, whose actions determined the national plot of awakening. Like ballads, it self-consciously appealed to an Irish folk audience, expounding with a stock nationalist vocabulary and incremental, repetitive phrases. And like the theater, it staged on its pages social and political conflicts, from the nationalist "Battle of the Rotunda" to the IWWU-supported Savoy strike, though the plot resolutions could rarely be resolved in a tidy five-act performance. Additionally, most of these journals not only resembled such literary genres: they also contained, within their pages, examples of the literary forms that made the cultural revival revered, from Celtic Twilight ballads and romances to allegorical drama.

Although it expressed political longings and assiduously documented the history of the years leading up to Irish independence, the advanced nationalist press shares many of the preoccupations of better-known literary forms. The *Shan Van Vocht* inaugurated many of the most important features of the advanced nationalist press at the onset of the revival; its signal contribution was, at every opportunity, to interlink cultural and political ambitions. An early essay, "Literature and Nationality," announced that "the man who sang or told of the past, who planned for the present, and who prophesied for the future was pre-eminent amongst his contemporaries."[19] In fact, for nearly every journal studied below, the writers of advanced nationalism returned repeatedly to these three related concerns: recovering nationalist stories and Gaelic myths and legends to understand or re-create a distinctive Irish identity; developing a flourishing cultural and political climate throughout the thirty-two counties to assert these singular characteristics; and preparing for the sacrifices necessary to transform Ireland into an autonomous state.

In a fashion more explicit than Celtic Twilight enthusiasts, the writers of the advanced nationalist press looked to the past for political, as well as cultural, lessons about Ireland's future. The *Shan Van Vocht, United Irishman,* and *Bean na hÉireann,* in particular, featured regular columns, poems, and stories that instructed readers about republican and Fenian exploits of the past, such as Milligan's play *The Green upon the Cape,* featuring Wolfe Tone in 1797, anonymous poems about the United Irishmen, and biographical profiles on memorable and forgotten activists. Several writers, such as Milligan, Gonne, and Markievicz, were particularly interested in retelling stories related to Celtic heroines, female nationalists, and "fighting women," such as Brigid, Maeve, Emer, Betty Fryers, Betsy Gray, Anne Devlin, Sarrah Curran, and Speranza (Lady Wilde). The *Irish Citizen* and *Irish Worker* also contained features about Ireland's past, but they were more often interested in parodying such a nostalgic approach. The *Irish Citizen* skeptically challenged Cumann na mBan's glowing reports of gender equality in the Brehon laws of precolonial Ireland. The *Irish Worker* also mocked the hagiographic approach of mainstream nationalist biographies by composing "Biographies in Brief" about tyrannical capitalists and petty plutocrats. In keeping with the Gaelic reclamations by William Butler Yeats, George Russell (AE), Augusta Gregory, and John Millington Synge, advanced nationalist journals dedicated significant space for essays, poems, stories, and plays about

Ireland's Celtic past; like this larger Celticist movement, the typical literary offerings—Milligan's "Tara Hill Is of Kings Forsaken" and Nora Hopper's "To Sheila na Gara (Ireland)"—were distinguished by recovery efforts rather than aesthetic innovations.[20]

Advanced Nationalism During the Revival

Women, Press, and Politics situates the study of the Irish press in a culturally vibrant, politically charged epoch, the Irish revival. It focuses in particular on the two decades prior to the Easter Rising (1896–1916), a period of increasing radicalization in Irish politics, when Irish poets and playwrights frequently crossed the cultural divide between high and low art by adopting the stance of street orators, revolutionary insurgents, and dissident journalists. Douglas Hyde called for the de-Anglicizing of Ireland; William Butler Yeats, Augusta Gregory, and Edward Martyn combined talents to form an Irish national theater; and James Connolly founded the first socialist party. By 1900, Maud Gonne and a small group of determined women established Inghinidhe na hÉireann (Daughters of Ireland), which combined cultural and political nationalism in an organization established expressly for women. The same year, Arthur Griffith, Maud Gonne, and other advanced nationalists founded Cumann na nGaedheal (League of the Gaels), an umbrella organization that sought to unify all existing separatist organizations. Within a few years, this group evolved into Sinn Féin (Ourselves).

During the decade that preceded the Easter Rising, militant organizations sprang up on a range of ideological fronts, demonstrating the potency of the nationalist (and Unionist), socialist, and feminist movements. Many individuals held membership or leadership roles in multiple organizations. While writing and editing *Bean na hÉireann,* Constance Markievicz and Helena Molony organized the Red Branch Knights (Na Fianna), later rechristened "Na Fianna Éireann"; together with Irish Republican Brotherhood (IRB) member Bulmer Hobson, the women trained these nationalist boy scouts in warrior arts that prepared them for membership in the Irish Republican Army. Having been revived by 1911, the secret, oath-bound IRB prepared the groundwork for a revolution, recruiting from a range of open militants in the working-class trade union body, the Irish Citizen Army, and the middle-class Irish Volunteers, both established in 1913 in response to the well-armed, Unionist-oriented Ulster Volunteers. Women were barred from membership in all these militant organizations except the Irish Citizen Army. Some feminists expressed their political activism in the militant Irish Women's Franchise League (IWFL), established in 1908 by Hanna Sheehy Skeffington and Margaret Cousins. By 1912, Irish suffragists in the IWFL were marching, heckling politicians, stone throwing, and breaking glass in an effort to force political leaders to consider their demands for political citizenship.

Part of the powerful mythology surrounding the Irish revival surely stems from a chronology whereby high literary achievement by writers such as Yeats, Synge, and Joyce preceded a militant movement based on the revival's searching preoccupation with Irish identity. *Women, Press, and Politics* understands the advanced nationalist press as "cultural politics," a phrase Sally Ledger and Scott McCracken have proposed to capture the instability of ideology and form during the fin de siècle, when "culture is never fixed or stable and cultural artifacts are the product of dialogue, debate and conflict."[21] The cultural revival, as many recent literary and historical studies have demonstrated, played an integral, rather than merely inaugural, role in revolutionary politics. This book contends that the women's writings in the advanced nationalist press constitute an essential part of the flourishing literary and revolutionary movements of the Irish revival. One can no longer claim to understand either the art or politics of Ireland's pre-independence years without an appreciation of how Irish women influenced both realms in myriad ways.

A recurrent preoccupation in recent studies about the revival is the need to distance literary scholarship from the heroic myths of Yeats, who positioned himself as the savior and savant of Irish culture when he declared that modern Irish literature sprang forth, fully formed, from the brain of a "disillusioned and embittered Ireland."[22] Revisionist historiography, most notably embodied in R. F. Foster's popular study, *Modern Ireland,* also refuses Yeats's theory of art filling the void created by "the vacuum in politics" following Parnell's fall.[23] *Women, Press, and Politics* shares such skepticism in Yeats's mythmaking. More centrally, it also reappraises revisionist literary history and historiography, by broadening the scope of inquiry to include women's cultural and political roles in canon formation and nation building, and by reexamining the conditions under which Irish nationalism assisted and advanced gender equality.

For well over a century, since Irish suffragists began to monitor and challenge the nationalist movement's treatment of women activists, feminists have lamented the failures of Irish nationalism to accommodate other emancipation objectives, such as gender equality.[24] Drawing on historical narratives of the emergent nation and a wide body of cultural documents, from editorials and epistolary writing to romances and drama, *Women, Press, and Politics* revisits how female journalists, political activists, and artists engaged in a long-standing, complex exchange of debates over the issues of feminism, trade unionism, and nationalism. At the same time, it reveals how women used diverse rhetorical and literary strategies, some more successful than others, as they adapted, revised, and sometimes discarded male theories and practices of Irishness.

Feminism and the Irish Revival

A vital context to a reappraisal of the Irish revival is the feminist challenge to late Victorian gender norms. Although critics frequently acknowledge that the idealism and the insecurities of the revival should be understood as manifestations of "the crises of the late Victorian period," such literary revisionism rarely explores how debates about Irish identity have a particularly gendered dimension.[25] When he chastised the New Journalism, Matthew Arnold adopted a coded vocabulary ("sensation, sympathy, generous instincts," "feather-brained") that disclosed his anxieties about feminism. Arnold was far subtler than some of his fellow critics in using the press to publicize a reproof of the New Woman, however. The popular press, in fact, proved to be a fertile generator in debates about "the woman question": in diverse formats—the editorial pages, serialized fiction, advertising copy, and cartoons—the press circulated competing ideals of femininity. As Patricia Marks has amply illustrated, even caricatures and satires inadvertently popularized the conduct and ideals of New Womanhood.[26]

The onset of the literary revival converged with a crisis about gender *and* nationalism, "two of the most powerful global discourses shaping contemporary notions of identity," as Andrew Parker, Mary Russo, Doris Sommer, and Patricia Yaeger assert.[27] In Ireland, the discourse of gender and nationalism can be detected in the earliest attempts by revival writers to delimit and define Irish identity.[28] Irish writers with often quite diverse attitudes about gender norms or Ireland's political future, for example, assumed feminine weakness or Irish dependence when they called up the feminine figures of the nation: Cathleen ni Houlihan, the Dark Rosaleen, Mother Ireland, or the Shan Van Vocht. In her illuminating study tracing the intersections of class, gender, and nationality in Yeats's writings, Marjorie Howes notes that, though these three categories have an "intimate relationship," the vigor and sustainability of such discourse owes more to fluid constructions than any particular manifestation of interdependence that might be revealed by a given writer or text.[29] *Women, Press, and Politics* is based on a similar desire to detect the supple and changing connections between the resilient discourses attached to one's class, gender, and national identity. It attends to the economic dimension in art and arguments written by Ascendancy or Protestant nationalist women such as Milligan, Gonne, Markievicz, and Gregory. It also traces the scrupulous monitoring of nationalism by feminists such as Hanna Sheehy Skeffington and Louie Bennett, as well as the criticism of middle-class women by Delia Larkin.

The journalism of women writers of advanced nationalism affords a corrective to essentializing claims that Irish nationalism is best understood as fascination with heroism and chivalry or as blind faith in a false cause.[30] Although nationalist discourse depends on rigid categories that demonstrate affinity and difference, the women writers of advanced nationalism could not easily agree on what shape these alliances might take. Alice Milligan and Anna Johnston, based in Belfast, chided Dublin readers not to forget Ulster's past and present sacrifices for the cause of Ireland, as Maud Gonne, frequently exiled in Paris, reminded Fenians of their friends in

France. Milligan, a Methodist nationalist, and Johnston, the Catholic daughter of an influential Fenian, sounded the chords of racial harmony and anti-sectarianism; Gonne often infused her anti-imperialist editorials with xenophobia and undisguised anti-Semitism. Constance Markievicz and Delia Larkin insisted on an economic analysis to Ireland's national struggle; Markievicz emphasized the expediency of a revolver, while Larkin suggested union organizing and cultural programming might better channel a suitably socialist nationalist spirit. Milligan, Johnston, and Gonne drew on the authority of the Shan Van Vocht or Cathleen ni Houlihan to legitimate their unwomanly roles as lecturers during the Centenary movement or leadership in the Transvaal Committee. Markievicz, on the other hand, radically refashioned the Dark Rosaleen into the militant image of herself during the Rising. Hanna Sheehy Skeffington, the most resistant writer of the lot, distanced herself from the capitulating pressures of nationalist discourse about femininity by refusing to draw on the ethos of motherhood in militant suffrage debates.

The figure of Ireland as a woman, a pervasive and long-standing image, is an ideological construct of a femininity commonly understood to be modest, passive, obedient, and submissive.[31] An irony of the Irish revival's fascination with this emblem is that it was increasingly invoked even as Irish women immodestly wrote in the advanced nationalist press, actively maneuvering through and around nationalist discourse. Irish women were not merely writing copy, however: during the years of the literary revival, Ireland's first wave of feminism was emerging as well, initiated by the educational reforms of the 1870s. Higher education had a radicalizing potential: it significantly broadened the economic and educational opportunities for middle-class urban women; it also mapped many of the routes other women would take into the revolutionary experiences that led to the founding of the Free State in 1922.[32] Whether educated or self-taught, of independent means or working-class, the women who wrote for the advanced nationalist press created public profiles as professional writers, while simultaneously participating in a flourishing cultural revival that included political debates about feminism, nationalism, and socialism.

Although the bulk of the writing in the advanced nationalist press took place in Dublin or Belfast, the transformation of female roles in Irish society was not merely an urban phenomenon. Even in rural areas throughout Ireland, locales that Éamon de Valera later nostalgically associated with the "laughter of comely maidens dancing at the crossroads,"[33] women experienced an important shift from the hard labor of field work to grueling, though less visible domestic housework. Although such shifts from the fields to the home had the effect of rendering women's labor increasingly imperceptible, some women argued in the pages of newspapers such as the *Irish Homestead* that their new identity as housewives and home industries workers established them as the heart of an ideal Irish body politic.[34]

Despite the gradual improvements for Irish women in the social context of education and rising professionalism, Irish women still lacked the vote and had limited opportunities for participation in the leading political organizations of the day. The Irish suffrage movement began in 1876 as a tiny group of less than fifty members; by the beginning of World War I the movement was enjoying prosperous renown. As suffragists broke glass, experienced imprisonment, and discovered the weapons of heckling and hunger strike, membership grew to over 3,000. In the years just prior to World War I, suffragists became embroiled in an intensified debate with nationalists over the Home Rule bill; at the same time, they demonstrated solidarity with socialists over aid to workers locked out during the seven-month Dublin strike.[35]

Whereas the Irish and British suffrage movements often worked shoulder to shoulder before the onset of World War I, their trade unionist counterparts did not. Even with the growth in "new unionism" and the modishness of socialism evinced in the Fabian Society in Britain, trade unionism was significantly underdeveloped in turn-of-the-century Ireland. Organizing among women workers was, moreover, hampered seriously by the socially conservative attitudes of working men who derisively dismissed women as "cheap labourers" who might undercut their trade union rates.[36] In Belfast, where the linen industry employed two to three times as many jobs for female workers as males, Mary Galway successfully founded a women's union among textile workers in the 1890s. It took two decades before such organizing reached Ireland's capital: not until 1911 did Delia and Jim Larkin succeed in founding the Irish Women Workers' Union in Dublin. Similarly, nationalist organizations at the turn of the century were exclusively composed of men. In 1888, when Maud Gonne attempted to join nationalist organizations such as the Contemporary Club, the Celtic Literary Society, and the National League, she was informed that women were excluded from membership.[37] Although she was allowed to work as a "freelance on the fringe," Gonne had to found her own organization, Inghinidhe na hÉireann (Daughters of Ireland), in 1900 to provide female nationalists a platform from which to work. By the time of the Easter Rising in 1916, women such as Constance Markievicz, Helena Molony, and Margaret Skinnider were members of the socialist-based Irish Citizen Army and saw action as snipers and soldiers; many more females joined Cumann na mBan, the women's council of the middle-class Irish Volunteers, smuggling intelligence, nursing the insurgents, and providing food on the run.

History of Irish Press

A valuable contribution in Eric Hobsbawn's influential study of nationalism is his recognition that, whereas nationalism is fashioned "from above," that is, produced and promulgated by an economic and political elite, nationalism "cannot be understood unless analyzed from below, that is in terms of the assumptions, hopes, needs, longings and interests of the ordinary people."[38] However culturally and politically influential its readership, the advanced nationalist press was never populist in the numerical sense. Nevertheless, to a far greater extent than mainstream Unionist or Independent journals, it allowed individuals from many walks of life—wealthy and working-class, Protestant and Catholic, male and female, urban and rural, from Leinster and from Ulster—to rehearse ideas and debates about the Irish nation that were later refined and polished in speeches, essays, poems, and plays. Moreover, even though some of its papers, such as *Shan Van Vocht* or *United Irishman,* relied on the labor of one or two editors, writing under numerous pen names, to create the impression of multiple voices, the advanced nationalist press was inherently a dialogic genre marked by an unstable discourse to which editors, authors, and the public could speak and respond.

The press remains a unique site for Hobsbawnian analysis of nationalist discourse because, in Ireland, its history and development so closely parallel the colonization of Ireland. The emergence of the press marked the imprimatur of British imperialism, but its growth and popularity coincided with the widespread demands of the Irish people for political and cultural autonomy. As Robert Munter's social history of the early Irish newspapers details, the advent of the Irish periodical press roughly coincided with the arrival of Oliver Cromwell, and for two centuries, these newspapers were primarily directed at an elite cadre of privileged, urban, Protestant, male readers.[39] During this early stage, circulation and distribution were constricted by the narrowly focused aims of the Ascendancy in Ireland. Yet, despite their limited, homogeneous audience, eighteenth-century Irish newspapers were the site of continuous experiment in format and style.[40] Not surprisingly, the rise in native readership followed the spread of literacy. As Niall Ó Ciosáin points out, though, the suppression of the Gaelic language due to the Penal Laws, the last vestiges of which were finally rescinded in 1829, and the subsequent Anglicization through the National Schools, which began operation in 1831, meant that the spread of literacy paralleled the spread of English.[41] By the mid-nineteenth century, in the wake of Gladstone's abolition of newspaper taxes in 1855 and of the paper duty in 1861, newspapers proliferated in the provinces and were thus increasingly written by and for the native population, albeit chiefly in English. Yet, as Marie-Louise Legg documents in *Newspapers and Nationalism*, the marked expansion in cheap newspapers coincided not only with a rise in English literacy but also with an upsurge in Irish nationalism after the famine.[42]

The popular appeal of newspapers in the second half of the nineteenth century also had significant class and gender implications. Arnold's contemporary, Sir John Pope-Hennessy, fretted in 1884 that the "reading public in Ireland is comparatively large and larger than the reading public in any country in the world." Most notably, he worried about the avaricious literacy of laborers, "the class who with an extension of the franchise will get a voting power that they do not now possess."[43] His correlation of literacy and the vote helps explain why British politicians and British cultural critics, such as Pope-Hennessy and Matthew Arnold, were openly anxious about a medium dedicated to the disenfranchised.[44] Though British parliamentarians might thwart the appeals of Irish nationalists, labor agitators, and suffragists in Westminster, they could not curtail the daily, weekly, and monthly onslaught of demands by what W. T. Stead called the "Government by Journalism."

By the end of the nineteenth century, the Irish periodical press was, according to Legg, "entering its golden days."[45] Virginia Glandon has counted 332 newspapers circulating in the thirty-two counties between 1900 and 1922, a figure that excludes the numerous pro- and anti-Treaty news sheets as well as the larger English newspapers.[46] Of these newspapers, a little more than half (172) espoused nationalist sentiments that ranged from constitutionalism (those who aimed for Home Rule) to revolutionary Fenianism (those who advocated a militant means to accomplish Irish independence).[47] Both schools of nationalist journalism could trace their lineage to the preeminent revolutionary journals of mid-nineteenth-century Ireland: the *Nation*, launched by Thomas Davis in 1842, and the *Irish People*, begun by James Stephens in 1863. In its advocacy of a cultural revival and political self-reliance, the *Nation* influenced the literary style and the self-reliant message of many later advanced nationalist journals, such as *Shan Van Vocht*, *United Irishman*, and *Bean na hÉireann*. The brash militancy and political self-sacrifice embedded in the IRB's *Irish People* likewise set the tone for later suffrage and labor newspapers such as the *Irish Citizen* and the *Irish Worker*. During the Irish revival, as historians and literary critics have shown, the advanced nationalist press became an increasingly important and diverse source of political and cultural education for the Irish citizenry.[48] Virginia Glandon explains that the influence of the press at this time was due to a number of causes: rising literacy, the British government's alternation between coercion and conciliation in its Irish policy, and the political climate following the failure of the Irish Parliamentary Party's long fight for Home Rule.[49] As we will see, the advanced nationalist press provided a unique public forum for debates about Ireland's future, and fertile ground for germinating ideas about what cultural and political organizations should develop.

Dedicated to agitating Irish readers to act on behalf of Ireland's political independence, the advanced nationalist press has sometimes been viewed as a distorting discourse rather than as a rhetorical or literary form. In his otherwise meticulous study of this press, for example, Ben Novick labels advanced nationalist writings "propaganda," implying that they relied more on distortion than on persuasion to convince their audience.[50] Yet, however rigid his political characterization of such writings, his readings of their language, imagery, and effect acknowledge their textual intricacy, shifting power dynamic, and rhetorical achievement.

Numerous canonical texts of the revival—Yeats and Gregory's iconic play *Cathleen ni Houlihan*, Anna Johnston's triumphant lyric "Rody McCorley," Pádraig Pearse's funeral oration for O'Donovan Rossa—share advanced nationalist journalism's absorption with the national question. George Bernard Shaw posited that persuasive art was to be expected during times of political longing for independence: "A healthy nation is as unconscious of its nationality as a healthy man of his bones. But if you break a nation's nationality it will think of nothing else but getting it set again."[51] Luke Gibbons contends that this "unfinished business" of Irish nationalism—political independence—resulted in a literary tradition that channeled creative currents into the stream called "national self-esteem."[52] This book contends that the formal and explicitly literary and rhetorical achievements merit study as well.

To a century's study of art composed during Ireland's most fractious social and cultural upheaval, in the last fifteen years, scholars have added new anthologies and collections that demonstrate women writers' longstanding, noteworthy contributions to Irish culture and politics.[53] Yet, even though many now appreciate Lady Gregory's central creative role in the Abbey Theatre and Elizabeth Bowen's considerable gifts to Big House fiction, few recognize how many women were also influential contributors to advanced nationalist journalism.[54] Alice Milligan and Anna Johnston edited and wrote most of the copy for the first advanced nationalist journals of the revival, the *Northern Patriot* and the *Shan Van Vocht.*[55] Helena Molony assisted James Connolly in editing the first socialist paper of the era, the *Workers' Republic,* in 1898. A decade later, Molony launched the first nationalist paper aimed at a female audience, the monthly *Bean na hÉireann* (Woman of Ireland), official organ of Inghinidhe na hÉireann (Daughters of Ireland), which served as a forum for many of the most significant feminist debates about nationalism. Constance Markievicz published her subversive feature on female militancy, "Woman with a Garden," in its pages; Hanna Sheehy Skeffington contributed scathing cautionary articles on the nationalists' disregard for women's equality. The trade union weekly *Irish Worker* provided one of the earliest sustained feminist-socialist commentaries in Delia Larkin's "Women Workers' Column." The premier Irish suffrage journal, *Irish Citizen,* featured brilliant repartee and Abbey Theatre reviews by Sheehy Skeffington, feminist-nationalist history by Constance Markievicz, artistic manifestos by poet Alice Meynell, theater criticism by Annie Horniman, and socialist commentary by Nora Connolly and Louie Bennett, who edited the journal during its last years of existence. Katherine Tynan, Nora Hopper Chesson, Dora Sigerson Shorter, and Eva Gore-Booth, among many other women writers, frequently contributed poems, plays, and short stories to these organs of advanced nationalism.

Profits of Recovery

Like earlier studies of the advanced nationalist press, *Women, Press, and Politics,* exhibits a miner's faith in the riches of sedimentary history. Sifting through obscure and neglected documents, one discovers a wealth of information about Ireland's cultural and political revival and a treasure trove of neglected women's art; indeed, on nearly every page, one can sense how writers were not merely recording but also promoting a flourishing revival of interest in the cultural and political autonomy of Ireland. There were Gaelic-language columns in *Shan Van Vocht, United Irishman,* and *Bean na hÉireann.* In the *United Irishman* and the *Irish Worker,* Gaelic-language classes were advertised and encouraged. Each journal also actively promoted cultural activities: *Shan Van Vocht* called for home reading circles and ran essays on literature and nationality; the *United Irishman* published meeting notices and minutes, as well as full-text lectures delivered at gatherings of Inghinidhe na hÉireann; the *Irish Worker* reminded readers of the biweekly rehearsals for the Irish Worker's Choir and the Irish Workers' Dramatic Society. Poems celebrated cultural and political movements, with Douglas Hyde's "Dan Mairseala na n Gaodhal" (Marching Song of the Gaelic Athletes) celebrating the Gaelic League, for example, and Constance Markievicz's "Hymn on the Battlefield," the Fianna.

However much their journalists may have embellished to heighten the vibrancy and uniqueness of the times, the advanced nationalist journals document the development not only of the best Irish writing during the revival but also of a distinctively Irish form of English. In keeping with the ferocious verbal virtuosity of Joyce, Arthur Griffith and Hanna Sheehy Skeffington proved to be among the most masterful debaters in print on questions of nationalism and feminism, respectively. Before Gregory popularized her Kiltartan dialect or Synge visited the Aran Islands, Milligan was writing poems and plays that sought to render the cadence and tone of Irish in her English-language stories, plays, and poems. Although some of the greatest works of the Irish revival, such as Joyce's "The Dead" and Synge's *In the Shadow of the Glen,* display deeply ambivalent attitudes about glorifying rural or western Ireland, advanced nationalist writers who celebrated the Irish countryside in mythic or nostalgic incantations embraced a theme widespread during the revival. For upper-class, Protestant-reared writers such as Milligan and Gonne, describing Donegal or windswept Howth proved an effective way of authenticating their nationalism. Gregory Castle observes that the Protestant imaginative "attempt to shift the grounds of Irish identity from race to locality" was a recurrent strategy by writers such as Synge and Gregory, who found Irish history "a painful accusation against their own people."[56] The *United Irishman* thus featured "Rambles in Erin," a serialized column on daylong walks in the countryside, and the *Shan Van Vocht* promoted restoring and decorating the gravesides of the republican dead and taking pilgrimages to monuments or localities associated with Ireland's nonsectarian republican past.

Undoubtedly, the advanced nationalist press depended on a symbiotic relationship between the idealized west of Ireland—a source of imagination and redemption—and gritty, turbulent Dublin, where the majority of writers were based. With the notable exception of *Shan Van Vocht*, most of these journals expounded on a particularly Dublin-based version of nationality. And although they were quick to delimit Irishness in terms of its rejection of the imperial Great Britain, all those studied in this book promoted a metropolitan identity that more closely resembled London than Limerick. Nonetheless, in a fragmented manner, many reminded readers of the work being done in the putative (newly industrialized, urbanized) provinces through notices such as "Notes from the North," "Derry Notes," or "Limerick Notes," "Ireland in London," "The Celt on the Clyde" (Glasgow), "Liverpool Irishmen," and "The Irish Cause in France."

Each of the journals of advanced nationalism, with almost palpable insistence, warned Irish men and women they must prepare for revolution—whether national, feminist, or socialist—in the near future. Many writers, in keeping with Yeats's play about hunger strike, *The King's Threshold*, or with Pádraig Pearse's eulogy for O'Donovan Rossa, endorsed the values of messianic self-sacrifice. The *Shan Van Vocht* featured retrospectives on prominent nationalists such as Henry Joy McCracken, William Smith O'Brien, and Thomas Davis, who sacrificed their lives for Ireland. The *Irish Citizen* marked the occasion of women's imprisonment and Irish suffrage's first martyrdom (the death of Marjorie Hasler) with photo galleries and extended remarks about the meaning of feminine militancy. The *Irish Worker* published poems on "The Coming Revolution," and Constance Markievicz wrote about militant slug-crushing gardeners to prepare women for the grislier tasks of warfare.

In 1915, Constance Markievicz noted the paucity of such women as she studied Ireland's distant and recent past: "Throughout later history, though Irishwomen have suffered and worked, they have as a rule taken no prominent part; there are no leaders."[57] In response, *Women, Press, and Politics* focuses on influential Irish women of the advanced national press, including Markievicz, who not only managed, edited, and wrote for weekly and monthly editions but who also played dominant roles in the nationalist, socialist, and feminist movements of the Irish revival.

Although, with the exception of trade unionist Delia Larkin, most women writers of the advanced nationalist press were born to social prominence, most of those studied below actively resisted the elitism that all too often attaches to such prominence. Their political commitment alienated them from the wealth and glamour in which they had been raised; they approached the task of running or writing for a newspaper with pragmatic, clear-eyed vision. As Sidney Gifford Czira recalled of Inghinidhe's first meeting to launch *Bean na hÉireann*, her expectation of working alongside "heroines" hardly prepared her for what she encountered that day:

> As I walked into the committee room, feeling rather overawed, I had a romantic picture in my mind of what these women would look like. They would be just like the heroines of '98 which I had often seen on the supplements to the *Freeman's Journal* I was sure. There was nothing dramatic, however, in the sight that met my eyes in that room. A few women were sitting round a table, earnestly discussing the plans for launching the paper.[58]

Such a quotidian picture of women writing in the nationalist tradition may not, at first glance, fairly compete with the familiar, heroic images and mythic lore attached to legendary women in Ireland's history. Yet Gifford Czira's nimble mental correction—from worshipping heroines to understanding them as creative, pragmatic writers—precisely models the transformation in thinking about women and nationalism that this book hopes to facilitate.

In recovering the largely overlooked political and cultural achievements of advanced nationalist journals, as well as the rhetorical and aesthetic facility of their women writers, *Women, Press, and Politics* focuses on a select group of journals and writers, with full knowledge that such recovery represents but a beginning, and that much work remains to be done.[59] Other influential writers and activists of the revival, such as Helena

Molony, Dorothy MacArdle, Rosamund Jacob, Maeve Cavanagh, Nora Hopper Chesson, Dora Sigerson Shorter, and Katharine Tynan, deserve their own reappraisals. Other critics can substantially enrich Irish cultural studies by mining the advanced nationalist press, a scarcely touched quarry of colonialism *and* independence, of what Carol Coulter once described as "the hidden tradition": the extensive, buried heritage of Irish women's rebellion as well as their entry into public life.[60]

1

Acts of Union

Political Desire, Protestant Nationalism, and the Shan Van Vocht

The Belfast-based monthly magazine *Shan Van Vocht,* in print from January 1896 to April 1899, was at the forefront of a new generation of advanced nationalist journals and popularized many of the political positions and cultural innovations we now associate with the Irish revival.[1] A decade before Sinn Féin had a name, the *Shan Van Vocht* promoted the nationalist ideals of economic and cultural self-reliance. Well before James Connolly had established the Irish Socialist Republican Party or emerged as a bridge between workers and militant nationalists, the journal afforded him a column for rehearsing many of his key arguments about a workers' republic. In an era when many nationalist organizations were Dublin-based and opened their doors to men only, the journal was edited and largely written by two Belfast women. Nevertheless, many critics have found it hard to praise the journal's innovations, describing its influence as "indirect" and its cultural nationalism as "generic" or "typical."[2] Indeed, the critical reception of the *Shan Van Vocht* among Irish literary historians could be characterized as the cordial but modest approval one normally reserves for a hardworking but average student.

Yet, as this chapter will argue, the achievement of Alice Milligan and Anna Johnston's *Shan Van Vocht* was significant, imaginative, and generative. Drawing on the long tradition of imagining Ireland as a colonized hag who promises to transform into a "girl with the walk of a queen" when Ireland is finally free, Milligan and Johnston named their magazine the *Shan Van Vocht* (Poor Old Woman) to signal the journal's nationalist political and cultural identity. Indeed, the *Shan Van Vocht* embodied the feminine potential for self-transformation, a persistent theme of romance, an illuminating, if little studied, narrative form the journal cultivated. The symbolic longing for an idealized girlhood reflected the radical desires of the Methodist Belfast woman Alice Milligan, whose interest in the romance also signaled a nostalgic project, aimed at evading, repressing, and uniting divisions in the present by focusing on a quixotic notion of the past, 1798. As the introduction has argued, feminine figures of Ireland are value-laden icons that manage both the release of suppressed political desires and the restraint of traditional gender roles. One must therefore be especially mindful of two discrete drives of sovereignty and sexual subservience when closely reading the political and cultural expressions of female iconography in the *Shan Van Vocht*. As we will discover, the gendering of the magazine's title and the frequent return to the romance genre were hardly accidental, for these two choices encapsulated many of the conflicted ideologies rooted in early advanced nationalist journalism.

Editing Out Factionalism: A Cultural History of the *Shan Van Vocht*

More than a pioneering journal of advanced nationalism, the *Shan Van Vocht* showcased Ireland's flourishing cultural revival and adopted a literary identity that shared the brash aspirations of William Butler Yeats in "To Ireland in the Coming Times" (1892):

> Know, that I would accounted be
> True brother of a company
> That sang, to sweeten Ireland's wrong.
> Ballad, and story, rann and song.[3]

Like the speaker in this manifesto of cultural nationalism, Alice Milligan (1866–1953) and Anna Johnston (1866–1902) modeled their journalistic efforts on the literary and political achievements of the United Irishmen, of an earlier era. Milligan and Johnston also intended their journal to be populist, offering readers Celtic Twilight ballads, revivalist stories, as well as nationalist news, meeting notices, and minutes. Yeats in the 1890s aimed at broad appeal, though he suggested readers would have greater rewards in his verse: "My rhymes more than their rhyming tell." The Belfast women expressed sure confidence in the literary ambitions of their journal, though Milligan cautioned that "a day will come when more than the poets' thoughts, more than the patriot-orator's moving words, Ireland will stand in need of arms strong to strike, and feet swift to pursue."[4] Thus the writings contained in the *Shan Van Vocht* were not simply "firmly cultural-nationalist," as critics have maintained.[5] In editor Alice Milligan's mind at least, the literary features, editorials, and notices were meant to embolden more than the Irish arts. Late in life, Yeats worried about the latent militancy of his early writings when he wondered, "Did that play of mine send out / Certain men the English shot?"[6] Milligan and Johnston impenitently acknowledged in their journalism of the 1890s that a Celtic revival would inevitably lead to physical conflict. Yet such certainty did not permit what Milligan called "anarchical methods"—"bomb throwing and blowing up buildings without aim or reason."[7]

The cooperative nature of cultural and political nationalism closely corresponded to the editorial vision of gender-inclusive Celticism. Whereas Yeats's poetry in the 1890s nourished a dependency on femininity that he, in Marjorie Howes's estimation, considered to be "Celticism's central problem rather than one of its distinguishing virtues," Milligan and Johnston betrayed little of Yeats's anxious, colonial masculinity.[8] Although they promoted the female virtues of patience, respect, and devotion as apt qualities for anti-imperial activists, they applied such essentialism with quiet irony. In an editorial shoring up support for a women's Centenary Committee, dedicated to commemorating the United Irishmen Uprising of 1798, for example, Milligan modestly ventured that "the women's committee will not intrude on the sphere of the committees already formed in Dublin and London, but there is a great deal of work which could best be undertaken by women." A few sentences later, however, she wryly underscored how sorely women's participation was needed in Irish nationalist politics after the fall of Charles Stewart Parnell:

> It is not too much to hope that in the present crisis of our country's history, occasion demands, when, alas! political dissensions are rife, that the women of Ireland, who are not called upon to have any opinion whatever as to who has the right to speak for Ireland in the British parliament, should form that *Union* which a historic occasion demands.[9]

Conjoining Celticism with femininity, as they had the literary with the political, legitimated Milligan and Johnston's unifying purpose in the *Shan Van Vocht.* To the many who claimed that women's conciliation and moderation, qualities ascribed to femininity by mainstream Victorian society, made them unfit for the rancorous and sordid world of politics, Milligan and Johnston pointedly responded, as did suffragists, that such a mollifying spirit—as well as their uniquely female condition as disenfranchised citizens—made women apt organizers in political movements embroiled in factionalism and debate.

As unifying women, Milligan and Johnston tapped many of the finest male poets, essayists, and short story writers of the era to contribute to their two-pence literary journal: William Butler Yeats, James Connolly, George Russell (AE), Lionel Johnson, William Rooney, Seumas MacManus, Douglas Hyde, and Cahir Healy. The majority of *Shan Van Vocht*'s writers were women, however: Katharine Tynan, Maud Gonne, Barry Delaney, Alice Furlong, Nora Hopper, Angela Loughrey, Regina Armstrong, Mairghead Keon, among others. Editor Alice Milligan and Secretary Anna Johnston, who adopted the pen names "Iris Olkyrn" and "Ethna Carbery," wrote most of the copy themselves—approximately sixteen pages of short stories, poems, biographical sketches, and editorials each month. Seumas MacManus, who married Anna Johnston in 1901, claims that Milligan and Johnston were responsible for every aspect of the operation: they "wrote almost all of the magazine. . . . They read the proofs. They kept the books. They sent the bills. They wrote the letters. With their

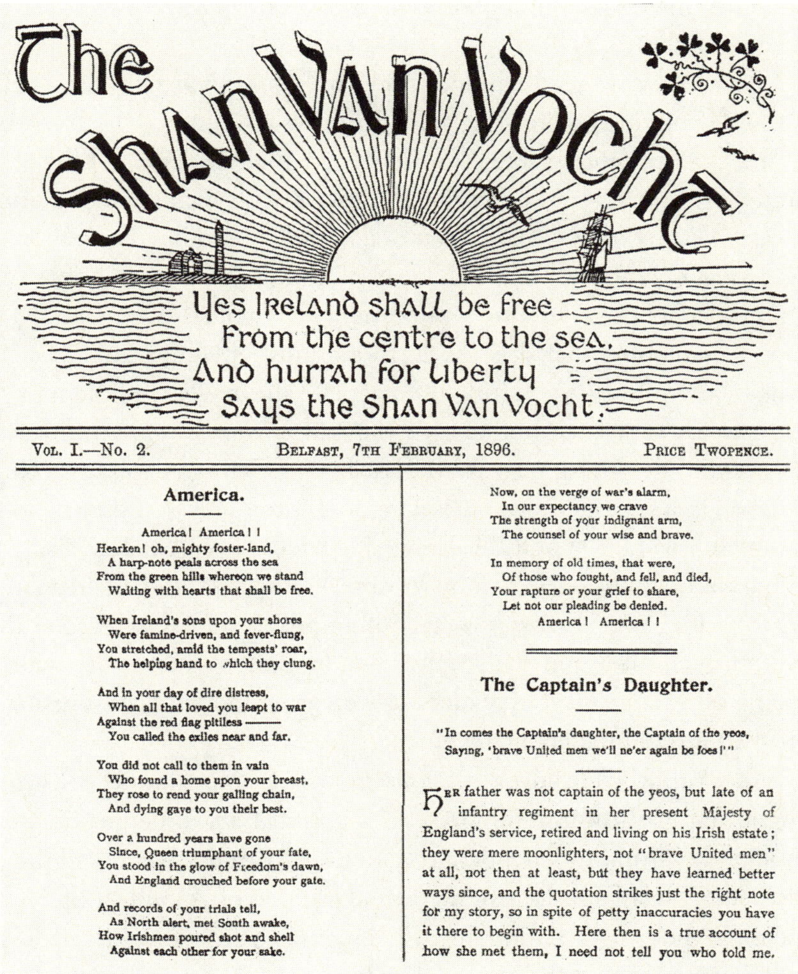

The Shan Van Vocht

Yes Ireland shall be free
From the centre to the sea,
And hurrah for liberty
Says the Shan Van Vocht.

VOL. I.—NO. 2. BELFAST, 7TH FEBRUARY, 1896. PRICE TWOPENCE.

America.

America! America!!
Hearken! oh, mighty foster-land,
A harp-note peals across the sea
From the green hills whereon we stand
Waiting with hearts that shall be free.

When Ireland's sons upon your shores
Were famine-driven, and fever-flung,
You stretched, amid the tempests' roar,
The helping hand to which they clung.

And in your day of dire distress,
When all that loved you leapt to war
Against the red flag pitiless ——
You called the exiles near and far.

You did not call to them in vain
Who found a home upon your breast,
They rose to rend your galling chain,
And dying gave to you their best.

Over a hundred years have gone
Since, Queen triumphant of your fate,
You stood in the glow of Freedom's dawn,
And England crouched before your gate.

And records of your trials tell,
As North alert, met South awake,
How Irishmen poured shot and shell
Against each other for your sake.

Now, on the verge of war's alarm,
In our expectancy we crave
The strength of your indignant arm,
The counsel of your wise and brave.

In memory of old times, that were,
Of those who fought, and fell, and died,
Your rapture or your grief to share,
Let not our pleading be denied.
America! America!!

The Captain's Daughter.

"In comes the Captain's daughter, the Captain of the yeos,
Saying, 'brave United men we'll ne'er again be foes!'"

HER father was not captain of the yeos, but late of an infantry regiment in her present Majesty of England's service, retired and living on his Irish estate; they were mere moonlighters, not "brave United men" at all, not then at least, but they have learned better ways since, and the quotation strikes just the right note for my story, so in spite of petty inaccuracies you have it there to begin with. Here then is a true account of how she met them, I need not tell you who told me.

1. Masthead of *Shan Van Vocht*, February 7, 1896. A frequent expression of optimism among nationalist writers of the day, the image of a sunrise later appeared in the banner of Inghinidhe na hÉireann (Daughters of Ireland), the masthead for *Bean na hÉireann* (Woman of Ireland), and the *Irish Worker*. Reproduced courtesy of the National Library of Ireland.

own hands they folded and addressed every copy that was to go out, and licked every stamp."[10]

Like many advanced nationalist journals, the *Shan Van Vocht* relied on a small coterie of writers. Its readership was also limited, both in number and socioeconomic status. Although, in its final issue, Milligan declared "a firmly-established connection with Irish workers in America," the vast majority of *Shan Van Vocht* readers were middle-class nationalist men and women in Belfast, Dublin, New York, and London. Yet its readers included some of the most prominent nationalists of the era. Maud Gonne proclaimed that she was "full of almost envious admiration" for Milligan and Johnston's "daring little paper"; she avidly read the monthly and regularly promoted her own Paris-based *L'Irlande Libre* in the *Shan Van Vocht*'s advertising pages.[11] Belfast Fenian Bulmer Hobson recalled that, even as a teenager, he was "saving up his pennies to subscribe to the *Shan Van Vocht.*"[12] When the Henry Joy McCracken Society dismissed Milligan and Johnston as editors of the *Northern Patriot* in December 1895, and they were left with no faction or political party to support their continuing efforts as journalists, they had to content themselves with depending on such dedicated readers, as well as on moderate advertising, to keep the journal financially solvent.[13]

Shan Van Vocht's advertisements especially appealed to consumers who viewed each simple purchase as a political act aimed at Irish economic and cultural independence from Great Britain. Nearly all the ads endorsed Milligan and Johnston's textual projects of embellishing on and educating about Irish nationality. Rectangular banners urged readers to invest in Irish-made accessories—Gaelic League '98 handkerchiefs and Wightman & Company's Irish jewelry, which were promoted as "real souvenirs of our Native Land." Readers were urged to cultivate their nationalist libraries by purchasing books such as *The Story of Wolfe Tone's Life* and *Irish Verses* by Thomas Mayne. Whereas a decade later, the *Irish Worker* advertised thrifty or trade union-allied venders, such as Larkin's Little Shop for Good Value, the *Shan Van Vocht* featured notices inviting readers to stay at the Prince of Wales Hotel and First-Rate Restaurant or the Imperial & Windsor Hotel, whose large hall was "suitable for Balls, Receptions, Dinners or Supper Parties." The journal thus implicitly appealed to middle-class Irish nationalists, though it aimed for a broader audience through international circulation. Nationalist expatriates, such as John MacBride in Johannesburg, Thomas Concannon in Mexico, and Patrick McManus in India, reported in the May 1897 edition their delight in finding copies of "The Shan" so far afield. Some readers, such as John Lavery, editor of *Coalfield's Gazette* in Middleburgh, South African Republic, and Patrick O'Byrne, editor of the *Gaelic Journal* in New York, also provided free advertisement for the *Shan Van Vocht* in their home papers, and urged Milligan and Johnston to "push circulation in the United States in a more business-like fashion."

As detailed in the chapters to follow, the *Shan Van Vocht* influenced later journals of advanced nationalism, notably the *United Irishman, Irish Worker,* and *Irish Citizen.* Starting in its second issue in February 1896, the journal featured a monthly column, "What Is Being Done," which alerted readers to new branches of nationalist societies, such as the Gaelic League, the Gaelic Athletic Association, and the Women's Union of the Centenary Committee; it publicized organizational meetings, reprinted their minutes, and often summarized lectures. Reproving dissension among nationalists when it arose, the column helped activists from London to Dublin and from Derry to New Delhi communicate with one another. "What Is Being Done" also provided a public forum for various writers to develop competing ideas about what Irish patriotism entailed: James Connolly made use of it several times to envision a socialist republic; Maud Gonne and J. P. Coughlan appealed for the humane treatment of political prisoners; and Thomas O'Brien lobbied for a "fight against the more grinding tyranny of the landlord class at home."[14]

Cultural and Political Plans in the *Shan Van Vocht*

The beliefs and methods of the nonsectarian United Irishmen strongly shaped the editorial content of the *Shan Van Vocht.* Milligan's editorials, in particular, advocated the seemliness of women promoting unity and overcoming factional party disputes. Given the split in the Irish Parliamentary Party over Parnell, the recent failure of the Ladies' Land League, and Milligan and Johnston's dismissal from the *Northern Patriot,* it is not surprising that *Shan Van Vocht* editorials promoted such conciliatory, unifying activism. The press of the 1890s could be, and often was, the venue for contentious exchanges over the Woman Question.[15] At the same time, even socially conservative women such as Eliza Linton and Margaret Oliphant used the press to publicize their political views, whether in savaging "the girl of period" in the *Saturday Review* or decrying the moral behavior of Sue Brideshead in Hardy's *Jude the Obscure.* Many traditional women chose to become journalists because they could do so within the domestic sphere. That so many middle-class ladies took on and ably performed the "womanly" tasks of writing for the press also indicates the early impact of first-wave feminism, notably in opening up secondary and university education to women.

Moreover, in the early 1880s, in the midst of social and economic discontent about land ownership—a conflict that led to the Land Wars between peasants, farmers, and landlords—the Land League's treatment of its sister organization, the Ladies' Land League, imparted a quiet lesson to Milligan and Johnston about Irish men's limited acceptance of women's independent nationalist action.[16] Within the confines of prison, the Land League leadership sought to control and to undermine the actions and strategies of the Ladies' Land League by repudiating its calls for direct action, such as a rent strike, against landlord power. The Ladies' Land League was finally suppressed, as the Tipperary Fenian John O'Leary famously remarked, "because they were honester and more sincere than the men."[17] Although James Connolly treated women such as Constance Markievicz and Helena Molony as equal members of the revolutionary movement, most male nationalists tolerated women in the struggle only during times of political urgency. Margaret Ward notes that women's prominence in Irish nationalism uniquely arises from an "exceptional political crisis" or emergency, such as the imprisonment and thus imposed absence of the Land League leadership or the Easter Rising, when a united front and backup support were needed.[18] Toiling in this context, in which even popular and successful female nationalists were gently suppressed, Milligan would have surely absorbed the message that feminine activism in Ireland would always be a highly scrutinized and potentially contested endeavor.

Quite likely, the most instructive lesson for Milligan in the necessity of editing out factionalism was her short-lived venture as editor of the *Northern Patriot*, a literary journal she and Anna Johnston founded in October 1895, only to be dismissed after three issues. Milligan's biographer, Sheila Turner Johnston, speculates that Milligan and Johnston were probably fired over a split on policy with the Henry Joy McCracken Society. Milligan and Johnston's open support for the Irish Republican Brotherhood and the amnesty campaign, two subjects that prominently appeared in the first three issues of the *Northern Patriot*, were likely the chief divisive subjects.[19] Catherine Morris explains, specifically, that the society resisted Johnston's involvement with the journal after they realized that her father was Robert Johnston, a founder-member of the Irish Republican Brotherhood.[20] In a loud, emphatic tone, the January 1896 editorial of the *Northern Patriot* proclaimed that the Northern nationalist movement had little tolerance for womanly writing if associated with the "party politics" of Fenian militancy:

> Our readers will observe that we have made a change. We were reluctantly compelled to take this step in order to *keep our journal from becoming the weapon of any particular party in Irish political life.* Since the foundation of THE NORTHERN PATRIOT *our policy has been to keep aloof from modern politics,* our object being to educate and elevate the minds of our youth; from that policy we have never deviated. THE NORTHERN PATRIOT is a journal of the people; *we shall never allow it to become an organ of faction.* (Emphasis original)

Although the *Shan Van Vocht* overshadowed and outsold the *Northern Patriot* (which, despite a reduced price, folded in November 1897), Milligan adopted an editorial voice that, at first glance, seemed much in keeping with the early non-factional dictates of the McCracken society. Yet, as we will see, the tone betrays less a "peace at all costs" mentality than a quiet indictment of the existing state of nationalist affairs, when women were too often pushed to the sidelines, while the men ceaselessly bickered. Milligan promoted women's inclusion in nationalist politics as a remedy for these ills. In a June 1896 editorial, for example, Milligan called for women's involvement in present nationalist organizations not out of a sense of gender inequality but rather because women were better suited for making alliances. Listing a host of activities, from caring for graves to selling home industries and sponsoring Irish concerts, she pointed out that such projects would induce "the women of Ireland [to] unite," thereby setting an example for the fractious men, who had created a political climate where "political dissensions are rife."[21] After having established that women were exemplary strategists who worked effectively in collective political projects, Milligan went on, in a July 1897 editorial, to remind readers that this feminine virtue was shared by the venerable United Irishmen of 1798, who, in her version of Irish history, "fought the strangers, not each other."[22] Still again later in February 1899, another editorial was dedicated to making peace in the Gaelic League: "The appearance of the slightest dissension at a time like the present will be a great hindrance to the movement, and in the name of our common cause we appeal to those who have influence with the Council to exert that influence in the interests of peace."[23]

Although Milligan took pains to advocate the traditional role of women as peacemakers, she did not therefore espouse feminine passivity. More often, she advanced women's role as unifiers out of a sense of feminine superiority. Milligan gleefully highlighted the successes of the Irishwomen's Centenary Union, a focused, effective body that contrasted with the ongoing wrangling in the men's organizations; at the same time, she underscored the political potential of women, who were the numerical majority, to advance their inherently minority position of overcoming factionalism.[24] Although she emphasized gender difference, Milligan challenged the idea of woman as "the weaker sex." She called for women and men to be trained equally, to prepare for the physical rigors of rebellion. One editorial, for example, supported the Gaelic Athletic Association's physical education program because it would prepare a national liberation army: "It is the bounden duty of every man, of every body, who dares to dream of freedom, to make himself in every way that lies in his power a soldier fit for Ireland's service."[25] The support of physical education in the context of the nationalist movement was also resolutely inclusive of girls and women, as Milligan made clear later in the same column: "Physical education has been given, for the last twenty years, a prominent place even in girls' schools. At the school in Londonderry where the Editor of THE SHAN VAN VOCHT spent many years, the smallest pinafored mite in the girls' kindergarten was drilled like a little soldier, and the parallel bars, the vaulting horse, and the Indian clubs were given as prominent a place in the school curriculum as the French or German Grammar."[26] In this commentary, in which a Methodist girls' school serves as a progressive model for feminine militancy, Milligan anticipated but came short of the subversiveness Constance Markievicz displayed in her gardening columns for the *Bean na hÉireann* (Woman of Ireland). As we will see in chapter 3, Markievicz's allegorical garden helped her normalize feminine militancy, a self-interested imperative for a woman who, as an expert shot, later served as second in command of Saint Stephen's Green during the Easter Rising. Whereas the expressly militant Markievicz sought to reimagine the Irish military so that it included women, Milligan more often invested her creative energies, as a fiction writer, in politicizing the Ascendancy girl's domestic realm. Like Markievicz's feminist recoveries of Irish nationalist women, though, Milligan's romances elaborate on the many ingenious forms that women's revolutionary activities might assume.

In keeping with the first nationalist organization of the cultural revival, the Gaelic Athletic Association, Milligan viewed sport as an important venue for the finer nationalist lessons in uniting Irishmen and women in a common goal: honor and dignity for the nation. A May 1896 editorial column emphasized the importance of orderly spectatorship and unified competition: "Let us then thoroughly understand this first principle—that every achievement in the athletic field is prompted by the ambition to have the country rather [than] the club or individual profiting the honour and glory."[27] A similar theme was present in a June 1896 editorial that advocated a new nationalist holiday, National Decoration Day, which was not to "be controlled by any society, or set of societies, or any political party in Ireland. It is simply suggested as a beautiful ceremony which we would desire to see grow into a custom, and which all who love Ireland and honour her patriot dead should observe, each caring specially for the graves in their locality."[28]

If the editor promoted orderly unity on the sports field as well as in the committee room, she displayed an unusual willingness to serve as an open forum for debates on Ireland's social, political, and economic future. In particular, Milligan proved to be far more responsive to the challenge of socialism than many of her nationalist contemporaries. In the November 1896 issue of *Shan Van Vocht,* Milligan began a new feature, "Other People's Opinions," which dedicated valuable space to "articles which we may not necessarily be in agreement with, but which in all cases are worthy of our earnest consideration." The inaugural column, James Connolly's "Can Irish Republicans Be Politicians?" was published within months of the establishment of the Irish Republican Socialist Party, a time when membership was tiny due to strong trade union resistance. Connolly went on to contribute four articles to the *Shan Van Vocht* on socialism, labor, and the efficacy of a republican party in Westminster. Critics such as C. L. Innes, Margaret Ward, and Nelson Ó Ceallaigh Ritschel maintain that Milligan and Johnston wanted to disassociate their journal from Connolly's socialist agenda.[29] The prominent publication of subsequent columns by Connolly and the Irish Socialist Republican Party, the conspicuous printing of letters endorsing Connolly's columns, and two commentaries by Milligan on Connolly's arguments suggest, however, that Milligan wished to downplay rather than dismiss Connolly's economic analyses. Like another cultural nationalist sympathetic to socialism, Maud Gonne, a woman who shared Milligan's socially mollifying disposition, Milligan tended to relegate social questions to the background in favor of broader nationalist projects.[30]

Another example of how Milligan navigated the merging paths of socialism and nationalism can be glimpsed in how she positioned herself and other readers in light of each of Connolly's polemics. In everything he wrote for the *Shan Van Vocht*, Connolly emphasized two related claims: first, that a successful Irish revolution required both a legislative and a military force; second, that a socialist republic had to be the goal of all Irish patriots seeking independence for their country.[31] In the issue following the publication of his first article, Milligan published a series of letters in response to it, most of which warmly praised and enthusiastically underscored elements of Connolly's argument.[32] Connolly's platform was also bolstered in subsequent columns by Thomas O'Brien, another member of the Irish Socialist Republican Party (ISRP), and Thomas Concannon.[33] Finally, Milligan twice appended a short paragraph to Connolly's column, indicating precisely what she did and did not endorse in his argument. After Connolly's column "Patriotism and Labour," for example, an editorial note discloses: "Whilst in full sympathy with Mr. Connolly's views on the labour and social questions, we are absolutely opposed to the scheme he puts forward for the formation of an Irish Republican party in the British Parliament. Any conscientious Republican would stick at the oath of allegiance."[34] Several months later, in October of 1897, Milligan publicly declined an invitation by the ISRP to lecture for them, offering instead to debate Connolly over whether Irish republicans should be politicians. Complimenting Connolly and his party for doing "good work for Ireland in preaching the gospel of democracy and spreading national principles," Milligan sidestepped his proposal to link socialism and nationalism.

In his submissions to the *Shan Van Vocht*, Connolly expressly acknowledged Milligan's persistent, latent anxiety about linking colonial and economic oppression. As he explained in his article "Socialism and Nationalism," dissension among Irish patriots need not be the end result of strategic alliances across class lines:

> This linking together of our national aspirations with the hopes of the men and women who have raised the standard of revolt against that system of capitalism and landlordism, of which the

> British Empire is the most aggressive type and resolute defender, should not, in any sense, import an element of discord into the ranks of earnest nationalists.[35]

Despite such assurances, however, Milligan's editorials studiously avoided addressing Connolly's main proposal and focused, instead, on a minor point, his call for a socialist republican party in Westminster. Such action, Milligan pointed out, would be "taking the broad road that leads to destruction, as such a party would inevitably be in alliance with the English labour party."[36] As we will see with Milligan's romances, these responses to Connolly's socialism—strategic and polemical as they were in articulating the nationalist praxis—consistently declined to answer his call for a united workers' republic. Of course, Milligan's reluctance to take up or fully endorse Connolly's ambitious ideals hardly sets her apart from other nationalists—whether female or male, Catholic or Protestant, wealthy or middle-class—of the day. Her challenges as a writer who sought to address more than one set of oppressions at once, however, will turn out to be a common trial for every female writer of advanced nationalism. Although many of the women studied in *Women, Press, and Politics* kept their eyes fixed on the "three great movements" of Ireland—nationalism, feminism, socialism—each writer fashioned a distinctive response in attempting to integrate these three emancipation movements.

Though Milligan's challenges as an upper-class Protestant nationalist were shared by other writers of her age, her eager but impossible wish to at once avoid and heal social divisions in the Irish nationalist movement are best understood in light of the growing sectarian and class divisions that emerged in the wake of the 1798 commemorations in Belfast. In Ulster, as Virginia Crossman has shown, the commemoration activities accentuated sectarianism.[37] Although Belfast was a wealthy city at the turn of the century, the workforce divided sharply along sectarian lines: Protestant cross-channel dock workers regularly earned two to two and a half times the salary of Catholic deep-sea dock workers.[38] The trade union movement in Belfast, moreover, was firmly controlled by the craft unions, whose membership was predominantly Protestant and Loyalist.[39] When Irish Parliamentary Party for West Belfast MP Joe Devlin sought to recruit working-class voters, he did so knowing the Conservative party could not hope for political survival with a labor program. Milligan's eagerness to subdue Connolly's socialism should thus be understood in the context of her desire to appeal to a religiously diverse, if economically homogeneous, middle-class audience. Her suggesting the political potential of Big House ladies, while remaining silent about domestic workers in her home or girls in the tenement rows, reveals a common middle-class habit of editing class divisions out of the nationalist movement. Though Milligan's aims were to unify nationalists, what she ended up doing was simply silencing and neglecting a critical group who, as her romances imply, had much to gain from a real revolution.

Milligan's Border Romances

The theme of alliance across the divides of religion, class, and ideology also suffused many of the literary features in the *Shan Van Vocht*. Perhaps the most memorable example can be read in Milligan's political romances, a popular literary form that shares the activist, interventionist impulses of late-eighteenth-century pamphlets, sermons, and speeches.[40] As Doris Sommer has written in the context of Latin America, political romances—which trace their lineage to nineteenth-century allegorical fiction—use the plot of heterosexual romance to sanction not only the destiny of females but also that of a nation in the making. Typically, these romances involve lovers, representing different regions, races, or economic backgrounds, whose "passion for conjugal and sexual union spills over . . . to win partisan minds along with hearts."[41] Like the romances studied by Sommer, Milligan's short fiction was composed during a period of intensive longing for nationhood. Living in Belfast, Milligan recognized that one of the most intractable obstacles to Ireland's achievement of national independence was divisive factionalism and sectarianism. Just as her editorials repeatedly admonished women readers in particular to cross the divides of party politics and religious difference to commemorate Ireland's patriot dead and to rally for a unified future, so, too, her fiction in the *Shan Van Vocht* looked to women to cross the divides of class, caste, and national perspective in order to transform Ireland.

Because Milligan set most of her narratives (and, indeed, lived most of her life) in Belfast, a city marked by sectarian divisions, the longing for reconciliation of warring constituencies (Unionists and nationalists, upper class and working class, northern nationalists and southern nationalists, Protestant nationalists and Catholic nationalists) is a driving force in every element of her political and cultural life. Not surprisingly, her adaptation of the romance—romances across the divide—reveals the tensions and conflicts that eventually led to the formal partition of Ireland in 1923. As Joe Cleary has argued, romances across the divide are an "anxious and contradictory literary mode," especially when set in partitioned places like contemporary Northern Ireland.[42] Because the political borders cannot be addressed, they are both literally and figuratively erased. The romance between members of two alienated communities thus enables the writer to imagine reconciliation that cannot be achieved in the political sphere. Cleary notes that one of the most remarkable features about literature set in partitioned nations is the "discursive invisibility" of the border, a political separation reimagined in the narrative as gender, class, religious, or behavioral differences.[43] Although Milligan set her stories and lived most of her life before the Government of Ireland Act partitioned six counties in the northeast of Ireland from the Irish Free State in 1923, her narratives structurally and thematically comment on long-standing imposed sectarian boundaries she navigated her entire life.

Alice Milligan and her collaborator Anna Johnston surely understood the concept of borders, living in a city marked by sectarianism. Despite their differences in background, Milligan, an upper-class Methodist, and Johnston, a middle-class Catholic, established a friendship and a cultural-political partnership on their shared commitment to Irish nationalism, a movement divided by factionalism and discord since the fall of Charles Stewart Parnell in 1891. Working in a climate of religious difference, political division, and class antagonism, Alice Milligan and Anna Johnston fixed on one abiding goal in their writings: unification. In essays, stories, and poems, the *Shan Van Vocht* expressed the political desire for consolidation, an end best achieved through feminine means: healing nationalist wounds, reconciling religious divisions, mending geographical borders, curing class conflict. These acts of unification advocated by the *Shan Van Vocht* masked unresolved divisions as well. Indeed, if we scrutinize the literary content of the journal—in particular, the thematic figures of unification—we can see that the journal advocated politically subversive if socially conventional roles for women in 1890s Ireland. As we will see throughout this book, Milligan's contradictory impulses about the possibilities and limitations of feminine political behavior were shared by many writers, both male and female, of advanced nationalism. Writers as diverse as Mary E. L. Butler, Maud Gonne, and Delia Larkin frequently diminished the social threat of feminine political action by emphasizing that women could effectively advance their cause within the home. As Milligan's fiction revealed the *Shan Van Vocht*'s long-standing political and social expectations for its readers, so, too, its editorials fixed on the aim to unite hopelessly divided communities. As we follow the quiet political work of pampered upper-class girls, who don symbolic slippers and teach Fenians how to fight, we will discover that Milligan's emphasis on Protestant nationalism represses, rather than rectifies, the class conflicts that her fiction seeks to repair.

That Milligan chose to express her nationalist desires for unity in narrative form is itself a formal manifestation of her impulse toward alliance. Deeply imbued with the values and aesthetics of the Irish revival, Milligan understood that the reception and canonization of Irish art was based on a text's ability to articulate national self-definition. In Ireland during the revival, two genres predominated: lyric poetry and drama. Milligan, in fact, viewed herself primarily as a poet, and was sorely disappointed when Yeats praised her as "a very effective prose writer" and advised her to try drama instead.[44] Although she followed his counsel, as least in part, designing innovative and germinal dramatic works such as *The Escape of Red Hugh* and *tableaux vivants* for Inghinidhe na hÉireann (Daughters of Ireland), she also developed her considerable talent in short fiction as well. Whereas the preeminent fiction writers of the day—Somerville and Ross (Edith Somerville and Violet Martin), James Stephens, George Moore,

James Joyce—used fiction to express strong ambivalence about the idea of the Irish nation, Milligan composed narratives that optimistically imagined a union of hearts, religions, and classes. Her romances make a strong case for reexamining the ideological and formal ideals of the Irish revival; her narrative subjects, thematic figures, and generic modifications of the romance plot challenge commonplace literary and political ideas about women in 1890s Ireland. Although, in the 1989 Attic Press pamphlet *A Kind of Scar*, Eavan Boland dismissed nationalist writing for "simplify[ing] women almost out of existence" through relying on "static, passive, ornamental figures" that do no credit to women or poetry,[45] her dismissal cannot fairly be said to apply to the fiction of Alice Milligan. With an ear tuned by the ballads of the United Irishmen and a mind trained by Methodist educators, Milligan rarely imagined her female characters as decorative embellishments to manly action. Moreover, as we will see, her protagonists adopted cunning strategies that many women in Irish history actually devised when they or their nation was under siege.

Milligan's desire for unity, especially among irreconcilable factions, and her unwillingness or inability to face conflicts based on religion and class help clarify the compelling nature of such a literary form. Nearly every romance she pens has a beautiful young protagonist whose political beliefs initiate the narrative conflict between landed authority and native rebellion. Although the plot of generational and ideological friction is tired and worn, Milligan animates the narrative by revealing the wily domestic strategies employed by her pampered rebel girls. Her protagonist subversively deploys the unexpected political tools of bourgeois life—the accouterments of leisured femininity—to undermine the colonizers. Nowhere do we see young girls taking up arms; rather, we observe them donning symbolic slippers and strumming nationalist harps. We learn, as a result, that every domestic gesture has the potential to contribute to the revolution.[46]

In one of Milligan's most representative stories, "The Little Green Slippers," which is set in Belfast in December of 1798, we meet the beautiful, impetuous Jessica Huston, a Protestant Northerner, who—against the autocratic command of her country gentleman stepfather—initially refuses to attend the Christmas Garrison Ball in protest of the recent executions of the United Irishmen.[47] After considerable threats by her stepfather and after ineffectually stamping her pretty little feet, she ultimately decides to attend the ball, but stirs a scandal by wearing "a pair of dainty morocco slippers of the rebel green, audaciously rosetted with crape." The green silk and the black crepe defiantly and, to the Garrison crowd, unequivocally, represent Jessica's inappropriate mourning for the executed Henry Joy McCracken, a leader of the United Irishmen. Moreover, as the green slippers were a gift from her beloved rebel on the run, Bernard Magennis, they represent to Jessica, and to us, her romantic desires, which are to reunite with her politically unacceptable lover. Jessica's name and plight, of course, recall Shylock's rebellious daughter, Jessica, who runs away to marry the Christian Lorenzo, in *Merchant of Venice*. By alluding to Jessica, Milligan is clearly signaling not only the close correlation of religion, race, and class in 1890s Ireland, but also the significant transgression Jessica's union with Magennis represents.

As do the national romances Doris Sommer describes in *Foundational Fictions*, Milligan's "The Little Green Slippers" effectively melds erotic and patriotic desires, for, as luck would have it, Jessica and her lover are reunited in the end because of her political defiance. Yet, for all its hopeful, quixotic impulses, even romances, when formed across the divide of politics, class, and religion, must face the practical limits of finding the lovers a home. Implicitly addressing the intractable divisions of Belfast, Milligan's romance across the divide requires a plot resolution that relocates the lovers outside the physical boundaries of Ireland in 1798. When she is banished from her stepfather's home for her "impudent rebel" act, Jessica is narratively rewarded with a "chance" meeting with Magennis, who had made one last stop at her aunt's home before sailing away from Ireland. Thus Jessica's "audacity in the wearing o' the green" is recompensed with the romantic resolution of marriage on the run. Her reconciliation with Bernard suggests the political challenges of reuniting Protestants and Catholics in facing down Britain, for this nationalized embrace can only take place away from Ireland's shores.

Reading "The Little Green Slippers," we learn that one source of feminine rebellion is a false-father's autocratic dictates. In another romance across the divide, "The Outlaw's Bride," Milligan locates the catalyst of political action in feminine subjection. This Christmas tale, based on Milligan's novel *The Cromwellians* (1893), returns to a theme that preoccupied Milligan throughout the 1890s: the historical discord between settler and native in the Cromwellian settlements of the early seventeenth century.[48] In Milligan's romance, the beautiful "dark-eyed" Eibhlin Og, a Dark Rosaleen, longs for escape from her opulent home and an arranged union with a captain of Cromwell's English army.[49] When the story opens at a Christmas eve ball, the wealthy "Puritan suitor" Captain Hosea Greatrex has come to the ball in hopes of winning Eibhlin's favor. Openly encouraged by Eibhlin's eager parents, Greatrex suppresses his Puritan guilt of "sinful pastimes" such as dancing in pursuit of a higher purpose, securing a bride. Eibhlin has other plans. Fully intending to "wound him by the power of her beauty," she tremblingly puts off his advances with "curt excuses to re-arrange her tumbled tresses," and slips tearfully to her room where she dreams of flight to the "unassailable mountains" in Connacht with her beloved, another politically inappropriate lover whom her mother dismisses as "that landless rogue Brian Connell."

With her title, Milligan announces the plot resolution of her romance, though this bride betrays her own penchant for outlaw exploits. Trying to dry her swollen eyes, she is startled by "a clanking on the window pane" and the sight, down below, of her sweetheart in a symbolic pose of male sexual potency: "a sword blade waving thereat like a white flame by the moonbeam." When Brian informs her that he is fleeing the area for awhile because of torching Greatrex's demesne, she is finally motivated to act on her own behalf. Coquettishly pleading for him to escort her to the "peace of the sanctuary," the convent of Athlone, she elicits the desired response from her lover: "There is no peace and sanctuary in the whole of Ireland. Nuns and friars alike are fugitives and outlaws. Soldiers quarter in their once holy places. There is no shelter for thee save with me." When his chivalry, prompted by the winter winds, prevents him from assisting an immediate escape, however, Eibhlin takes matters into her own hands. In her silk gown and light slippers, with nary a wrap around her bare, white shoulders, she slips out of her window and nimbly drops onto his waiting steed.

The narrator tells us "in a moment she was safe in shelter near his heart," but not until the final paragraph do we discover the allegorical lessons of Eibhlin's brazen union with her "tall outlaw" in exile. Unlike "The Little Green Slippers," this union of hearts takes place on Irish soil, but beyond the pale of colonial rule: the harsh, rocky, and wind swept region that Cromwell relegated the native Irish when he reputedly commanded them "to hell or Connaught." After days of riding in the winter snow and ice, Connell finally delivers Eibhlin "straight into the firelight," and places our hoary heroine directly in his mother's chair, whereupon her thawing face blooms into a transformed Dark Rosaleen: "She blushed, as she looked upon Brian, till the face that had been pale, was like a lovely rose." Milligan implies, thus, that union across the divide, like marriage to a bachelor still living at home, will involve power exchanges between women, for an aging Mother Ireland must give way to the revitalized Dark Rosaleen. Several years later, Milligan would revisit this scene of the Dark Rosaleen supplanting Mother Ireland in her dramatic legend *The Last Feast of the Fianna* (1899). Whereas, in "The Outlaw's Bride" as in her *Shan Van Vocht* editorials, she had projected a harmonious redistribution of power between nationalist players, in her later play, Milligan proved more willing to explore the inevitable struggles between two forceful females who proved inexperienced in sharing anything of value. As we will see in chapter 2, Milligan's critical appraisal of women competing for power would later influence Maud Gonne's writings about female collaboration.

Several important lessons about gender are embedded in Milligan's tale of Eibhlin Og. First, feminine powerlessness in the face of a coerced marriage settlement fuels Eibhlin's rebel sympathies. In her room, she first spills tears over the realization that "her heart was not her own to give." Feminine bonds across religious and class divides also provide Eibhlin lessons in political agency. Speculating on her daughter's disappearance from the ball, Eibhlin's mother bitterly remarks, "She has stolen away, no doubt, to be with old Brigid her nurse, who will humour her and incite her to rebel against us." Like the Ascendancy playwright Augusta Gregory, whose Fenian sympathies were first awakened by nightly tales from her nurse, Eibhlin opens her heart to a rebel, thereby demonstrating her allegiance to her surrogate rather than her birth mother. Like the "red revolutionary" Constance Markievicz, who gave up her Dublin Castle parties and her silk gowns to help bring about a workers' republic, Eibhlin Og leaves behind her sparkling jewels and her opulent Big House for marriage to a Son of Erin. Unlike Markievicz, however, who traded in her role as posh bohemian for a far edgier part as Marxist countess, Eibhlin assumes a similar social role, albeit an economically reduced one, from potential wife of a Cromwellian soldier to bride of a landless rebel.

In such stories as "The Little Green Slippers" and "The Outlaw's Bride," Alice Milligan endeavored to achieve reconciliation between communities at odds by composing nationalist narratives more often than lyric poems or plays; but the antirealist aspects of her romances also reflect her solidly Irish credentials. Terry Eagleton has provocatively suggested that Irish writers' long-standing alienation from realism stems, in part, from the sensationalism of Irish history, which always seemed to trump the most spectacular of tales; by equal measure, Irish fiction writers spurned realism in a generic response to the conditions of a divided society, which precluded the Olympian standpoint that realism requires.[50] The genre of romance thus proved an enticing narrative form because it allowed Milligan to comment formally and structurally on the past and simultaneously project utopian desires for the future. Milligan's romances, in other words, narratively trace the historical processes of subjugation, rebellion, and Union that 1650, 1798, and 1801 represented. They also envisage a political revolution cum social union that threatened Britain's imperial prestige but not Protestant class supremacy. For a writer caught up in the fervor of the approaching centenary of 1798, Milligan's choice of romance also makes sense because the standard elements of the chivalric romance, a precursor to Milligan's political romance, easily align themselves with the *aislingi* lyric poems of eighteenth-century colonized Ireland. Whereas the chivalric romance features a hero of high birth who undertakes a dangerous, lonely quest to gain his lady's favor, the *aisling* sublimates the desire of sexual union with the yearning for political sovereignty. Most strikingly,

Milligan's revisionist romances center on the agency of the female protagonist. Unlike the romance of earlier ages or the *aisling*, both of which presumed a universal male as the primary active agent who achieved the transformation for which the story yearned, Milligan's political romances contemplate woman as the speaking, acting, and desiring subject of each text.

The *Shan Van Vocht* used a generically innocuous form, nationalist romance, as well as socially benign characters, Protestant girls, to conceal far more threatening, if ideologically conflicted, content. So, too, its editorials ardently supported nationalist activities, from the Gaelic League to the Gaelic Athletic Association, and managed to evade censorship and suppression by Dublin Castle, a rarity for such a prominent nationalist journal. Yet such careful, cunning use of bourgeois femininity had its limits: though they employed silk slippers and well-polished beauty for nationalist ends, Milligan's privileged heroines held back from actively dismantling the comforts and advantages enjoyed by their families, who benefited from this ancestral conquest of Ireland. Keeping a steady focus on a surprising group of rebels, Milligan deliberately provided only bit parts and nonspeaking roles to the dispossessed women and men who had the most to gain from a revolution. As a result, the economic dimension to rebellion—Brian's landlessness, Brigid's working conditions—could be quietly edited out of the story. Milligan's choice to keep class analysis out of her fiction was also evident in her editorials for the *Shan Van Vocht*. As we have seen, Milligan's editorial voice imparted a sense of class privilege and class insecurity about the place and purpose of Protestants in an emergent, sovereign Ireland. Like Big House fiction, a kissing cousin of Milligan's border romances, the *Shan Van Vocht* expressed a host of anxieties over the conquest of Ireland.[51]

Alice Milligan and the Female Protestant Literary Tradition

In 1890s Ireland, both Alice Milligan and Anna Johnston were held in tender regard among nationalists for their collaborative achievements in the *Shan Van Vocht* and for their individual talents as revival writers. Alice

Milligan, in particular, was recognized as a haunting lyric poet, an innovative dramatist, and an influential nationalist figure. Thomas MacDonagh called her "the most Irish of living Irish poets, and therefore the best."[52] Susan Mitchell, writing from the distance of several decades after the *Shan* was no longer in print, argued that Milligan served as "the infant nurse" of the revival, someone who "looked after it while it was yet inarticulate and who expressed its wants."[53] Critics today consider her dramatic legend *The Last Feast of the Fianna,* the first example of Celtic Twilight drama, inspiring William Butler Yeats, Augusta Gregory, and Edward Martyn in their early efforts to found an Irish national theater.[54] Milligan's *tableaux vivants* are now also recognized as early instances of feminist drama.[55] And, late in her life, the *Irish Press* declared her pivotal to the Irish cause: "Nobody, at the turn of the century, saw with clearer eyes than Alice Milligan that of the two sides of the Nationalist movement—the cultural and the political . . . she vigorously supported every phase of the revival—the language, the feis [festivals], the dramatic and literary renaissance."[56] As editor of the *Northern Patriot* and the *Shan Van Vocht,* Milligan is also a founder of a new generation of nationalist journalism, one of the most influential weapons in the anticolonial arsenal.[57] Yet her writings, together with the poetry and prose of her collaborator Anna Johnston, are today "not so much underrated now as . . . almost completely forgotten,"[58] largely because their literary and political efforts are primarily visible in the advanced nationalist press.

Alice Milligan's multiple identities—as an upper-class, highly educated, Protestant, female nationalist from Belfast—reveal one reason why her writings are still so little studied. Of course, other Anglo-Irish cultural nationalists, such as Augusta Gregory, William Butler Yeats, and J. M. Synge, addressed the putative problems of their Ascendancy ancestry by highlighting their deep roots in places beyond the pale of colonial influence, such as Galway, Sligo, or the Aran Islands. As Yeats later claimed, "from that / Contact everything Antaeus-like grew strong."[59] Milligan, however, declined to apologize for her Belfast origins or her wealthy, Methodist pedigree. Her strategy, instead, was to take permissible upper-class qualities of femininity, such as munificence and self-sacrifice, and expend them in the service of Ireland, rather than for God, Britannia, or family. In her autobiographical lyric of national awakening, "Ode for 6 October," for example, Milligan reclothed wifely duty and Christian atonement in the garments of nationalist service: "O Ireland dear, of my whole life's love for thee / . . . . O Ireland dear, thy redemption come to thee!"[60] However, whereas Milligan's pursuit of alliances influenced her rejection of Unionist politics, her peacemaking impulses inhibited her from renouncing the social and economic supremacy her family and her class enjoyed. Howes has suggested that such conflicts and contradictions distinguish Anglo-Irish Celticism.[61] The longing for harmony among Protestants and Catholics, Northerners and Southerners, men and women effectively diverted Milligan and her readers from the class conflicts of industrial fin de siècle Belfast. Milligan's narrative subjects, cosseted upper-class girls, surprise the imperialist men in the stories—and *Shan Van Vocht* readers—by their political convictions and agency. Yet left unexamined is the hierarchy of class that allows her affluent heroines to take advantage of such privileged opportunities at all.

Milligan's mediating philosophy is indebted to a prominent female writer of the Ascendancy class, novelist Maria Edgeworth (1768–1849). Like the Unionist Milligans, in whose well-appointed hallway a gilded portrait of Robert Emmet hung, the liberal Anglo-Irish Edgeworths occupied a minority position within their class. Determined to practice a kind of benevolent paternalism, Richard Lovell Edgeworth managed his estate and treated his tenants in a style meant to repudiate the kind of practices that the fictive Rackrent family deplorably represented.[62] Maria Edgeworth initially assisted and eventually supplanted her father in many of the practical and literary practices of such "ameliorating" efforts. Indeed, both women served their literary apprenticeships at their fathers' knees. An important difference was that, whereas Edgeworth studied economics with exacting French Enlightenment rigor, Milligan took in folklore and legends from an antiquarian Fellow of the Royal Irish Academy, who published on the archaeology of the countryside.[63]

In Edgeworth's *Castle Rackrent,* the narrative promotes multivalenced, conflicting messages: the economic elite is praised for its commitment to the rational supervision of property and populace and strongly remonstrated for abusing its patrician privileges. Mary Jean Corbett argues that, to make sense of these inconsistent messages—and of the widely divergent critical responses to Edgeworth's oeuvre—one must historicize Edgeworth by reading her work through the lens of Edmund Burke, whose writings served as a model of colonial discourse and enlightened magnanimity toward the native population.[64] My reading of Milligan, for its part, aims to unsettle and qualify her resistance literature by scrutinizing it through two lenses: upper-class benevolence and advanced nationalist journalism. As we will see, although Milligan ultimately endorsed rebellion, especially when conducted by intrepid, discerning, affluent girls, her thematic figures of union across the divide share important commonalities with the ambivalent "insider-outsider" perspective of Edgeworth and Burke, who could never approve such revolutionary ends. Milligan's writing in the *Shan Van Vocht* thus marks a transition from colonial to postcolonial literature: although her narrative subjects were "Empire girls," clothed and schooled in the Anglo-Irish tradition, the political pining for national independence, and the sexual desire for the rebel, led them further astray than their parents had ever envisioned.

In her centenary activism, her historical retrospectives, and her romances across the divide, Alice Milligan leaned far closer to a revolutionary than to the mediating stance Corbett finds in Edgeworth's fiction. In large part, this was because Milligan's late-nineteenth-century nationalism looked to the example of the United Irishmen, a political society that, fostered the century before in the North and originally dedicated to Catholic civil rights and parliamentary reform, quickly transformed into a physical force movement. The United Irishmen Uprising proved to be a fertile inspiration for a Protestant nationalist like Milligan, offering her, as Mary Helen Thuente and Nancy Curtin compellingly document, an important model for melding political and cultural nationalisms.[65] Founded in 1791, the United Irish Society emerged, like the *Shan Van Vocht* a century later, out of middle-class desire to achieve an independent, unitary, nonsectarian Irish republic. Many poems and songs of the era, such as Henry Joy

McCracken's "The Social Thistle and the Shamrock," record the society's resolute ambition for a united resistance to England by the Presbyterian Scots and Catholic Irish:

> The Scotch and Irish friendly are, their wishes are the same,
> The English nation envy us, and over us would reign. . . .
> Our historians and our poets, they always did maintain,
> That the origin of Scottishmen and Irish were the same. . . .
> Now to conclude and end my song, may we live long to see,
> The Thistle, and the Shamrock, entwine the olive tree.[66]

A telling detail in McCracken's concluding stanza is the prediction of harmony between these two competing flora of Northern Irish nationalism. Many of the United Irishmen songs, in fact, argued that England's political might emerged from the old method of divide and conquer. Wolfe Tone's song "Ierne United" provides a popular rendition of the linkage between discord and imperialism:

> But soon—ah! Too soon, did fell discord begin;
> Our domestic dissensions let foreigners in,
> Too well they improv'd the advantage we gave,
> Whom they came to protect they remain'd to enslave. . . .
> Then let us remember our madness no more,
> What we lost by dissension, let Union restore;
> Let us firmly United, and our covenant be,
> Together to fall, or together be Free.[67]

Another important contribution of the United Irishmen to advanced nationalists a century later was their aim to unite nationalists across geographical borders through the political-cultural project of nationalist journalism. The society supported the publication of four newspapers—the *Northern Star* (Belfast), the *National Journal* (Dublin), the *Press* (Dublin), and the *Harp of Erin* (Cork)—rooted in three of Ireland's four green fields. These newspapers, like the *Shan Van Vocht*, combined cultural features such as poems and songs with political articles and editorials, and used cultural nationalism—songs, poems, a Gaelic magazine, a harp festival—to entertain, educate, and influence their readers in political nationalism. For her part, Milligan believed it imperative to incorporate the tumult and excitement of national politics in her writing; in an 1893 letter to *United Ireland,* she set forth her strong view of the larger, formative role of political strife in

> Irish literature[, which] cannot be developed in any hedged-in peaceful place, whilst a conflict is raging around. It must be in the thick of the fight, and if brought apart from it and commanded to declare spiritual gospels to an awaiting world, the silence will come at last.[68]

Milligan found it hard, however, to meet that imperative, and harder still to fulfill her goal of unifying partisans while staying "in the thick of the fight," as we have already seen in her romances.

In one important sense, the *Shan Van Vocht* differed from its forebear in its sexually inclusive ideal of citizenship. The anonymously authored United Irishmen song "Paddy Evermore" characteristically described masculine Irishness when it intoned,

> UNITE, UNITE, UNITE, my boys, quell discord, live in peace
> Forget your Feuds in mutual love, and brotherly embrace
> Let each man freely chose his way, our maker to adore,
> And tell the world as Irishmen, we are PADDIES and no more.[69]

Editorials and historical features in the *Shan Van Vocht* also fostered the manly virtues of Irish patriotism. A typical Celticist column implored, "Think of the ideals of manhood and chivalry she [Ireland] has cherished through the long ages," and went on to recall for readers the virile exploits of Cuchulainn, Brian of Banba, and Red Hugh O'Donnell.[70] At the same time, the literary features prized open a place to imagine girls and women, not just boys and men, as Irish patriots. Next to the unsigned laudatory poem "Our Irish Girls," Milligan reminded male poets that "praise of the women of Ireland need not be left out of the songs of freedom."[71] Just as Milligan's romances imaginatively envisioned Empire girls' contributions to the revolution, Milligan's editorials frequently outlined how women could contribute to the emancipation of their nation, whether in the home, on the dais, or in the committee room.

Despite the many indications of support for militant nationalism in the *Shan Van Vocht,* Alice Milligan was deeply invested in the popular memory of the United Irishmen as a consolidating, rather than radical, political force. In keeping with her upper-class, Protestant background, Milligan drew inspiration from a popular, if selective, memory of 1798, one shared by other Protestant nationalists such as Yeats and Gregory. In Milligan's mind, the eighteenth-century society united patriots and poets, Catholics and Protestants, Southerners and Northerners, the wealthy and the poor. An executive member of the Belfast branch of the Irish Women's Association and a cofounder of the Henry Joy McCracken Society, Milligan spent much of the late 1890s traveling throughout the country, lecturing extensively for the Gaelic League about her version of United Irishmen. Each issue of the *Shan Van Vocht* also featured numerous editorials, historical retrospectives, poems, plays, and short stories about the heroics of men such as Wolfe Tone and Henry Joy McCracken, who crossed the social and political divide to embrace the nationalist cause.[72] Even the source of the journal's title—the eighteenth-century ballad "The Shan Van Vocht"—was edited in the opening issue to remove the divisive sectarianism of the original song. In the opening stanza of one well-known version of the ballad, the speaker, the Shan Van Vocht, anticipates a French invasion to help destroy the Orange Order:

> Oh! The French are in the Bay,
> They'll be here without delay,
> And the Orange will decay,
> Says the Shan Van Vocht.

In another version, the speaker focuses upon Saxon and Danish invasion, and blames these plundering people for "profaning" the "sainted isle of old." The ballad quoted in Milligan's opening number, on the other hand, judiciously edits out these sectarian lines and quietly obscures which countries might serve as Ireland's allies:[73]

> There is news from o'er the sea . . .
> From the land of liberty,
> Brings the best of news for me,
>   —Says the Shan Van Vocht.[74]

In her imaginative writings, just as in this version of the ballad, Milligan betrays vestiges of Edgeworth's Ascendancy project to find a middle path between the aristocratic abuses of power and the native violence of insurgency.

A large proportion of Milligan's literary efforts, from her play *The Daughter of Donagh* to her most memorable lyric, "When I was a Little Girl," evince a sustained investment in the theme of alliance, consolidating past and present, Unionist and nationalist, Protestant and Catholic, working-class and upper-class, cultural and revolutionary activism. Whereas Edgeworth created unstable characters such as Thady Quirk, who faithfully serves and is cruelly subjugated by the Ascendancy Rackrents, Milligan devised heroines who enjoy the doting service of a houseful of servants yet dream of emancipating their country. The well-raised speaker of "Little Girl," who embodies upper-class femininity and impudent rebellion, obeys her nurse, who nightly cries out:

> Come in! for it's growing late,
> And the grass will wet ye!
> Come in! or when it's dark
> The Fenians will get ye

And, though she listens attentively by the fire to her nurse's Cromwellian adages about God and the British Empire, by the poem's conclusion, we learn that her femininity and her youth, rather than the privileges afforded her class and caste, determine her political sympathies:

> But one little rebel there,
> Watching all with laughter,
> Thought "When the Fenians come
> I'll rise and go after."
>
> Wished she had been a boy
> And a good deal older—
> Able to walk for miles
> With a gun on her shoulder;
>
> Able to lift aloft
> That Green Flag o'er them
> (Red-coats and blackpolice
> Flying before them);
>
> And, as she dropped asleep,
> Was wondering whether
> God, if they prayed to Him,
> Would give fine weather.[75]

This early lyric, which was well known during her career as a journalist, indicates that Milligan's ideas about feminine behavior, ostensibly conventional upper-class passivity, always contained a resistant, activist component.

Although Milligan's stories and editorials promote a variety of active roles for Irish girls and women bent on Irish liberty, they do not at first glance seem to agitate for gender equality. Indeed, even as critics have held up the *Shan Van Vocht* as a model of journalistic nationalism and an early example of feminine editorship, they have underscored the conventional gender roles promoted on its pages. Sheila Turner Johnston, for example, laments that Milligan was "much too busy to pause over gender issues."[76] Yet the editors' silence about suffrage, admittedly a preeminent cause for feminists at this time, is shaky grounds for dismissing the commitment to gender equality of these writers. After all, the icon of modern femininity, the New Woman, took many different forms, as well. In Ireland and across the Irish Sea, New Women might be wild or womanly, organizing or anarchist, fallen or pure, nationalist or orientalist, leisured or working, bicycling or bookish. So, too, in the columns of the *Shan Van Vocht*, feminine agency and activism are ubiquitous, albeit not uniformly expressed.

Indeed, the roles for political women in the *Shan Van Vocht* foreshadow what Louise Ryan has called "the dual roles of 'girl on bicycle' and 'sniper on the roof' " adopted by the Cumann na mBan (the women's council of the Irish Volunteers) during the Easter Rising of 1916.[77] Although the journal's editorials and features, poems and romances rarely envision a girl with a gun, nearly every issue contained examples of how ladies of the past and women of the day chose to do their bit for Ireland. Alongside recollections and histories about male patriots such as Wolfe Tone and Robert Emmet, there were features about female contemporaries, such Anne Devlin, Lady Fitzgerald, and Speranza (Lady Wilde). The *Shan Van Vocht* also reminded readers about the life of female activists from the North, such as the prophetic Betty Fryers, and retold tales of heroic battles fought by the valiant Betsy Gray.[78] The majority of these female features detail the lives and activism of aristocratic or Ascendancy women who, through patriotic husbands, sweethearts, or distant heroes, became committed to the cause. Yet, in each in these features, Milligan and Johnston emphasized little about the revolutionary men in these women's lives; instead, they recounted how women—despite their political, social, and gendered upbringing—risked more to dedicate themselves to Irish independence. Such a focus, though, promoted a value-laden scale, whereby the contributions of wealthy, Ascendancy ladies were worth more than the risks undertaken by laboring native men and women.

One example of the Milligan's approach to the valuation of women can be seen in her short biographical essay about Speranza, pen name of Lady Wilde, the Ascendancy patriot-poet and mother of Oscar Wilde. In this sketch, the author regrets that, given the confines of space, "justice [cannot be done] to the worth of Lady Wilde's poetry. . . . To-day the best we can do is to draw attention to her life, to the persistent and consistent course which she followed to the risks that she dared and to the matchless spirit which in a time of doubt, danger, and despair, she brought to the service of Ireland."[79] The choices made in this essay, however, are less a matter of space than a dependable strategy of the journal for recruiting readers to be writer-activists. Just as *Shan Van Vocht*'s readers learns how Lady Wilde first grew interested in Irish culture, so, too, they might recognize, as a young Speranza did, that "she had a country, that it had certain demands upon her, that it would be a crime to neglect the duties which Nature had placed upon her." As readers of the *Shan Van Vocht*, they also shared an important bond with Speranza, who subscribed to the premier nationalist journal of her day, the *Nation*, and who "studied its contents and learned something of the state of Ireland, and the causes responsible for its state." Implicitly, then, Speranza's life represented a positive and possible model of feminine activism, one that directly linked benign, cultural activities, such as reading nationalist journals, with direct action, such as speaking out at Fenian trials.

Although the *Shan Van Vocht* failed to promote gender equality in the overt fashion of later newspapers such as the *Irish Citizen*, it upheld a consistent ideal of feminine behavior as forthright, strong-willed, and politically committed. And although it implored women to show their nationalism in conventionally feminine ways, the domestic tools they were to use turned out to be effective forms of political resistance. Crossman has pointed out that the editors of the *Shan Van Vocht* aimed "to operate the magazine as a 'literary factor in the National cause,' " inspiring and educating at the same time.[80] Milligan's wealthy girls adapted this model of feminine nationalism, though their choices and actions were hardly passive. The lessons of Milligan's romances, which envisioned women's activism within domestic borders, transformed the genre and the ideals of bourgeois femininity at the same time. Unlike the revolutionaries Maud Gonne and Constance Markievicz, who left behind the comforts and the trappings into which they had been born, Milligan's romantic protagonists demonstrated how women could as plausibly espouse revolution from the Big House as from the tenement rows. That she left unexamined the class privileges assisting her protagonists in their national rebellions in no way negates the subversive elements in each girl's activism.

We can witness Milligan's proto-feminist lessons in two of her stories, "The Harp That Once—!" and "The Captain's Daughter."[81] Indeed, the first reveals her increasing willingness to parody and to critique the romance plot through dramatizing the undesirability of heterosexual union. In this narrative, Milligan wryly revises the well-known nationalist emblem of the weeping woman with a harp, a popular emblem of the United Irishmen, into an aristocratic activist who uses the customs of chivalry to her political advantage. Despite being an eminently marriageable granddaughter of her Ladyship the Dowager, Mabel possesses rebel blood that "had been warmed to flame in this year '98 by the stories she heard of the people's suffering."[82] Like the impudent Eibhlin of "The Outlaw's Bride," Mabel learns her nationalist lessons early in life from her Gaelic-speaking nurse, a familiar path for Protestant nationalists whose introduction to Irish nationalism was through enchanting stories and songs that their native nurse or governess taught them. In this anti-romance set in 1798 Dublin, Mabel plays the coquette in order to foil a British army captain, who is on his way to find and punish rebel United Irishmen. Joining forces with her nurse, Mrs. Kelly, whose son Denis was among those hiding on the outskirts of Dublin, Mabel sets out to detain Captain Warren while her nurse alerts the rebels to flee to safety. Beautiful, unmarried heiresses rarely have trouble entertaining eligible bachelors, but Mabel has her work cut out for her in the disciplined Captain Warren. Nonetheless, he finds he cannot deny Mabel's offer to play the harp for him. Of course, "he had not reckoned on the time a harp takes in tuning." Nor had he realized when a string, by chance, had popped, that "the fixing of a string was a more tedious process than the tuning." He will never forget, however, how long a simple parlor piece could take to finish, especially when the harpist insists on playing the refrain of an unfamiliar native ballad, "The Coolin," over and over again, in hopes, the narrator tells us, that "the enchanting melody would haunt his ears till death." As the captain squirms uneasily in his chair, he realizes too late what Mabel understood from the start: "it was not a very wise thing" to allow pretty young ladies to distract when raids are so close at hand. Though the captain won't admit it to himself, his men recognize the "mockery in her smile" and the "mischief in her eyes." And, of course, as they go to raid the rebel homes, they discover that none are to be found.[83]

In Milligan's most overtly feminist short story, "The Captain's Daughter," we can detect not only her initial flirtation with realist fiction, but also her early interest in narrating the lives of autonomous, activist girls. Serialized in the earliest issues of the *Shan Van Vocht*, from February to April 1896, "The Captain's Daughter" teaches its audience that feminine agency could also mean advocating sensible, not terrorist, activism by elaborating on one of Milligan's sternest editorials, which denounced "senseless violence," such as bombing buildings "without aim or reason other than mere desire of vengeance."[84] Both the editorial and the moral of her story share a solid Enlightenment foundation, groundwork established by Edmund Burke in his *Thoughts on the Cause of the Present Discontents* (1770), which was composed in the wake of perceived parliamentary corruption and the public disturbances caused by the Wilkes affair.[85] As Burke promoted the rational stewardship of land and sternly rebuked indiscriminate, emotional violence, Milligan's literary and editorial voice instructed readers in discerning, rational rebellion. A mock romance, "The Captain's Daughter" also generically deviates from many of the formal features of her earlier stories. The narrative lays bare and plainly mocks many of the conventions of the chivalric romance, from the bumbling "knight" Captain Moonlight to the daring damsel who foils the ineffectual men. The story also relies on recent events and real people, taking place during the 1888 Land Wars and modeling its protagonist, Millicent O'Brien, on Charlotte Grace O'Brien (1845–1905), whose father William Smith O'Brien helped to lead the abortive Young Ireland revolt in 1848.[86] Indeed, Millicent proves to be far more attentive to gunpowder than marriage plots.

The political project of Milligan's mock romance can be viewed best by setting it next to the popular Ascendancy novel she was surely seeking to revise, Mabel Morley's *Boycotted* (1889). In Morley's political novel, the narrative sought to incite outrage about agrarian violence by linking Fenian terror, embodied in "Captain Moonlight," with the threats of rape of Ascendancy ladies. Milligan's "The Captain's Daughter" shares many of the same plot features but importantly replaces the feminine helplessness in Morley's novel with Ascendancy agency. Like Morley's novel, its narrative is set during the Plan of Campaign, not in 1798; its action takes place in a rural area between Cork and Kerry, rather than in the urban landscape of Belfast or Dublin, in order to heighten female vulnerability, especially during moments of political conflict over land rights. These details prepare us immediately for a genre quite distant from the historical romances discussed earlier. Although another beautiful, pampered daughter of the upper class, Millicent O'Brien will prove to be quite a different model of bourgeois, feminine activism, someone closer to the New Women readers of the *Shan Van Vocht*. Through the example of her Gaelic-speaking nurse, Molly Breen, the young Millicent has learned to rebel from the "stern English disciplinarians" at her English boarding school by brandishing her rule-breaking tongue, an increasingly familiar weapon for New Women, as we will see in chapter 2. Millicent utters English when French was compulsory, German when French was required. In the corridors between lessons and at night in the dark, Millicent "smashed the rules into fragments" by speaking loudly and wildly of Irish myths and lore, Fenian history and heroic tales.[87]

As the story opens, Millicent has returned from England only to find her family estate about to be attacked by a band of "moonlight" rebels, who had hoped to obtain the captain's guns for some vague, future uprising. In her encounter with moonlight rebels, she is caught alone in her unattended house in the rural hinterland. Unlike the cowering female who fearfully encounters Captain Moonlight in Morley's novel, however, Millicent bravely faces the challenge of matching wits with real, live rebels. Yet, though her Irish heart sympathizes with the native men's goal of Irish independence, her Ascendancy mind resists giving them what they have come for. What she observes is not merely poor planning and unproven exigency:

> It wasn't anything in the way of a rising that was afoot in that winter season of eighty-eight, with a parliamentary agitation in full swing. . . . This wasn't Rory of the Hills and his brethren who stood below her on the frosty ground. . . . These were people whom she feared had no higher motive than a fierce one of vengeance against some poor wretch of a land-grabber. . . . The capture of arms, the deadly use of them, in this case meant nothing for Ireland; nothing but more desperate hate between class and class.[88]

Surprising the rebels, who had expected to find the home empty, Millicent ends up outwitting and then shaming the men for being "moonlighters." Refusing to give them her father's guns, yet swearing her silence, Millicent talks of politics and parliamentary strategy, revealing along the way that she, too, was a Fenian sympathizer. When one of the Moonlighters, Jim Shaugheny, exclaims, "Divil a wan, Miss, but why didn't ye tell us ye were that way av thinking' at the first. . . ? Shure who wud have looked for the like in the captain's daughter?" Millicent replies, "Ah, I see you don't know the Wexford song about the captain's daughter," and rewards the men with books rather than guns to prepare more intelligently for war.[89]

Like Robert Dwyer Joyce's ballad "The Boys of Wexford," to which she refers, Millicent prompts the men (and the *Shan Van Vocht* readers) to consider allies of the revolution in unexpected places. As Millicent challenges conventional wisdom about class and political sympathy, she also confronts her audience with the nature of feminine agency as well. In this and other attempts to recast the revolutionary, if passive, Mother Ireland as the conventional, if activist, coquette, Alice Milligan inevitably revised what it meant to be a nationalist in late-nineteenth-century Ireland.

Conclusions: The Demise of the *Shan Van Vocht*

Alice Milligan's fiction deepens and complicates many of our assumptions about gender, genre, and nationalism at the end of the nineteenth century. Repudiating the passive feminine emblems of Ireland, Milligan imagined feminine subversion through unexpected political agency. Challenging the standard approach to the Irish revival, which privileges two genres—poetry and drama—that were favored by its most effective propagandizer, William Butler Yeats, Milligan's innovations to the romance teach us that Irish popular fiction, like Irish modernism, was often a vibrant, intricate site for debates about nationalism. Reading Milligan's romances, we can discover that Milligan's alternate image of the nationalist Irish woman, the activist coquette, represents an enduring figure in Irish fiction. When placed alongside other memorable nationalist females, from Glorvina in Sydney Owenson's *Wild Irish Girl* (1806) to Millie Kinnard in Iris Murdoch's *The Red and the Green* (1965), Milligan's privileged heroines reveal how she was writing in an expressly feminist, as well as nationalist, tradition. Milligan's romances and mock romances articulated an overarching political project of the *Shan Van Vocht* to encourage women in nationalist activism, even as their unifying plots enabled her to bury or evade important questions about social or religious differences among nationalists, and among the Irish more broadly.

With the closing of the *Shan Van Vocht* in April of 1899 and its subsequent resurrection, in Dublin, under the newly masculinized name of the *United Irishman*, Milligan's proto-feminist message was quickly lost. Critics have argued that the journal folded because of financial insolvency, caused, in part, by the editors' conscientious avoidance of party or factional politics.[90] In the editorial of the final, April 1899 issue, Milligan pointedly blamed the *Shan Van Vocht*'s demise on "the unfortunate sectional policy which is shattering the forces of Ireland at present." As we will see in chapter 2, Arthur Griffith learned from such failure: his Dublin-based *United Irishman*, and its successor, *Sinn Féin*, depended heavily on financial supporters who condoned his journal's strong separatist approach to nationalist politics, an approach that sharply diverged from the scrupulously nonsectarian editorial voice of the *Shan Van Vocht*. By holding high the example of the United Irishmen of 1798 and by stressing the seemliness of peacemaking for Irish women, the *Shan Van Vocht* hoped to unify nationalists across region, class, sex, and religion and fuse them into a mass revolutionary movement. Sadly, there was little public support for such a hope. Nonetheless, the *Shan Van Vocht*'s political project and subsequent failure help account for the rhetorical strategies later used by female journalists engaged in the nationalist, feminist, and socialist movements of early-twentieth-century Ireland. In the end, the journal failed largely because of its unifying spirit, most apparent in the romances that filled its pages: romance across the borders might delight, but firm factionalism was what kept a journal in business. Although the stories and the very existence of the *Shan Van Vocht* testified to the agency and centrality of female activists in the nationalist campaigns of the 1890s, the journal's mollifying editorial and fictional counsel ensured its ultimate demise.

2

Voices for Erin

Maud Gonne, Inghinidhe na hÉireann, and the United Irishman

The Dublin-based weekly newspaper *United Irishman*, like the *Shan Van Vocht*, used its title to announce its political lineage and cultural aspirations. Drawing on the example of 1798 (as well as on John Mitchel's mid-nineteenth-century revolutionary weekly), the journal anticipated a broader movement that would use fresh cultural expressions and innovative social activities to help enliven and engage Irish men and women to act decisively for Irish political independence. Whereas its name alludes to a solitary male, the *United Irishman* owes its rhetorical and cultural strength less to the individual talents of its gifted editor, Arthur Griffith, than to his openness to a collaborative process that especially accommodated Irish women. Indeed, as this chapter will argue, the contributions of the journal's women writers, most notably its most prolific female commentator, Maud Gonne, are in large part responsible for its broader influence and more enduring success.

Literary critics and historians have often viewed Maud Gonne (1866–1953) as a beautiful inspiration or as a dangerous distraction, depending on their viewpoint, rather than as an activist, writer, or literary collaborator. Although her case is exceptional, Gonne's critical reputation suffers in a way that resembles the case of many women involved in Irish nationalism. Maria Luddy recently summarized what many feminist critics have been suggesting for over a decade: "Women, when associated with nationalist uprisings . . . are generally seen in symbolic terms and rarely acknowledged as playing an active role in the practical or theoretical formulations of these organisations."[1] In an effort to wrest Gonne from her usual symbolic role within Irish literary history, this chapter places her within the context of her activist and journalist peers. Such a process certainly alters our perception of Gonne, for we must reconsider her as an author, rather than as an object, of the Irish revival. Surprisingly, by examining Gonne's writings within the context of the advanced nationalist press, we also are confronted by the discovery of how collaboration proved to be an influential and generative model, both for the *United Irishman* and for a woman who is, still today, widely characterized as solipsistic and self-aggrandizing. By exploring women's writings in the *United Irishman*, we can thus view how such early, often tentative feminism in this fin de siècle newspaper suggested even more pronounced collaboration of the kind that is most frequently associated with the advanced feminist commentary featured in *Bean na hÉireann* (Woman of Ireland) and the *Irish Citizen*.

Cultural History of the *United Irishman*

In print from March 1899 to April 1906, the *United Irishman* rose phoenixlike out of the ashes of the *Shan Van Vocht*. Soon after Arthur Griffith and William Rooney formed their modest halfpenny weekly, Alice Milligan and Anna Johnston ceased publication of their Belfast monthly and forwarded their list of subscribers to the men in Dublin.[2] Very quickly, the *United Irishman* was recognized by its Irish readership to be one of the most significant nationalist newspapers of the day. R. M. Henry, in his 1920 study of Sinn Féin, praised the journal's "remarkable" editing, literary "excellence," and distinguished contributors, many of whom "were not (or did not remain) in sympathy with its political propaganda."[3] In her memoirs, Mary E. L. Butler quoted the editor of a "large English daily newspaper," who hungered to have Griffith on his staff because "he has the power of killing his adversaries with the point of his pen."[4] In the midst of the civil war (and a year after Griffith's sudden death from a cerebral hemorrhage in 1922), George A. Lyons emphasized the *United Irishman*'s "probity and dignity in public affairs." Griffith's political eloquence, in Lyons's mind, "ultimately dislodged the political mountebanks from their strongholds."[5] Also in 1923, James Stephens enthused that "the best poetry and literary criticism in the English language was written weekly by us in the *United Irishman*."[6] Even a political detractor such as Augustine Birrell, chief secretary of Ireland, acknowledged that Griffith was "an extraordinarily clever journalist."[7] Later scholars have also highlighted the cultural consequence of Griffith's writing and his journalistic enterprise in the *United Irishman*. Revisionist historian F. S. L. Lyons called the *United Irishman* "as potent a force as the *Nation* had been for contemporaries of Thomas Davis."[8] Ben Novick, in turn, described Griffith as the "supreme propagandist of the Irish revolution."[9]

William Rooney and Arthur Griffith established the newspaper the *United Irishman* in 1899, in the wake of the centenary of the United Irishmen Uprising. The 1798 centenary commemorative movement not only inspired the title and frequent topics contained in the new journal but also, as we have seen in chapter 1, developed a talented cadre of women to serve as voices for Erin. The movement sought to legitimate nationalism, to unite its various factions, and, through promoting women's visibility in politics, to foster the emergent feminist movement. Numerous nationalist women got their first experience as public activists when they traveled the country on public speaking tours, explaining the *United Irishman*'s "ideal of an independent Irish republic uniting all its people regardless of their religion."[10]

Like the *Shan Van Vocht*, the *United Irishman* promoted the Irish-Ireland movement, a diverse consortium of political and cultural organizations that repudiated Ireland's political union with Great Britain. Unlike groups such as Douglas Hyde's ostensibly apolitical Gaelic League, however, Griffith's journal promoted Ireland's literary revival only so long as it served the purpose of advancing Ireland's "absolute independence from foreign control."[11] Its editors did not advocate the methods of armed revolution, though many of the writers published in its pages did; instead, as R. M. Henry observes, the journal aimed "to build up a kind of national

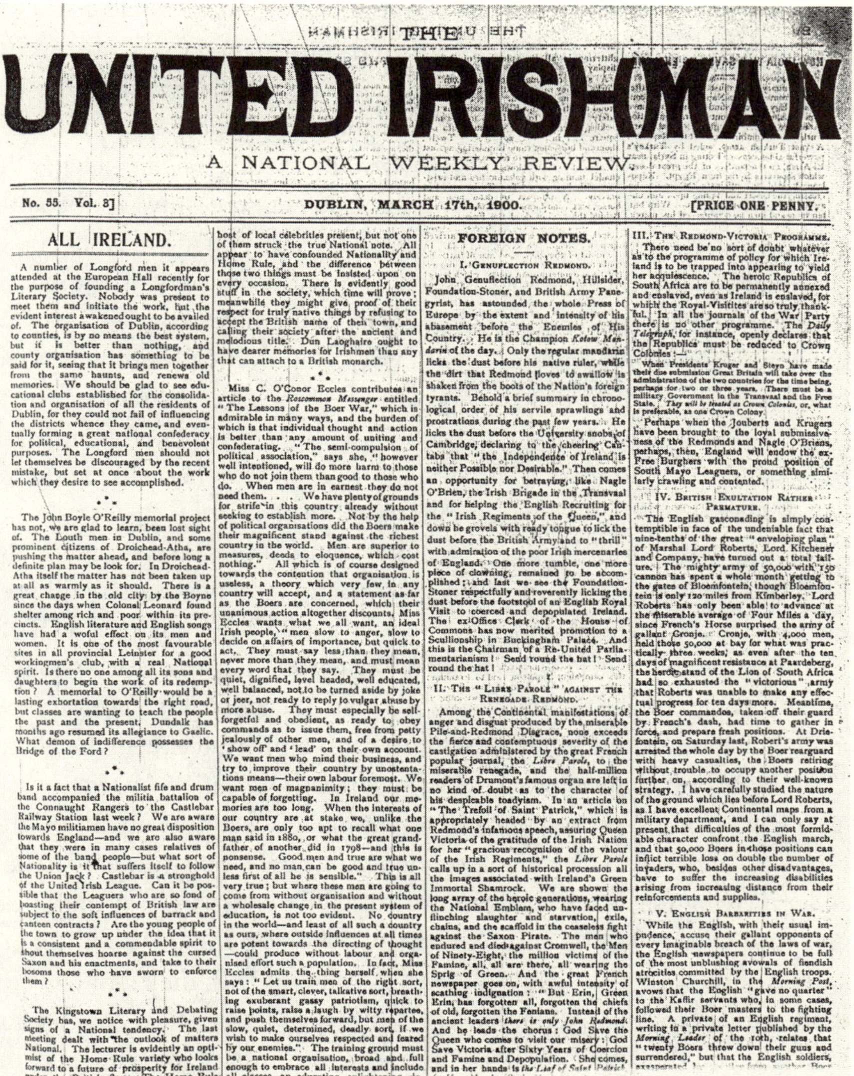

UNITED IRISHMAN

A NATIONAL WEEKLY REVIEW

No. 55. Vol. 3] DUBLIN, MARCH 17th, 1900. [PRICE ONE PENNY.

ALL IRELAND.

A number of Longford men it appears attended at the European Hall recently for the purpose of founding a Longfordman's Literary Society. Nobody was present to meet them and initiate the work, but the evident interest awakened ought to be availed of. The organisation of Dublin, according to counties, is by no means the best system, but it is better than nothing, and county organisation has something to be said for it, seeing that it brings men together from the same haunts, and renews old memories. We should be glad to see educational clubs established for the consolidation and organisation of all the residents of Dublin, for they could not fail of influencing the districts whence they came, and eventually forming a great national confederacy for political, educational, and benevolent purposes. The Longford men should not let themselves be discouraged by the recent mistake, but set at once about the work which they desire to see accomplished.

* * *

The John Boyle O'Reilly memorial project has not, we are glad to learn, been lost sight of. The Louth men in Dublin, and some prominent citizens of Droichead-Atha, are pushing the matter ahead, and before long a definite plan may be look for. In Droichead-Atha itself the matter has not been taken up at all as warmly as it should. There is a great change in the old city by the Boyne since the days when Colonel Leonard found shelter among rich and poor within its precincts. English literature and English songs have had a woful effect on its men and women. It is one of the most favourable sites in all provincial Leinster for a good workingmen's club, with a real National spirit. Is there no one among all its sons and daughters to begin the work of its redemption? A memorial to O'Reilly would be a lasting exhortation towards the right road, but classes are wanting to teach the people the past and the present. Dundalk has months ago resumed its allegiance to Gaelic. What demon of indifference possesses the Bridge of the Ford?

* * *

Is it a fact that a Nationalist fife and drum band accompanied the militia battalion of the Connaught Rangers to the Castlebar Railway Station last week? We are aware the Mayo militiamen have no great disposition towards England—and we are also aware that they were in many cases relatives of some of the band people—but what sort of Nationality is it that suffers itself to follow the Union Jack? Castlebar is a stronghold of the United Irish League. Can it be possible that the Leaguers who are so fond of boasting their contempt of British law are subject to the soft influences of barrack and canteen contracts? Are the young people of the town to grow up under the idea that it is a consistent and a commendable spirit to shout themselves hoarse against the cursed Saxon and his enactments, and take to their bosoms those who have sworn to enforce them?

* * *

The Kingstown Literary and Debating Society has, we notice with pleasure, given signs of a National tendency. The last meeting dealt with the outlook of matters National. The lecturer is evidently an optimist of the Home Rule variety who looks forward to a future of prosperity for Ireland under the British flag. The Home Rule idea cannot for any length of time delude [illegible] host of local celebrities present, but not one of them struck the true National note. All appear to have confounded Nationality and Home Rule, and the difference between those two things must be insisted upon on every occasion. There is evidently good stuff in the society, which time will prove; meanwhile they might give proof of their respect for truly native things by refusing to accept the British name of their town, and calling their society after the ancient and melodious title. Dun Laoghaire ought to have dearer memories for Irishmen than any that can attach to a British monarch.

* * *

Miss C. O'Conor Eccles contributes an article to the *Roscommon Messenger* entitled "The Lessons of the Boer War," which is admirable in many ways, and the burden of which is that individual thought and action is better than any amount of uniting and confederating. "The semi-compulsion of political association," says she, "however well intentioned, will do more harm to those who do not join them than good to those who do. When men are in earnest they do not need them. . . . We have plenty of grounds for strife in this country already without seeking to establish more. Not by the help of political organisations did the Boers make their magnificent stand against the richest country in the world. Men are superior to measures, deeds to eloquence, which cost nothing." All which is of course designed towards the contention that organisation is useless, a theory which very few in any country will accept, and a statement as far as the Boers are concerned, which their unanimous action altogether discounts. Miss Eccles wants what we all want, an ideal Irish people, "men slow to anger, slow to decide on affairs of importance, but quick to act. They must say less than they mean, never more than they mean, and must mean every word that they say. They must be quiet, dignified, level headed, well educated, well balanced, not to be turned aside by joke or jeer, not ready to reply to vulgar abuse by more abuse. They must especially be self-forgetful and obedient, as ready to obey commands as to issue them, free from petty jealously of other men, and of a desire to 'show off' and 'lead' on their own account. We want men who mind their business, and try to improve their country by unostentations means—their own labour foremost. We want men of magnanimity; they must be capable of forgetting. In Ireland our memories are too long. When the interests of our country are at stake we, unlike the Boers, are only too apt to recall what one man said in 1880, or what the great grandfather of another did in 1798—and this is nonsense. Good men and true are what we need, and no man can be good and true unless first of all he is sensible." This is all very true; but where these men are going to come from without organisation and without a wholesale change in the present system of education, is not too evident. No country in the world—and least of all such a country as ours, where outside influences at all times are potent towards the directing of thought—could produce without labour and organised effort such a population. In fact, Miss Eccles admits the thing herself, when she says: "Let us train men of the right sort, not of the smart, clever, talkative sort, breathing exuberant gassy patriotism, quick to raise points, raise a laugh by witty repartee, and push themselves forward, but men of the slow, quiet, determined, deadly sort, if we wish to make ourselves respected and feared by our enemies." The training ground must be a national organisation, broad and full enough to embrace all interests and include all classes, an educating, enlightening, de- [illegible]

FOREIGN NOTES.

I. Genuflection Redmond.

John Genuflection Redmond, Hillsider, Foundation-Stoner, and British Army Panegyrist, has astounded the whole Press of Europe by the extent and intensity of his abasement before the Enemies of His Country. He is the Champion *Kotow Mandarin* of the day. Only the regular mandarin licks the dust before his native ruler, while the dirt that Redmond loves to swallow is shaken from the boots of the Nation's foreign tyrants. Behold a brief summary in chronological order of his servile sprawlings and prostrations during the past few years. He licks the dust before the University snobs of Cambridge, declaring to the cheering Cantabs that "the Independence of Ireland is neither Possible nor Desirable." Then comes an opportunity for betraying, like Nagle O'Brien, the Irish Brigade in the Transvaal and for helping the English Recruiting for the "Irish Regiments of the Queen," and down he grovels with ready tongue to lick the dust before the British Army and to "thrill" with admiration of the poor Irish mercenaries of England. One more tumble, one more piece of clowning, remained to be accomplished; and last we see the Foundation-Stoner respectfully and reverently licking the dust before the footstool of an English Royal Visit to coerced and depopulated Ireland. The ex-Office Clerk of the House of Commons has now merited promotion to a Scullionship in Buckingham Palace. And this is the Chairman of a Re-United Parliamentarianism! Send round the hat! Send round the hat!

II. The "Libre Parole" against the Renegade Redmond.

Among the Continental manifestations of anger and disgust produced by the miserable Pile-and-Redmond Disgrace, none exceeds the fierce and contemptuous severity of the castigation administered by the great French popular journal, the *Libre Parole*, to the miserable renegade, and the half-million readers of Drumont's famous organ are left in no kind of doubt as to the character of his despicable toadyism. In an article on "The Trefoil of Saint Patrick," which is appropriately headed by an extract from Redmond's infamous speech, assuring Queen Victoria of the gratitude of the Irish Nation for her "gracious recognition of the valour of the Irish Regiments," the *Libre Parole* calls up in a sort of historical procession all the images associated with Ireland's Green Immortal Shamrock. We are shown the long array of the heroic generations, wearing the National Emblem, who have faced unflinching slaughter and starvation, exile, chains, and the scaffold in the ceaseless fight against the Saxon Pirate. The men who endured and died against Cromwell, the Men of Ninety-Eight, the million victims of the Famine, all, all are there, all wearing the Sprig of Green. And the great French newspaper goes on, with awful intensity of scathing indignation: "But Erin, Green Erin, has forgotten all, forgotten the chiefs of old, forgotten the Fenians. Instead of the ancient leaders *there is only John Redmond*. And he leads the chorus: God Save the Queen who comes to visit our misery: God Save Victoria after Sixty Years of Coercion and Famine and Depopulation. She comes, and in her hands is *the Leaf of Saint Patrick* [illegible]

III. The Redmond-Victoria Programme.

There need be no sort of doubt whatever as to the programme of policy for which Ireland is to be trapped into appearing to yield her acquiescence. The heroic Republics of South Africa are to be permanently annexed and enslaved, even as Ireland is enslaved, for which the Royal-Visitites are so truly thankful. In all the journals of the War Party there is no other programme. The *Daily Telegraph*, for instance, openly declares that the Republics must be reduced to Crown Colonies:—

> When Presidents Kruger and Steyn have made their due submission Great Britain will take over the administration of the two countries for the time being, perhaps for two or three years. There must be a military Government in the Transvaal and the Free State. *They will be treated as Crown Colonies*, or, what is preferable, as one Crown Colony.

Perhaps when the Jouberts and Krugers have been brought to the loyal submissiveness of the Redmonds and Nagle O'Briens, perhaps, then, England will endow the ex-Free Burghers with the proud position of South Mayo Leaguers, or something similarly crawling and contented.

IV. British Exultation Rather Premature.

The English gasconading is simply contemptible in face of the undeniable fact that nine-tenths of the great "enveloping plan" of Marshal Lord Roberts, Lord Kitchener and Company, have turned out a total failure. The mighty army of 50,000 with 150 cannon has spent a whole month getting to the gates of Bloemfontein, though Bloemfontein is only 120 miles from Kimberley. Lord Roberts has only been able to advance at the miserable average of Four Miles a day, since French's Horse surprised the army of gallant Cronje. Cronje, with 4,000 men, held those 50,000 at bay for what was practically three weeks, as even after the ten days of magnificent resistance at Paardeberg, the heroic stand of the Lion of South Africa had so exhausted the "victorious" army that Roberts was unable to make any effectual progress for ten days more. Meantime, the Boer commandos, taken off their guard by French's dash, had time to gather in force, and prepare fresh positions. At Driefontein, on Saturday last, Robert's army was arrested the whole day by the Boer rearguard with heavy casualties, the Boers retiring without trouble to occupy another position further on, according to their well-known strategy. I have carefully studied the nature of the ground which lies before Lord Roberts, as I have excellent Continental maps from a military department, and I can only say at present that difficulties of the most formidable character confront the English march, and that 50,000 Boers in those positions can inflict terrible loss on double the number of invaders, who, besides other disadvantages, have to suffer the increasing disabilities arising from increasing distance from their reinforcements and supplies.

V. English Barbarities in War.

While the English, with their usual impudence, accuse their gallant opponents of every imaginable breach of the laws of war, the English newspapers continue to be full of the most unblushing avowals of fiendish atrocities committed by the English troops. Winston Churchill, in the *Morning Post*, avows that the English "gave no quarter" to the Kaffir servants who, in some cases, followed their Boer masters to the fighting line. A private of an English regiment, writing in a private letter published by the *Morning Leader* of the 10th, relates that "twenty Boers threw down their guns and surrendered," but that the English soldiers, exasperated [illegible]

2. Front page of *United Irishman*, March 17, 1900. The *United Irishman* communicated the privileging of politics over art with its first page format. Notice, in particular, its spare masthead, lack of imagery or illustrations, and four columns of prose in very small font. Reproduced courtesy of the National Library of Ireland.

forum in which all 'real' Nationalists might have their say."[12] The guiding principle of the *United Irishman* was separatist nationalism, advocating Irish self-reliance and patriotism.[13] Early on, Griffith emphatically distanced the journal's editorial policy from the political philosophy of Home Rulers. Whereas the Home Ruler, in Griffith's words, "acknowledges the right of England to govern this country," demanding only "facilities for purely local Irish matters in Ireland," the *United Irishman*'s ideal nationalist "totally rejects the claim of England or any other country to rule over or interfere with the destinies of Ireland."[14] Even the advertisements revealed the newspaper's philosophy of economic autonomy: nearly every item featured—cradles, corsets, cigarettes, crucifixes—were "guaranteed Irish-made." Like the gendered subtext of Alice Milligan's short fiction, many of the ads encouraged readers to consider domestic, traditionally feminine activities such as household shopping as political action.

A year after Griffith penned his first editorial proclaiming the ambitions of a new generation of advanced nationalists, a new nationalist society and cover organization for the Irish Republican Brotherhood (IRB), Cumann na nGaedheal (League of the Gaels) emerged, expressly to promote the causes most frequently discussed in the pages of the *United Irishman*. As Maud Gonne, one of the founding members, recalled, the aim of Cumann na nGaedheal was "to link up all existing National societies into an open Separatist movement."[15] Cumann na nGaedheal members thus promoted the cause of Irish independence through as many means as possible: reviving Gaelic culture, training Ireland's youth in Irish sports, developing and promoting Irish industries. Still, even though both Rooney and Griffith were members of the secret, militant IRB, the editorial voice of the *United Irishman* did not preach immediate revolution. Instead, following *Shan Van Vocht*'s editorial and fictional counsel, the editors of the *United Irishman* acknowledged that, though war was the necessary precursor to Irish freedom, their readers needed first to providently prepare for that eventuality.

As the *United Irishman* developed over time, its editorial voice more faithfully reflected the pragmatic political philosophy of Arthur Griffith (1872–1922), who after the death of Rooney in 1901, took over full editorial duties. Although Griffith remained committed to Ireland's independence, he frequently advanced moderate means to achieve it. Characteristic of his belief that Ireland needed to advance to independence by careful steps, not reckless leaps, was Griffith's "Hungarian policy."[16] In "The Example of Hungary," first published in the *United Irishman* and later reissued in pamphlet form as *The Resurrection of Hungary*, Griffith suggested that Irish members of Parliament resign en masse, as Hungarian deputies had done from the imperial Austrian parliament in the 1860s, creating a "dual monarchy," based in both London and Dublin. Such a proposition had as its final ambition an independent Irish state, but without the radical transformations in Irish society that militant republicans, socialists, and feminists envisioned.[17] His role in the Sinn Féin movement, which Griffith launched in 1905, provides another illustration of Griffith's careful political positioning. Sinn Féin functioned initially as an umbrella for several Irish separatist nationalist organizations—Cumann na nGaedheal, the National Council, and Dungannon Clubs—that promoted Griffith's idea of abstention from Westminster. Griffith's political vision of a British government painted green—complete with a king, House of Lords, and House of Commons—had far less influence on the movement, however. Virginia Glandon argues that this was in part due to Griffith's personal "reluctance" to assume full leadership responsibilities in the Sinn Féin administration, a reluctance, Glandon adds, "which he demonstrated throughout the greater part of his career" because he doubted he possessed the charisma to lead a national movement.[18]

If Griffith lacked a dynamic presence on the dais, he effectively employed his talents as a journalist: the *United Irishman* extended its political sway well beyond Ireland's thirty-two counties. Two series written by Griffith, "The Resurrection of Hungary" and "The Working Policy," were reissued as pamphlets; *Resurrection* was translated into several Indian languages and sold over 3,000 copies. Indeed, Mahatma Gandhi explained that he found Griffith's proposals valuable in planning nonviolent noncooperation *(satyagraha)* in India.[19] The *United Irishman* was surely not, as nationalist historian Francis Jones claims, one of the most widely read papers in Ireland;[20] instead, its influence was felt because its writers and readers were many of the same writers and activists who would shape the literary and political future of the country in the twentieth century. The *United Irishman* sent out weekly subscription copies to Anna Johnston, Alice Milligan, Maud Gonne, John O'Leary, and James Connolly; many members of the Gaelic League and the Irish Republican Brotherhood also read and publicly supported the newspaper.[21] Initially relying on '98 clubs to promote its sales, the newspaper later attracted a notable list of contributors: William Butler Yeats, J. B. Yeats, John Millington Synge, Oliver Saint John Gogarty, Frank Fay, George Moore, John Eglington, Edward Martyn, Éamon Ceannt, Michael Davitt, John O'Leary, James Connolly, Seumas MacManus, Anna Johnston (Ethna Carbery), Alice Milligan, Maud Gonne, Nora Hopper, Jennie Wyse-Power, May Curran, and Mary E. L. Butler. Although Griffith and Rooney wrote most of the copy, using numerous pseudonyms to disguise how much of the weekly was penned by only two men, they counted on public figures in the myriad cultural and political movements active in Dublin to contribute poems, plays, and reviews; to discuss and to develop a new Irish literary style; and to debate nationalist politics.

Gender in the Discourse of Nationalism in the *United Irishman*

From its inception to the present, the *United Irishman* has received scholarly attention, though few critics have commented on the extent to which women's writings and women's concerns were showcased in its pages. When historian Margaret Ward published her feminist study *Unmanageable Revolutionaries* in 1983, few contemporary scholars knew about the political work of the Ladies' Land League or the nationalist cultural projects of Inghinidhe na hÉireann (Daughters of Ireland). The *United Irishman* assisted Ward's study in two different respects: by featuring commentators who sought to narrate the eighteenth- and nineteenth-century history of women and nationalism and by modeling the kind of feminist recovery that Ward's historical study would later join. The weekly journal recorded the ongoing cultural and political activities of organizations led by women, such as the Irish Transvaal Committee, an anti-enlistment organization founded in 1899, in the wake of Britain's Boer War, by Maud Gonne and Anna Johnston, among others. It offered weekly minutes of the Patriotic Children's Treat Committee, a "ladies' committee" designed to provide a free treat to Dublin children who had refused to attend a celebration honoring Queen Victoria during her 1900 visit to Ireland. Having successfully fed and entertained 30,000 Dublin children with nationalist songs, stories, and speeches, the ladies disbanded their committee in July of that year to launch Ireland's first nationalist organization for women: Inghinidhe na hÉireann (Daughters of Ireland). Thus Griffith's weekly served as a valuable archive that Ward and other historians would study in assessing the political and cultural atmosphere of Dublin at the fin de siècle.

Best known as a nationalist-separatist weekly newspaper, the *United Irishman* in effect served as a nationalist women's studies primer. Building on the quiet feminism of the *Shan Van Vocht*, the *United Irishman* highlighted Irish women's history and culture, though commentators varied widely in their selection and interpretation of what sorts of women and action deserved the attention of its readers. The newspaper discussed the literary, historical, and political contributions of nationalist women from the past and present; it provided reviews and commentaries about female artists; it featured poems and plays written by women; and it included numerous opinion pieces, features, and weekly columns by female journalists.[22] It also alerted its readers to the nationalist writings of women featured in other newspapers.

The *United Irishman* lacked the multivoiced nationalism of Inghinidhe na hÉireann's *Bean na hÉireann* (Woman of Ireland; 1908–11), whose nationalist writers were strongly sympathetic to labor and feminism; its gender analysis certainly fell short of the forthrightly militant suffragist monthly the *Irish Citizen* (1912–20), each of which is discussed in greater detail in chapters 3 and 5. Examining the weekly in light of the late-twentieth-century debates about nationalism among Irish feminists, though, one cannot help but be struck by the *United Irishman*'s exuberant response to women's involvement in the nationalist activities of fin de siècle Dublin.[23] Indeed, the *United Irishman* disproves a familiar feminist criticism of Irish nationalism as a movement of failed potential: it documents how the feminist, socialist, and nationalist movements drew strength from each other. Women such as Maud Gonne, Constance Markievicz, Nora Connolly, Barry Delaney, Kathleen Clarke, Alice Milligan, Ella Young, Anna Johnston, Mary E. L. Butler, May Curran, and Hanna Sheehy Skeffington wrote for the journal and were avidly discussed as autonomous participants in cultural and political affairs of the day.

Though certainly not all of its commentary was nourished by the kind of feminist sensibility that would characterize the philosophy and writings of Irish feminism's fiercest champion, Hanna Sheehy Skeffington, the *United Irishman* focused increasing attention on women as readers, writers, and activists. Mary E. L. Butler, for example, wrote the four-part series "Womanhood and Nationhood," which promoted a conservative vision of gender roles in the "Nationalisation of the Irish homelife."[24] Repeating many of the key points made in her Gaelic League pamphlet *Irishwomen and the Home Language*, Butler's series aimed to attract previously apolitical women to the cause of Ireland, "to enlist the aid of the home-maker as a nation-maker."[25] She sought to reassure women that they need not "mount a platform" or even leave the home to help "make the homes of Ireland Irish." In another column, "Irishwomen's Work," Butler rejected the feminist stridency of suffragettes who "clamour[] for 'Rights' " and "ape [men's] fashions." Instead, Butler implored women to use their influence as mothers, sisters, wives, and maidens to "work well for Ireland, each in your own sphere."[26] Although, just a decade later, such commentary would exemplify the opposition for activist women such as Constance Markievicz and Hanna Sheehy Skeffington, at the turn of the century, Butler's insistence that Irish nationalism need not draw women outside of their domestic sphere represented a positive step for Irish women inclined to take an interest in their nation's march toward independence.

Maud Gonne also concentrated many of her articles on women's life within the domestic sphere, though, as this chapter will argue, her strategic essentialism served more as a stepping-stone to broader activism of the kind that Butler deplored. In this way, Gonne's early writings about gender roles paralleled Griffith's nationalist editorials proposing the example of Hungary. Both Gonne and Griffith, in other words, used their journalism to build a base of devoted Irish patriots who, they hoped, would be prepared, down the road, for more extreme activism. Drawing on the "old prophecy which says that Ireland will be saved by the women," Gonne revised Irish myth and lore to help women discover their potential as wives and mothers, and later as activist sisters, in revolutionizing politics and society.[27] Like Butler's columns, which accepted the middle-class expectations of women as primary inculcators of children's spiritual and moral values, Gonne's column encouraged Irish mothers to be activists within the home by teaching their children nationalist politics: to "*know* as well as *love* Ireland . . . her history, her language and her literature" in order "to serve [Ireland] intelligently."[28] Gonne's commentary assumed traditional roles for women, as did many female writers of advanced nationalism, such as Delia Larkin, whose writings are examined further in chapter 4. Gonne's acceptance of sexual difference, however, shared the values of many nineteenth- and early-twentieth-century feminists who drew on and developed such ideas of difference for the cause of woman's emancipation. As we will later discover in chapter 5, Butler's and Gonne's rhetorical strategy, in reminding women that because they "make the home atmosphere . . . women are the chief nation-builders," shares a similar warrant with many suffragists who proclaimed that women's scrupulous housekeeping predicted their proficiency in Parliament.

Other articles in the *United Irishman* were considerably more forthright in advocating public and independent-minded activism for women. One weekly column glowingly described the political action and poetry of the women of the Young Ireland movement, offering more details and literary excerpts one hundred years ago than the initial three-volume *Field Day Anthology of Irish Writing* (1991) contained.[29] Two others focused in particular on women's contributions to economic nationalism.[30] The populist, propagandistic goals of the newspaper meant that art was submitted to political judgment, as D. E. S. Maxwell observes.[31] The sustained interest in topics about women and the ubiquity of female writers in its pages strongly suggest that the values of emerging feminism—promoting women as equal (if sometimes separate) participants in political activism—were beginning to influence the broader nationalist movement.

Even though the emergent women's movement in Ireland had achieved important advances in education and economic autonomy, most openly political nationalist organizations of the day barred women from membership. As Maud Gonne later recalled in her autobiography, *A Servant of the Queen* (1938), "None of the parties in [1890s] Ireland want women; the National League, the Fenians, the Celtic Literary Society, the Contemporary Club, have all refused me membership because they accept no women members."[32] Whereas the British feminist movement at this time was a visible political force and mobilized around a host of issues, such as the campaign against the Contagious Diseases Act, the Social Purity Crusade, the Married Women's Property Acts, the militant suffrage crusades, and working women's struggle for decent working conditions, Ireland in 1899 had few women's organizations expressly created in order to fight for the emancipation of the female sex as a whole. Irish and British feminists initially shared many of the same political concerns; over time, though, the two groups began to diverge and develop differently in their campaigns for employment, education, and the vote.[33] As the suffrage movement was slowly gathering pace, a growing number of women gained admittance to higher education. By the early 1890s, both Catholic and Protestant middle-class women had access to (though not equal standing in) higher education as a result of the 1878 Intermediate Education Act and 1879 Royal University Act. Many middle-class women could also claim greater economic autonomy as a result of the Married Women's Property Acts of 1870, 1874, and 1882. By the turn of the century, women could sit on Poor Law Boards and Local Government Councils, two important opportunities that prepared Irish women for full political participation. The centenary commemorative movement also proved instrumental in providing a whole new generation of women the opportunity to master public speaking and political discourse. As Cliona Murphy points out, these gradual advances, which enabled Irish society to "grow accustomed to the idea of women in public life," served as the critical steps for feminist activism in early-twentieth-century Ireland.[34]

The promotion of women in the pages of the *United Irishman* undoubtedly owes much to the flourishing cultural movements that increasingly admitted women to Dublin's cultural societies in the 1890s. The Gaelic League, founded in 1893, and the Irish National Theatre, established in 1897, conspicuously included women among its members and founders. When Inghinidhe na hÉireann was established in the fall of 1900 after the success of its Patriotic Children's Treat Committee, the *United Irishman* prominently published announcements of meetings, the minutes to same, and even summaries of lectures; it also printed the society's objectives, rules, and membership lists. The *United Irishman*'s committed interest in Inghinidhe's activities may, in part, explain why feminine collaboration figured so largely in the weekly.[35] Initially established to give women a forum for nationalist activities, Inghinidhe soon developed a budding feminist agenda as well. Evening lectures and entertainment, such as *tableaux vivants,* often focused on powerful, self-reliant women of the past such as Brigid, Maeve, Anne Devlin, Grania Mhaol, Sarah Curran, and Ihghean Dubh. In less than a decade, as we will discover in chapter 3, Inghinidhe's monthly journal, *Bean na hÉireann* (Woman of Ireland), made more explicit the organization's urgent debates about the relationship between nationalism and feminism.

Unquestionably, the growing acceptance of political women, in large part achieved because of women's activism on a number of related fronts, helped create an environment where male advanced nationalists were receptive to women's equal participation. The editorship of Arthur Griffith may also have played a part. Although several biographers suggest he behaved with shyness and chivalry toward the "fairer sex," Arthur Griffith wrote frequently in both the *United Irishman* and *Bean na hÉireann* (here under the under the pseudonym "Ier") about women as "intellectual comrades and helpers in various concerns of public life . . . in morals, no stronger and no weaker in the main than men, and worthy of frank, full confidence and trust, and of the highest and best education."[36] Griffith's promotion of female equality may have been influenced by one particular woman with whom he worked closely during the years he edited the *United Irishman:* Maud Gonne. From 1899 to 1901, Griffith collaborated with William Rooney in writing and editing the newspaper. When Rooney died suddenly in May 1901, Griffith was left without a partner in a political-intellectual venture he always viewed as collaborative.[37]

Maud Gonne may have served as the indispensable figure whose philosophy, writings, activism, and political-social network helped broaden Griffith's perspective on women and workers. In 1899, the year before Rooney's death, the *United Irishman* published eight articles, in addition to Gonne's six, written by or directly addressing women. Meanwhile, Gonne was spending less time writing and editing her Parisian monthly *L'Irlande Libre*. Instead, she was submitting columns to the *United Irishman* and other nationalist newspapers, as well as serving as a liaison between Griffith and other important nationalists such as John O'Leary, William Butler Yeats, Michael Davitt, and James Connolly.[38] Margaret Ward and Antoinette Quinn suggest that during the weekly's initial years, Gonne functioned less as a writer than as a financial supporter of the *United Irishman*, her contributions ensuring that the newspaper publicized her activism and the projects of Inghinidhe.[39] At this time, Gonne did pay Griffith an editorial subvention of twenty-five shillings a week, and her fund-raising in the United States certainly helped keep the newspaper afloat. Yet a mere catalogue of articles by or about women tells a slightly different story. Over the course of the first three years of the journal's existence, articles authored by or focused on women increased almost sixfold in number.[40] Thus it is more likely that the newspaper's frequent reportage of Gonne's speeches, lecture tours, and political organizing was due less to her financing of the paper than to Gonne's persistent predilection to unite all of her many nationalist projects.

Collaborative Example of Maud Gonne

In her autobiography, Maud Gonne neatly summarized her working philosophy: "I never willingly discouraged either a Dynamiter or a constitutionalist, a realist or a lyrical writer. My chief preoccupation was how their work could help forward the Irish Separatist movement."[41] As a close friend of Arthur Griffith, and one who brought him in contact with nationalists as diverse as Connolly and Yeats, Milligan and Butler, Gonne may have simply, naturally introduced Griffith to another untapped resource vital to the Irish cause: women. Patrick Colum remarked that, by 1904, when Gonne began to remove herself from nationalist politics because of her divorce from nationalist hero John MacBride, Griffith lost a contact who enabled and embodied collaboration, "a certain largeness" that broadened and enriched Griffith's political and intellectual perspectives:

> Maud Gonne's marriage had removed not only an inspiring figure, not only one who brought something of the great world to him, but one who had kept him close to notable people. . . . The group of intellectuals whom he had mingled with at Maud Gonne's reunions in Nassau Street were dispersed or were no longer on good terms with him.[42]

Indeed, in 1905, a year into Gonne's absence from Dublin politics, at least one faithful reader of the *United Irishman* expressed dismay at the weekly's decreasing focus on political columns directed at women readers; implicitly registering frustration at advanced nationalist journals' low estimation of its female readership, the writer sarcastically lobbied for a women's nationalist journal that would be "frankly and fully national, brightly and not too solidly written [with] fashion articles which I suppose would be its strong point—indispensable for the capture of the female seoinini."[43] Not until 1909, when Helena Molony established *Bean na hÉireann*, with strong support from Maud Gonne, did nationalist women mobilize to produce a newspaper for women, founded, as Molony later remarked, expressly to "counteract" the conservative nationalist views of Griffith, as promulgated in the *United Irishman* and its successor, *Sinn Féin*.[44] From the perspective of some members of Inghinidhe na hÉireann, in serving Griffith's national agenda, his socially conservative views about women and the working class, and his proposed pathway to Irish independence through the dual-kingdom model of nineteenth-century Hungary, neither of these journals sufficiently attended to the demands of the Irish feminist and socialist movements.

That Gonne was both a famous beauty who inspired and infatuated numerous men and a secretly unwed mother in Catholic Ireland sharply influenced the poetics of her nationalist discourse. As I have argued elsewhere, Gonne's journalism of the 1890s suggests that she identified strongly with the sorrows of many of the impoverished women she met on her fact-finding missions.[45] For much of her journalistic career, Gonne in fact was struggling with a central challenge for women writing in the Irish nationalist tradition: she could never decide whether she was speaking *as* or *for* Ireland.[46] Gonne used many different strategies in her attempts to attract readers, inspire activism, and remedy what she perceived to be injustices. Critics have been quick to pick up on her self-aggrandizing moments—in her letters to Yeats, in her autobiography, and in her public performance as Cathleen ni Houlihan, for example—and to use these to discredit Gonne's political discourse. Although these moments are significant,[47] this chapter intends to explore another, little commented on dimension of Gonne's career as a nationalist: her collaborations with women.

In recent scholarly work on the subject of collaboration, literary critics have charted a new set of maps for understanding the creative process. From Jack Stillinger, who influentially challenged the myth of solitary genius, to Wayne Koestenbaum, who emphasized that literary partnerships were often covert eroticized "double-talk," we can now recognize that the literary process is rarely a solitary venture, and these hidden alliances were frequently valued by the participating writers for the subversive potential of using and undercutting conventional expectations, whether about gender, sexuality, or national identity.[48] Such collaborative authorship is certainly evident in the drafting and production of Milligan and Johnston's *Shan Van Vocht*. This modest literary magazine, as we have seen, had wide-reaching influence for Irish nationalists of the 1890s; such a two-woman collaborative venture may have additionally served as a inspiring model for the women who only a few years later founded Inghinidhe na hÉireann. Milligan and Johnston were founder-members of Inghinidhe. Many other members subscribed to the *Shan*; indeed, Maud Gonne publicly remarked on how she treasured the journal, reading it well after it had gone out of circulation.[49]

In her recent study on feminine collaboration, Holly Laird traces a fusion model of feminine collaboration that, though often uncritically celebratory, proves useful in examining the generative political and cultural work of Maud Gonne and her sisters in Inghinidhe na hÉireann. Exploring how feminist collaborators frequently employed the group assembly as a place for dialogue and exchange, Laird remarks, "For feminist collaborators, what is notable . . . is the room it creates for them to talk together."[50] As Ward's history of Inghinidhe na hÉireann discloses, the fifteen women who came together in the rooms of the Celtic Literary Society after Easter Mass in 1900 began their groundbreaking political organizing with idle girl talk about a gift for a man (Arthur Griffith, who had broken his African sjambok in defense of Maud Gonne's nationalist virtue) and anticolonial fashion (black and khaki clothing to demonstrate alliance with the Boers in their war with Britain).[51] The monthly reports in the *United Irishman* disseminated to a wider audience how this nationalist women's collaboration involved "very hard work to be gone through, which would take a great deal of time."[52] Based on the wide-ranging views about women and nationalism that were published in the *United Irishman*, some of this "hard work" undoubtedly involved disputes and disagreements about women's role in the anticolonial struggle.

Inghinidhe's dedicated space also afforded nationalist women a previously unknown opportunity to draw together as women and as nationalists to devise their own creative responses to British colonialism. One of the particular strengths of this collaborative, creative exchange lay in Inghinidhe's ability to attract women from diverse backgrounds: journalists Anna Johnston and Alice Milligan, actresses Maire Quinn, Molly Walker (later Maire nic Shiubhlaigh), Sara Allgood, and Maire O'Neill, teacher Sinead O'Flanagan, and professors Mary Macken and Hanna Sheehy (later Sheehy Skeffington) were some of the "working girls" who established Inghinidhe in the inaugural meeting in October of 1900. Like the textual exchanges and literary partnerships studied by Laird, this sisterhood of Irish nationalists collectively constructed a rigorous policy regarding membership that emphasized common concerns and shared allegiances: candidates had to make a serious commitment, submit to a public vetting process, and adopt a new Gaelic persona to join. Once in the sisterhood, members of Inghinidhe met regularly, planned creatively, and learned from each other how to develop their own and other women's abilities to talk, write, and act privately and publicly about Ireland's national future. The opening lecture delivered at Inghinidhe's first ceilidhe, later reprinted in the *United Irishman*, discloses some of the character of this women's collaborative project. Written and delivered by Maud Gonne, the subject (the goddess Brigid) and content owed much to the women-sponsored occasion:

> MY SISTERS AND FRIENDS—Each branch of Inghinidhe ha hÉireann is called after some Celtic heroine, who becomes the patron of the branch, and one of our objects is to revive the memories of the Irish heroines, which have been too much forgotten of late years.[53]

Stepping delicately around the Christian saint, Gonne proceeded to construct a proto-feminist emblem for Ireland, a deity that typified feminine autonomy and national beauty. When Gonne maintained, for example, that "the Celts, differing widely in this from the Semitic race, have always reverenced the feminine equally with the masculine principle,"[54] she was disclosing not only the race-based foundations of her anticolonial nationalism but also an imagined genealogy of Irish feminism. Her rediscovery of a mythic Celtic past can thus be read as a searching aim to find empowering alternatives to imperial and patriarchal models of femininity. Her anti-Semitism (an implacable racism that she took to her grave) might be understood, in particular, in relation to widely circulating ideas of Celticism.

Characterizing the colonized cultures of Ireland and India as "exotic," "primitive," or "barbaric" certainly assisted colonial administrators and proponents of Empire in their efforts to justify Britain's imperial presence there.[55] Yet both Celticism and Orientalism have sometimes afforded women a means of empowerment, for both discourses, as C. L. Innes notes, highlight social practices of a distant culture or land in order to distinguish it from the patriarchal West. Celticism, in particular, assisted Irish women writers because it offered them "an empowering alternative tradition" that opposed the patriarchy of the established churches and the British Empire.[56] Gonne's interest in highlighting the goddess Brigid's beauty and wisdom thus valuably discloses Gonne's (and her female collaborators') imagined community, a sisterhood that recovered or re-created examples from the mythic past to help differentiate Ireland from its colonial masters. Such "donning of historical garb," as Declan Kiberd has pointed out in the context of Gonne's contemporaries Pearse and Connolly, may be more radical and long-standing than previously acknowledged.[57] Gonne's reviving the stories and practices of Celtic ancestors was a widespread pursuit for writers of the revival, though the women who studied and recovered heroines of Irish myth and history shared more than anticolonial principles in differentiating Celtic culture from that of the colonizers. A half century earlier, in 1846, "Mary" of the *Nation* proposed a collection on the "Illustrious Women of Ireland."[58] Milligan and Johnston, in the *Shan Van Vocht*, also highlighted prominent nationalist women in their monthly features. Milligan's play *The Last Feast of the Fianna* (1899) returned to the banqueting hall of Fionn MacCumhal to challenge the masculine supposition that "it is by the cunning wiles of love a woman alone can triumph."[59] Lady Gregory revisited the cultural memory of Brigid (the saint) as well as the legendary Grania; in her essay on the saint, she hinted at how this feminine figure could serve both as a conventional model of good works and a demanding ideal for social justice.[60] In her finest three-act play, *Grania*, Gregory sympathetically dramatizes the dilemma of a powerful woman who acts on sexual desire rather than passively accepting her function as a decorative pawn controlled by men. And, as we will see in chapter 3, Constance Markievicz dedicated numerous columns to the project of recovering well-known if often-forgotten stories of nationalist girls and women of Ireland's past, overtly challenging Irish history to broaden its scope to include Irish women's myriad roles in the ongoing revolution.

Thus, for Gonne, the attraction of Brigid depended on her pagan origins, her Celtic lineage, and the sex-segregated customs in honor of her feast day. Indeed, central to Gonne's lecture was delineating the ways women in the old Highlands of Scotland or in small villages in Ireland worshipped Brigid or Bride as she was sometimes called during her feast day *(feis)* on the first of February. As described by Gonne, the *feis,* "undoubtedly of Pagan origin," draws on the particular talents and resources of women who created statuary of Bride from sheaves of corn, shells, and winter foliage, allowed men to "make obeisance to her," then "barr[ed] the door" so that the women could worship alone, breaking bread "very sparingly, in order to have more to give among the poorer women of the place."[61] Though Gonne acknowledges her intellectual debt to Alexander Carmichael's *Carmina Gadelica*[62] in relating these customs, Gonne's lecture reads less as a mythological or anthropological report than a deft proposal of what a woman's nationalist organization (such as Inghinidhe na hÉireann) might offer to women of Ireland: a forum that would develop women's artistic talents, attend carefully to women's material needs, and accord women the central authoritative role in the community.

A number of Gonne's articles, as well as frequent notices and advertisements in the *United Irishman,* helped record the ways that Inghinidhe fostered creative expression, economic awareness, and female autonomy. A week after Inghinidhe's highly successful production of George Russell's (AE's) *Deirdre* and Yeats and Gregory's *Cathleen ni Houlihan,* Gonne submitted a mournful eulogy for Anna Johnston ("Ethna Carbery"), who had died suddenly from acute gastroenteritis on the plays' opening night, April 2, 1902.[63] In her fresh grief, Gonne remembered Johnston for many of the qualities that she privileged in describing the devotees of Brigid: imagination, solidarity, and devotion. Johnston—"our friend, our comrade, bound to us . . . in a bitter struggle for a holy cause"—demonstrated particular talent, in Gonne's remembrance, as a "fellow worker" and writer: coproducing the *Shan Van Vocht,* Johnston "brought the breath of home and a wild longing to return while it taught [emigrant readers] to work for the freedom of our Motherland."[64] Gonne noted that Johnston also dedicated "many hours of her busy life" writing letters to Irish emigrants, sharing with homesick and often impoverished correspondents "some of the beauty and fragrance of our land." Johnston's poetry, in Gonne's imagination, also owed its genesis to the Celtic muse of the land itself: "Her love for Ireland was the passion of her life" (a curiously insensitive remark given that Johnston had only months earlier married the Donegal folklorist Seumas MacManus).

In her final words to comfort her shocked and grieving readers, Gonne sought solace in "the Spirit World" and the "Ever-living ones," where Johnston was now "working and guiding still as she worked and guided here . . . I believe that the communion of those banded together in a bitter struggle for a holy cause can never be broken." Gonne returned to the utopian female community of the devotees of Bride, the "communion of those banded together," a Celtic woman-centered Eucharistic rite that seems particularly vested in notions of female martyrdom. Read in the context of the recently performed *Cathleen ni Houilihan,* where the iconic Cathleen inspires men to die for love of her, Gonne's closing words about Anna Johnston imply that one woman's journalism, poetry, and long-standing activism functioned as a critical part of the revolution. Like Michael Gillane's determination to join the uprising in Killala in the Yeats–Gregory play, Anna Johnston's commitment was to be "remembered for ever," not least because Johnston shared Gonne's commitment with a sisterhood in Inghinidhe.

Gonne's repeated appeals for feminine, often feminist, collaboration took many forms during the years she wrote for the *United Irishman.* A favorite topic was inculcating nationalist values in Irish children; this was not surprising, given that what brought Inghinidhe together in the first place was a patriotic children's treat to reward Dublin children who had refused to attend a celebration in Phoenix Park honoring the queen. In "The National Education of Children," Gonne argued that both men and women should be involved in a range of activities—from forming boys' brigades to organizing winter history classes, when it would be too cold to march outside—to resist "the Anglicization of Irish children."[65] Stressing that both men and women were suitable military trainers, Gonne opined that educating children would be "especially suitable for the women," a view that, as we have seen, advocated revolutionary militancy without necessarily contesting gender roles. Gonne's columns also suggested concrete ways that her Irish readers could reject British control over their daily lives. One column, for example, encouraged Irish merchants to cultivate economic partnerships outside of Britain.[66] Gonne also reminded her readers that if they wanted freedom, they needed to foster frequent and direct communications with Irish Americans, many of whom relied on the biased British press for their news about Ireland.[67]

As a journalist and a critic of the press, Gonne well understood the dynamic of exchange between newspaper and readers. In one telling article, Gonne described the Irish press as an explicitly literary form that shouldered the responsibilities of cultural revival, as "a great educative force," and as a primary source for cultural regeneration and civic instruction.[68] Endorsing a principal philosophy of the Irish revival, Gonne imparted to the Irish press the creative achievement, political significance, and combative command of Ireland's heroic, militant past. Her description draws on many of the same qualities as those she ascribed to the devotees of Brigid: "The Irish Press should be bright and sharp and keen, like the sword of the Gael, and following the true tradition and mission of the sword which is to inspire as well as to defend."[69] Though her imagery depends on a masculine tool of power and resistance, her interpretation of the "true tradition and mission" of the sword, "to inspire as well as to defend," inserts a place for female models of action as well. Her ideal of the Irish press turned out to be especially accommodating to the nationalist journalism of women. Indeed, in tracing the history of the "national" press, Gonne highlighted "the Irishwomen whose verse also enoble[d] its pages," nationalist writers and activists such as "Mary" (Ellen Downing) and "Eva" (Mary Anne Kelly) of the *Nation*, Ellen O'Leary, and Fanny Parnell.

Gonne viewed the press as a primary source of education in all countries, though she noted that its influence was more pronounced in Ireland given "the want of public libraries in most of the country towns and villages of Ireland, and the want of educational advantages, such as are found in free countries." She was thus also eager to emphasize to her Irish readers the economic dimension of the newspaper market. Painting a stark contrast between the starving poet who "sings a noble song [and] may have dined off a crust of bread" and the fat millionaire who "digests with difficulty his superfluous and lengthy dinner, yawns and wonders how he may fill the weary time till he can sleep," Gonne argued that readers should be alert to a similar polarity between the "imitative" English press and "noble, heroic" national journals. Such values can hardly be surprising from the first president of Inghinidhe na hÉireann, which had explicitly adopted as one of its goals "to discourage the reading and circulation of low English literature, the singing of English songs, the attending of vulgar English entertainments at the theater and music hall, and to combat in every way English influence, which is doing so much injury to the artistic taste and refinement of the Irish people."[70] Here, then, we can witness a familiar feature of Gonne's Celticism, a practice that Kiberd has described as a "fatal willingness to take the colonizer at his word and convert every insult into a boast."[71] Anti-Semitic paranoia aside, Gonne's analysis offers a glimmer of insight into how the market helps to shape the news:

> The [English] Press is generally the expression of some great money or vested interest; in serving that interest it is sincere, if usually lying, and when dealing with other matters it expresses not necessarily what anyone thinks, but what the Editor thinks his readers are thinking. . . . It is our duty to carefully watch the advertising of our papers, and see that no such immoral [imperialist] advertisements find their way into them.[72]

For Gonne, the mainstream newspapers of the day disqualified themselves as objective dispensers of the news because their relationship to the marketplace strongly determined how issues were framed. This analysis offers an understanding of the mass media that anticipates the propaganda model later famously characterized by Edward Herman and Noam Chomsky as "manufacturing consent."[73]

Whereas much of the writing in the *United Irishman* remained anonymous or pseudonymous, Maud Gonne always signed her work, a detail that suggests her comfort in claiming a public, autonomous identity. Although Gonne certainly used her beauty and fame for political purposes, she also used the unwanted attention she received from the Crown's spies to protest the surveillance of her anticolonial activities and to deride common ideas about both feminine and national weakness. She frequently highlighted her gender to great political effect. In one letter to the editor, for example, Gonne effectively draws attention both to the sexual and national dimension of her political status. Alerting readers to the "delicate attention" she received by members of the G division (an observation amply documented by several thick files in the Dublin Castle Special Branch Files, housed in the Public Record Office in Kew), Gonne goes on to complain:

> I would point out that it is reckless extravagance to devote two, and sometimes even three, men to my service. After all, I am a woman, and can only do one woman's work in the day, and it seems to me that a man who is doing no work, only watching my work, ought to be able to stand as much fatigue myself. I therefore protest in the interest of taxpayers against this extravagance.[74]

Here her literalist irony calls into question the Victorian double standard regarding women, the putative "weaker sex." Her emphasis on the "extravagance" of Her Majesty's spies also cleverly parodies middle-class Unionism, which so often cloaked its conservative ideology in the garb of prudent concern for the bottom line. Her rhetorical success thus owes as much to her natural gifts of eloquence as to her reputation as a beautiful, fashionable lady who always dressed for the occasion. And though she surely enjoyed the attention her regal splendor and Parisian clothes received, Gonne viewed these as merely a "passport" that allowed her to move in a wider arena.

Gonne's signed articles, public lectures, street protests, and private soirées provide us with ample evidence that Gonne accepted and relished the spotlight. Yet she also dedicated a great deal of her creative energy to bringing women together and organizing, acting, protesting, and educating. Her skill and success on platforms where at first few of her sisters in Inghinidhe would stand invited serious scrutiny of her unwomanly behavior, and Gonne was quick to offer familiar Celtic lore in her defense. To her critics who clucked over her anomalous behavior, Gonne reminded readers of the prophecy of Brian Ruadh, in which "there would be a famine and that a woman dressed in green would come and preach the revolt. After that, men would rise and there would be fighting and many killed but that the English would in the end be driven out."[75] Even before her memorable performance as Cathleen ni Houlihan in Yeats and Gregory's 1902 play, Gonne's lectures and essays returned repeatedly to her fascination with the symbolic power of a woman leading men to freedom. Though there was undoubtedly an element of self-aggrandizement in evoking such an image, Gonne's belief in the old prophecy that Ireland would be saved by a woman legitimated not only her public activism, but also the activism of all Irish women doing their part for Ireland. Thus, hoping "to revive the memories of Irish heroines," Gonne lectured and wrote about women such as Brigid, Maeve, and Emer because she sought to enlist other women in the nationalist movement, too.

To examine another iconic feminine figure who, in Gonne's view, declined to use her national authority to serve her community's most vulnerable members, Gonne also dusted off an earlier commentary on Queen Victoria, first published in *L'Irlande Libre*. Composed near the end of Victoria's reign, in the jingoistic year of Victoria's Diamond Jubilee (1897), Gonne translated her most incendiary article, "The Famine Queen," from the French and republished it in the *United Irishman* within days of the queen's arrival in Dublin in 1900. In "The Famine Queen," readers can hear many of the characteristic qualities of Gonne's most stirring articles and speeches: oratorical flourishes and anaphoric phrases, pathos-filled appeals to nationalist values such as pride, courage, and chivalry, and emblematic scenes that contrast a withered English ruler with a blossoming Irish maid. Certainly her most rousing choice, though, involved replacing England's characteristic national icon, the vigorous, bowler-hatted John Bull, with the feeble, eighty-one-year-old reigning queen, who, in Gonne's words, grasps "the shamrock in her withered hands" in order to recruit soldiers for the Anglo-Boer War. Gonne highlighted Victoria's sovereign status and her maternity. Suggesting the misuse of both, she invited unfavorable comparisons with the iconic nobility of Brigid and Mother Ireland, as well as with the conventional view of devoted Irish mothers. By describing Victoria as a queen and a mother, she thus reminded readers of the failures not only of the female sovereign but also, by implication, of the whole nation:

> And in truth, for Victoria, in the decrepitude of her eighty-one years, to have decided after an absence of half-a-century to revisit the country she hates and whose inhabitants are the victims of the criminal policy of her reign, the survivors of sixty years of organised famine, the political necessity must have been terribly strong; for after all she is a woman, and however vile and selfish and pitiless her soul may be, she must sometimes tremble as death approaches when she thinks of the countless Irish mothers who, shelterless under the cloudy Irish sky, watching their starving little ones, have cursed her before they died.[76]

Gonne's ad hominem attack on the "pitiless soul" of the queen provoked the censors to seize copies on grounds of libel. Yet, as controversial as her statements were, Gonne's attack merely reversed the British nationalist adulations heaped on the queen during the Jubilee. Read next to her sympathetic portrayal of the devotees of Brigid and her sisterhood in Inghinidhe, Gonne's savage characterization of Victoria marks out the queen's greatest failure as her neglect of the most vulnerable in her realm: women. Where British high and popular culture praised the queen for her womanly decorum, her selfless service, and her generous heart,[77] Gonne held up to view what the queen—and the British nation—had done for Ireland. However devoted a mother to her British progeny, Victoria was a ruthless, contemptible stepmother toward the Irish race.

Gonne's aggressive critique of Victoria depended on the familiar oppositions invoked by Celticism and colonialism alike. Although Gonne's use of Celticism allowed her to provide a stirring, sharp-tongued defense of shelterless Irish mothers, her dependence on this binary system of thought not only essentialized Irish mothers but also discouraged her from critically examining how such a racial theory assisted imperialism elsewhere, such as in Southern Africa. Perhaps the most memorable example of the limits of Gonne's feminist anticolonial politics can be viewed in her article "The Boer Women," where she celebrates anti-British wives and daughters such as Hedrina Joubert, who was married to Afrikaans Commandant-General Piet Joubert, and whom Gonne praises for braving bullets and loneliness in the African veld in order to "personally provide for [her husband's] table."[78] Indeed, Hedrina Joubert was well known for accompanying her husband on commando raids, and according to Byron Farwell, it was she who was considered "the soldier in the family."[79] In Farwell's retelling of the Anglo-Boer War, Hedrina is credited with first sounding the alarm when British troops arrived at the disastrous Battle at Majuba.

Gonne and many Irish nationalists interpreted the Anglo-Boer War (1899–1902) as a key contest against imperial Britain. Christopher Saunders and Iain R. Smith have called that war "the greatest test of British Imperial power since the Indian Mutiny and . . . the most extensive and costly war fought by Britain between the defeat of Napoleon (1815) and the First World War."[80] Radical nationalists such as Maud Gonne and Arthur Griffith, who founded the Transvaal Committee in Dublin in 1899 to galvanize Irish nationalists, considered the Boer cause a parallel to their own efforts toward national independence. By 1900, when Lord Kitchener entered the brutal scorched-earth phase of the campaign, rounding up Boer women and children into concentration camps, where more than 20,000 died, Gonne embarked upon a second lecture tour to the United States to publicize her outrage against the British war on an international stage. In many of her lectures, she lauded the efforts of a small band of Irish soldiers, including her future husband, John MacBride, the leader of the Irish Brigade, which fought on the Boer side to advance the cause of anti-English solidarity and to train for their own resistance struggle at home.[81]

Published only months before the founding of Inghinidhe na hÉireann, "The Boer Women" expresses a decidedly different attitude about anticolonial feminine activism. It also suggests that Gonne was indebted to many of her surrogate daughters in the movement in developing her later, more advanced ideas about gender equality. Rather than promoting a sisterhood that pledged solidarity as workers, educators, artists, and activists, Gonne celebrates another sisterhood in her opinion piece: the Boer women "are not essaying the role of Amazons. They are only trying to soften some of the horrors of battle, to ease the pangs of suffering and cheer and comfort the well."[82] Anxiously rejecting feminine militancy, whether on behalf of nationalism or feminism, the article approvingly endorses, instead, a conventional view of the domestic wife, with one small alteration: the wife shows her devotion to husband and home by serving him creature comforts while he is away fighting as an anticolonial soldier. We will witness a similar dynamic in the trade union journalism of Delia Larkin in chapter 4, where Larkin simultaneously advocated union rates for working girls and upbraided married women who neglected their duties at home. Though many women writers of advanced nationalism could not countenance the extremism of woman's militancy, at least one anonymous contributor to the *United Irishman* did. In a poem published a month later in the *United Irishman*, "H. S." declared that if women are not the first line of defense, they will, if necessary, keep the cannons booming:

> We, Boer women, too can fight;
> —We, too, can die. Should our men fall
> *Our* guns shall thunder from the height,
> —Our bodies line the latest wall.[83]

Instead, Gonne's vision of feminine support for a nationalist campaign anticipates the limited political opportunities for many women in Cumann na mBan (Irishwomen's Council), who saw action, supplied intelligence, and nursed the wounded during the Easter Rising, the War of Independence, and the Civil War.[84]

Like many of Gonne's articles, "The Boer Women" gestures in two directions at once: rebuffing Victorian expectations of woman's domestic place in the private sphere of hearth and home, Gonne nevertheless singles out Hedrina Joubert's part as "the faithful wife, the devoted mother, the fearless companion—who braves the awful carnage of war and amid whistling bullets and bursting shells provides, like the careful housewife that she is, for her husband's table. For the Boer women go to battle with husbands and fathers." In this passage, then, we can witness Gonne's familiar shifts regarding public and private femininity at the fin de siècle. Gonne begins by offering praise of Joubert's traditional womanliness as a loyal wife and selfless mother; at the same time, Gonne declares that the meaning of femininity radically alters when placed in new contexts, such as the battlefield. Just as Alice Milligan proposed that Ascendancy girls in silk slippers could make sacrifices for their nation, Maud Gonne's opinion piece here maintains that middle-class ladies might deserve war medals, too. Although she carefully distances herself from the militant feminism of suffragettes, Gonne nevertheless attempts to highlight a model of feminine political activism that many Irish women could imagine replicating at home.

If Gonne's celebration of the Boer women reveals the limits of her feminist nationalist expression, her portrait of analogous feminine pioneers also indicates the shortcomings of her racial perspective regarding transnational solidarity in the anticolonial struggle. Having just returned from a lecture tour to the United States, Gonne exuberantly declared that the Boer women had foremothers among the white settler wives in the colonial America frontier, since they were women who "were ever ready to protect their homes" from the "savage enemies." As Gonne saw it, "The women of the [American] frontier also embodied many of the characteristics of the Transvaal women. In their constant fear of the Indians they were ever ready to protect their homes. The Boer women have likewise had to dread their savage enemies—the Kaffirs and Matabeles—ever on the watch to despoil their homes."[85] In revealing her alliance with white settlers such as Boer women and American colonialists rather than with those resisting the cultural, political, and economic mastery of their native lands, Gonne laid bare a persistent, thinly disguised element of racial chauvinism in her nationalist outlook at the turn of the century. Indeed, Gonne's racism was shared by other advanced nationalists such as John MacBride and Arthur Griffith, who published his outrage in the pages of the *United Irishman* over Britain's violation of "the white man's tradition" by joining up with "native races against the brother-white."[86]

Gonne's analysis displays what Chandra Mohanty has labeled "the authorizing signature of western feminist writings," critical commentary that stresses "third world difference" and neglects important variances in class, caste, and religion within the "singular monolithic subject" called "colonized women."[87] Gonne's efforts to establish an anticolonial sisterhood with Boer women and with American frontierswomen thus confront readers with the limitations of essentialist claims about transnational feminist solidarity. Her writing, like that of Milligan and Johnston in the *Shan Van Vocht,* is thus at once resistant to and complicit in both imperialism and nationalism.

The strain between Gonne's anticolonial efforts in Ireland and her racial alliances elsewhere parallels a common tension in women's collaborative processes, some of which grow out of cultural, racial, and sexual differences between authors. As Lorraine York forcefully argues, women's collaboration more frequently than not expresses a "widely varying dynamic" of exchange based as much on "unshared reality" as on women's perceived commonalities.[88] Critiquing the "celebratory" and "idealistic" accounts of feminine collaborators, York notes that women's collaborations are far less unitary and harmonious than critics have allowed, especially if the effect of power and property in shaping the dynamic of exchange between collaborators is taken into account. We will examine a similar struggle between playwright Augusta Gregory (Lady Gregory) and trade unionist and amateur actress Delia Larkin in chapter 4, when we witness an ardent debate over the competing claims of art and labor in the wake of the Dublin Lockout of 1913. Whereas Gregory and Larkin's dispute highlights the efficacy of different rhetorical styles, Gonne's attempts at solidarity and collaboration reveal how unstable such alliances often are.

Staging Feminine Collaboration: Gonne's *Dawn*

York concedes that "collaborative groups can occupy many spaces, sometimes simultaneously, on the spectrum that runs from fusion to difference."[89] One of Maud Gonne's final submissions for the *United Irishman*, and her only expressly literary contribution, neatly exemplifies York's observation. In 1904, Gonne shared her docudrama *Dawn* with *United Irishman* readers.[90] Still today an unstaged play, *Dawn* enacts both the generative spirit and unequal relations of feminine collaboration as it returns to the fulsome convictions that animated her first lecture for Inghinidhe na hÉireann. Starring the iconic Bride (Brigid), *Dawn* dramatizes the potency of a Mother Ireland who successfully rallies her children to fight the Stranger who had dispossessed them of their land. Concentrating on the lives of starving, dispossessed peasants during the recent Land Wars, the play also thematizes the economic dimension of rebellion. And drawing on the principal performative features of the Inghinidhe's many ceilidhe, *Dawn* incorporates song, documentary-style realism, and stylized tableaux that reflect its collaborative genesis.

A nationalist allegory that returns to the figure of Ireland as a woman, *Dawn* expresses a recurrent feature in Gonne's nationalist vision: her wish for women both to embody Erin and to serve as her voices. When Gonne wrote about eviction and rack-renting, she frequently shifted between two personae, Mother Ireland and a Daughter of Erin.[91] In *Dawn*, she reconciles this dilemma by casting two lead characters, Bride and her daughter, Brideen, to dramatically illustrate the collaborative function of female nationalism. *Dawn*'s drama centers on a symbolic Mother Ireland, Bride, who speaks with hope and defiant pride, and also on a realistic daughter, Brideen, who vividly reminds her audience of the impoverished despair Gonne had recently witnessed in Gweedore, County Donegal. The regal Bride, a woman "of about forty," closely corresponds to the thirty-seven-year-old Gonne and to her descriptions of the Goddess Brigid. Bride's name is interchangeable with Brigid; it also bears a strong resemblance to the new surname Gonne used to sign her play, MacBride.[92] Brideen, the devoted daughter of Erin who dies before her time, shares important qualities with Anna Johnston, whom Gonne had memorialized just two years earlier. Where Brideen "will never leave" her mother or "the place I was born," Johnston stayed rooted in the North, first in Belfast then later in Donegal, working tirelessly as a journalist, poet, and activist in the Henry Joy McCracken Society, the Commemoration Committee, the Gaelic League, and Inghinidhe. In Gonne's telling, the death of both Johnston and Brideen serves as a redemptive act of martyrdom. Brideen's selfless suffering and starvation initiate "the dawn" of rebellion and resistance. The "loss" of Johnston bequeaths the "Spirit World" a greater "gain."

Tellingly, Bride, Brideen, Gonne, and Johnston all expressed their political agency best through exercising their voices. To fully understand the feminist implications of women speaking out, it is well worth recalling that popular culture of the day commonly associated a woman's public voice with suffragist agitation.[93] Detractors of female activism frequently maligned political women by focusing on their inappropriate voices. As Jane Marcus drolly observes, even Edwardian women were raised to be "she who may be interrupted." For women in Catholic Ireland, speaking out was doubly transgressive: it meant dismissing a female's most important model, the Virgin Mary. After the Great Famine (1845–52), Irish culture underwent a devotional revolution; the number of shrines dedicated to Mary increased markedly. In the nineteenth century's most striking manifestation of Mariolatry, the Apparition at Knock in 1879, Mary's presence was defined by her silence. Indeed, her muteness came to embody ideal femininity for all Irish women.[94] For many, merely speaking out was in itself a radical act. Suffragettes went much further, however. Learning that "*the interruption of male discourse*" was "the real key to the genius" of militant feminine activism, they perfected Christabel Pankhurst's fine art of disrupting political swagger.[95]

Yeats and his contemporaries have helped us remember Gonne's theatrically trained voice, a dramatic sound that Francis MacManus recalled had "witchcraft" in it.[96] Her willingness to use her voice publicly to lecture, rally crowds, and educate the masses set an example that many other women chose to emulate. As we have seen in her first lecture for Inghinidhe, Gonne emphasized woman-centered culture and political action;

such activities routinely involved both the worship of a noble, exceptional woman (such as herself) and the creative labor of other women. By 1904, when *Dawn* was first published in the *United Irishman*, more and more women in Inghinidhe were learning how to speak and perform in public. They were giving lectures, enacting *tableaux vivants*, reciting famous political speeches, and even lobbying men on the streets and saloons of O'-Connell Street to resist enlistment. This work, as Mary Trotter argues, afforded nationalist women "an organized public voice in the discourse of Irish nationalism."[97]

Gonne's unusual combination of allegorical tableaux with realistic settings owes a debt to Inghinidhe na hÉireann's popular ceilidhe; the dramatic realism of *Dawn* anticipates what would become the hallmark of the Irish National Theatre.[98] The different kinds of musical, discursive, and dramatic styles manifested in the ceilidhe represent some of Ireland's most enduring traditions, however jarring Gonne's combination of them may seem in its final effect. Gonne's two favorite modes as a journalist, lyrical allegory and fact-finding reportage, are present in *Dawn:* a small cast of two-dimensional characters representing good (the peasants) and evil (the Stranger) and the machinations of plot—evictions, famine, death by starvation—graphically remind the audience of the reasons behind the physical force movement. Gonne's unusual dramatic combination was also evident in her speech-making style, where she routinely juxtaposed lantern slides that documented evictions in famine-ravaged Mayo in 1898 with heated rebukes against the injustice of evictions, the wrongs of the relief works, and the barbarity of the battering ram. Later Abbey plays, such as Sean O'Casey's *Juno and the Paycock* (1925) and T. C. Murray's *Autumn Fire* (1924), contain a similar combination of realism and melodrama.

Bride's energies are focused on ridding her land of the "Stranger." In certain passages, she sounds like Gonne's idea of the Woman of the Sidhe, the "Queen" to whom Gonne dedicates her autobiography and who serves as the dramatic model for Gonne's public performances as a nationalist. In the first tableau, "Sunset," when an old friend, Michael, awakens from a hunger-induced faint, he tells her, "Bride, Bride of the Sorrows, it is your service I took, I have been faithful. I thought one time I might have been one of the stones your foot would rest on when you walked to Freedom—when you will drive the Stranger out—but I am too little a stone."[99] When Bride's daughter, Brideen, despairs about hunger and the prospect of the workhouse, Bride echoes Gonne's earliest columns in the *United Irishman* in replying: "Daughter of mine, take courage, the night is coming on, and it is very dark, but the day will dawn, and little Eoin will laugh in the dawn and the sunlight because you did not leave the country because you have been faithful to me."[100] Gonne scrupulously records the material consequences of Brideen's "faithful" service, too. Though revolution glows on the horizon, Brideen's obedience to Bride will cost her her life.

It is tempting to read Gonne's play in light of *Cathleen ni Houlihan*, the play that solidified her career as a theatrical nationalist. To do so, however, reveals several important differences in the origins and outcomes of sovereignty claims. Whereas Yeats and Gregory set their play in the iconic year 1798, Gonne sets hers in recent history, during the Land Wars, in order to highlight the way political liberation movements were punished by British injustice and cruelty in the form of evictions and relief works. In the Yeats–Gregory play, domestic disruption ensues when Michael Gillane forgets his betrothed, forfeiting the comfort assured by Delia's dowry of a "whole hundred pounds" for the lure of Cathleen's romantic talk of nationalist lovers "who will be remembered for ever." Gonne's play advocates revolution for less idealistic, more material reasons: human survival in the face of mass suffering and genocide.

A more instrumental influence on Gonne's lone theatrical endeavor is Alice Milligan's dramatic legend, the *Last Feast of the Fianna* (1899), which many regard as the first example of Celtic Twilight drama.[101] Milligan's *Last Feast*, one of the inaugural productions of the Irish Literary Theatre, was first performed in Dublin with Edward Martyn's *Maeve* on February 19, 1900; subscribers of the *Daily Express* obtained a first reading of this play a year earlier, when it was published as a two-week serial.[102] An accomplished producer of *tableaux vivants*, Milligan adapted the spare, still form of this amateur genre into a stirring one-act play that recalls the noble characters of Irish legend. Anticipating Inghinidhe's interest in recovering the stories of Celtic women of Ireland's past, she also inserted a feminist reappraisal of male-dominated warrior culture. The play tightly focuses on a well-known story, the departure of the bard Oisin to the land of everlasting youth, Tir na nOg. Milligan's retelling, however, is less concerned with the dissolution of the Fianna than the power exchange between two women who, alternately, entice Oisin and push him to leave. It also contains an unmistakable feminist lesson, later picked up in Gonne's *Dawn* and Inghinidhe's creative activities, about the potency of a woman's voice:

> Dreaming poet, have you not learned three things are not to be looked for—leaves in winter, snow in summer, and the silence from a woman.[103]

Though Fionn delivers this adage with a patronizing air, his words prophetically disclose the theme of the play: with merely her voice, woman can change the course of clan.

The two female leads in the play, Grania and Niamh, closely correspond to the generational divide between Bride and Brideen—which, as we have already seen, suggestively captures Gonne's matriarchal relationship to younger activists in Inghinidhe. The regal Grania, we learn, has "whitening tresses whose beauty has faded like the leaf in Samhain." The beguiling fairy princess Niamh enjoys the radiant beauty of everlasting youth. The spare details disclosed about each legendary woman also recall allegorical Ireland in her two most familiar guises, Cathleen ni Houlihan and the Dark Rosaleen. Of Grania, we discover that "many have died for her sake." In turn, the preternaturally dewy Niamh recalls the renewal of national resolve; her symbolic complexion, Fionn tells us, is "like roses, like the dawning day."[104] Milligan's play also returns to the question of power exchange between women, a theme that concludes her border romance, "The Outlaw's Bride," discussed in chapter 1. Where her short story only hints at the potential challenges in women's collaborations over power, Milligan's play acknowledges the messy underbelly of women competing with one another, providing particular insight regarding the pettiness of an aging queen who fears displacement by a desirable, youthful nymph. At the same time, her dramatic legend cunningly clothes a contemporary dynamic in period dress. In Milligan's presentation, Grania and Niamh's public pursuits of power and passion look not so different from the more familiar competitions among men. Celtic women, Milligan informs us, can be immodest, sexually ravenous, narcissistic, ambitious; Irish women, by implication, can be, too. Placing Milligan's play next to Gonne's, we can better glimpse how Gonne edited factionalism of a different kind out of her own writings. She persistently, if quixotically, viewed women as collaborative workers, rather than as competitors, in the nationalist movement. Though Maud Gonne's early writings for the *United Irishman* encouraged many women to feast at the Fianna's table, she never forgot to reserve a special place for the queen.

In her discussion of *Dawn*, Antoinette Quinn has argued that Gonne's play is better understood as a theatrical response to *In the Shadow of the Glen*, J. M. Synge's realist dramatization of marital unhappiness in the rural west, than as an imitation of *Cathleen ni Houlihan*.[105] Gonne famously walked out on the premiere of Synge's play, remarking that the play's representation of peasant marriage was incompatible with a theater supposedly dedicated to national pride.[106] Gonne's two characters, Bride and Brideen, visibly resist the feminist action of Synge's female lead: they will never leave the home, even when it is destroyed by the battering ram. Yet that is not to say that Bride and Brideen lack political agency of their own. If one understands Gonne's allegory as related to Milligan's legend and the dramatic project of Inghinidhe's *tableaux vivants*, which presented strong, defiant female models of national resistance, Bride and Brideen resemble more the sisterhood of Inghinidhe, especially as it was outlined in their original goals and in Gonne's harmonious account of the devotees of Brigid. Typified as Mother and Daughter of Erin, Bride and Brideen display admirable physical endurance and intellectual vigor, which is required now that their men have departed, through death, emigration, or desertion, and their home has been destroyed. Forced as head of the family to work on the roads, Bride angers the Stranger by remaining on her land, "wander[ing] round the fields that was hers."[107] Brideen, who "has the look of death on her," deftly resists the malevolent aid of the Stranger, thereby reminding her audience of the domestic disorder that has resulted from British misrule in Ireland.

As the play opens at sunset, Neil Durkan and his mate Mike O'Hara are toiling on the famine relief works. Neil observes to Mike that "it's a long, hard road" on the famine road: "two hours to Clovagher, and then nine hours on the works, and the hunger on us all the while, and only to get this, for all the hardship, . . .fi' pence worth of Indian meal for a day's wage."[108] The detail of "Indian meal" is small, though significant. Although readers of the *United Irishman* would no doubt be connecting this reference to folk memories of the Indian meal distributed during the Great Famine of mid-nineteenth-century Ireland, Gonne may have also hoped to link Irish suffering with that of other nations colonized by Britain, such as the Indian subcontinent, which was, at the time of Gonne's writing, also experiencing a devastating famine in Bengal. This famine and India's plight as a colonized land were topics Gonne and other *United Irishman* contributors often discussed in their columns.[109]

When the Stranger first appears, in the second tableau, "Night," he reveals the sly trickery and cruelties that have guaranteed him a hated memory in the Irish imagination. After reminding Brideen that her husband, Eoin, had not sent back money from America as promised, the Stranger, sounding like the morally corrupt, white plantation owners in nineteenth-century American slave narratives, attempts to use her maternal instincts to try to get her under his lecherous clutches:

> You had better take my offer and go up to my farm. There is food and good shelter waiting for you, and you may take the child with you if you like. It is cruelty leaving him out in the cold this bitter night. You have not a mother's heart to leave your child shelterless, a night like this. There are not many who would do for you as much as I am ready to do, in spite of all the hard things you and your people have said of me. But I like you, Brideen, and I have a fancy to have Bride's daughter for my servant.[110]

As a faithful daughter of Bride, Brideen refuses, but that evening, she quietly dies of starvation. Brideen's death becomes the catalyst for the peasant revolt that concludes the play, but her passing is hardly passive, ornamental, or static. In fact, as the scene with the Stranger suggests, her decision to resist the Stranger's accommodation—like the hunger strikes by suffrage activists—was politically motivated action. In fact, as Bride watches her death approaching, she envisions Brideen as part of a militant atmosphere that drives away the cold, obscuring British presence in the land: "See, Brideen, see, the dawn is coming, the red dawn. The river of blood must flow, but there is freedom on the other side of it, and the Strangers are driven away like clouds before the sun. Brideen, it is you and the mighty dead who are driving back the clouds."[111]

In the final tableau, "Dawn," Brideen's death causes the people to awaken from their starvation and passivity to fight the Stranger. As the orphaned Eoin puts apple blossoms in Brideen's hands, Bride sings a dirge that is also a defiant battle cry:

> It is dark the land is, and it's dark my heart is,
> But the red sun rises, when the hour-heart is come,
> O the red sun rises, and the dead rise, I can see them
> And it's glad they are and proud.
>
> . . . .
>
> They have bright swords with them that clash the battle welcome
> A welcome to the red sun that rises with our luck.[112]

Repeating her vision of a new dawn, a frequent expression of optimism among nationalist writers of the day and the image emblazoned on the banner of Inghinidhe na hÉireann,[113] Bride also revises the symbolic power of redness, from the cartographic emblem of the British empire to the metonym for Irish revolution. Although Mike realizes, "Now the dead are speaking to us, they cry for vengeance," it takes the words of little Eoin to direct the people's grief. Defiantly resisting the offer of adoptive parents and a standing home, he clings to Bride and replies: "No. I will not leave her. I will stay and fight for her." The play then closes with a macabre scene of near-starving neighbors joining together to fight for Bride and their land, while Bride repeats her fighting song: "They have bright swords with them that clash the battle welcome, / A welcome to the red sun, that rises with our luck."[114]

Neither a lyrical, a complex, nor an intricately plotted play, *Dawn* nonetheless offers a decisive feminist and materialist vision for the emerging Irish national theater, although not all critics of the play would agree. Even a sensitive feminist interpretation such as Quinn's, for example, laments the play's "strains between nationalism and feminism" because Gonne resorts to traditional, patriarchal models whereby women suffer and men act.[115] As *Women, Press, and Politics* has shown—and will continue to show—female writers of advanced nationalism, from Alice Milligan in the 1890s to Louie Bennett at the onset of World War I, found that addressing, let alone resolving the tensions between nationalism and feminism would prove their most intractable struggle. Each woman answered the challenge differently. Milligan buoyantly devised stories where women could use the trappings of traditional upper-class femininity to subversive ends. Adapting Coventry Patmore's treacly veneration of the domestic woman in "Angel of the House" for radical Irish ends, Gonne's *Dawn* teaches its audience that even a worshipped woman can have radical agency. Although Bride inspires a rebellion in which the remaining peasants—all male—are expected to fight, revolution would never occur if not for the potency of her voice. Bride, moreover, is hardly a devouring lover who uses men to get back her good looks and her four green fields, as is the case in *Cathleen ni Houlihan*. Bride's purpose for urging an uprising is practical: if they do not fight, they will surely perish. Bride's language is indeed modeled on such realistic pragmatism. Her idealistic, superstitious language emerges from the extreme poverty Gonne saw firsthand on her travels throughout Ireland when she spoke out against landlord evictions. Quinn also regrets that Gonne's *Dawn* reverses her personal experiences as a tireless canvasser for Irish liberty. In fact, unlike the sharpshooters Constance Markievicz and Margaret Skinnider, Gonne never took up arms herself; she picked up her pen and raised her stirring voice instead. *Dawn*'s original context, in the pages of the *United Irishman*, suggests that both Gonne and her nationalist audience understood that nationalist ventures included—indeed, required—rhetoric as well as action. Thus, in its focus on the revolutionary power of a woman's voice, *Dawn* emulated rather than contradicted Gonne's exemplary life.

Conclusions: Reassessing Gonne as a Literary Collaborator

In her study of women's collaboration, Holly Laird has argued that "literary collaborators blur the boundaries not only between each other in writing, but between text and speech, between a text and its contexts."[116] We can confirm this in the case of Maud Gonne, most of whose opinion pieces were first delivered as speeches, and only later published in the *United Irishman.* Though primarily studied as accounts of the first women's nationalist organization, Gonne's published speeches represent only one of the most visible parts of a broader feminist and nationalist movement. Understanding them as part of a larger literary collaboration, one that involved lectures and journalism, pep talks and meeting notices, strategy sessions and playful conversations, reveals how easily Gonne's work as writer and political organizer blurred such boundaries between text and performance, individual and collective action.

Thus Gonne was not only, as she once claimed, a "freelance on the fringe."[117] She also worked, and worked productively, with other women in a variety of creative, political, and personal collaborations—illustrating Ella Young's mythological stories, performing and producing Inghinidhe's amateur theatricals, and staging and starring in myriad political protests. She focused her energies in shared philanthropic efforts, such as clothing drives, school meal campaigns, and nursing the wounded during wartime. In committee work, Gonne collaborated with women—and men—in the 1798 centenary commemorations, the Transvaal Committee, the Patriotic Children's Treat, and, of course, Inghinidhe na hÉireann. She later helped found a female body of dissidents, the Women's Prisoners' Defense League, popularly called "the Mothers," which drew on the creative and practical activism that characterized Inghinidhe. She even tried her hand at a collaborative business venture, the Roebuck Industries, a cottage industry cooperative for unemployed members of the Irish republican movement. Because of Gonne's literary, political, and popular status—as the muse of Yeats, the estranged wife of John MacBride, as the Woman of the Sidhe or Cathleen ni Houlihan—Gonne's relationship to feminism and to the feminist movement has been frequently misconstrued. It is now time to reconsider her work in light of how she developed, recorded, and participated in women's collaborations in the nationalist movement *and* the literary revival.

3

Allegory as Resistance

Constance Markievicz, Bean na hÉireann, *and the* Irish Citizen

Poets, historians, and biographers have kept alive the memory of Constance Markievicz (1866–1927) largely because of her status as an "exceptional woman." She was a rebel soldier during the Easter Rising of 1916 as well as the founder of Na Fianna Éireann, earlier known by the English name "Red Branch Knights," the first paramilitary organization of the revolutionary years, which later evolved into the junior training ground for the Irish Republican Army. More than a soldier, Markievicz represents to postcolonial and feminist critics one of Ireland's most notorious anticolonial New Women, an activist who visibly supported feminism, socialism, and nationalism alike. Well known as the protégée of James Connolly, she achieved much on behalf of women and workers in her own right. She was the first woman elected to the British Commons (1918); as the minister of labor, she was the only woman to serve in the cabinet of the first Dáil Éireann (1919–21). Despite these concrete accomplishments, Markievicz is still remembered today more for her shrill voice, her facile zeal, and her theatrical flair as a sharpshooter wearing an ostrich plume. Markievicz's contemporaries, such as William Butler Yeats and Sean O'-Casey, memorably rebuked her revolutionary spirit as "ignorant goodwill," her mind as "a bitter, an abstract thing," and her voice as "soar[ing] into a still-born scream."[1] Later biographers and historians perpetuated many of the earlier myths. D. J. Smith viewed her as a laughable "lady amusing herself" with a "talent for scene-stealing."[2] Sean O'Faolain claimed she had "instinct not ideas."[3] Arthur Mitchell concluded that her "socialism was more emotional than theoretical."[4] It is no wonder, Elizabeth Coxhead remarked, that Markievicz "is remembered for the wrong reasons, in the wrong way. . . , regarded with a curious ambivalence, accused of undue fanaticism and bitterness, blamed for much that was not her fault . . . hers is not the image of Irish womanhood we want to present to the outside world."[5]

Although her drive was exemplary, we can now see that Markievicz resembled many female activists of early-twentieth-century Ireland in speaking out and actively participating in the three leading political movements of the day—nationalism, feminism, and socialism. Like many of her sister activists, she also wrote for several influential journals connected with these movements, most notably, the nationalist-feminist monthly *Bean na hÉireann* (Woman of Ireland) and the suffragist weekly the *Irish Citizen*. Upon her release from prison during the general amnesty in 1917 and up until her death in 1927, Markievicz contributed editorials and poems, letters and speeches to preeminent nationalist, feminist, and socialist journals such as the *Workers' Republic, Irish Worker, Sinn Féin, Poblacht na hEireann, Éire, An Phoblacht*, and the *Nation*.[6] And she did so despite involvement in underground governmental operations, imprisonment, and the need to go into hiding during the War of Independence (1919–21) and Civil War (1922–23).

Although O'Faolain has influentially maintained that the "printed material" about Markievicz's life "is small, the oral testimony copious as a legend,"[7] Markievicz herself left behind a significant body of writing that simultaneously challenges and helps account for persistent, negative portraits of her. Unlike Alice Milligan and Maud Gonne, she never wrote regularly for the press, often choosing more physical means of expressing her activism. Markievicz's intermittent contributions to nationalist journals nevertheless demonstrate a significant rhetorical and theoretical achievement in which she linked the three most influential political movements of the day.

This chapter will explore the ways that Markievicz used the forum of the advanced nationalist press to enlist women in the cause of political activism, to heal significant divisions between the suffragists and the nationalists during the years when these two groups were often at odds, and to promote the idea of the "Armed" New Woman, an activist who would be equipped with the historical background, visionary ideals, and military weaponry to bring about the liberation of Ireland, women, and the poor. As many revival writers and activists would discover, "identity is seldom straight-forward and given, more often a matter of negotiation and exchange."[8] Reading Markievicz's press writings teaches us how, through subversive use of allegory, nationalist identity could be persistently and intricately bound up with notions of gender equality.

Revolution and the Vote

For the past two decades, feminist historians have sought to understand the complicated, often divisive relationship between nationalism and feminism in early-twentieth-century Ireland. These historians have documented how the Home Rule struggle damaged the credibility and popularity of the suffrage movement, causing a decade-long rift between nationalists and feminists in the critical years leading up to independence.[9] Other commentators have noted how such divisiveness largely dissipated in the aftermath of the Easter Rising. Both the Irish Women's Franchise League and Cumann na mBan (the women's council of the Irish Volunteers) were fundamentally altered as suffragists committed to the nationalist cause and as nationalist women developed explicitly feminist demands.[10] In the politically charged period leading up to the Easter Rising, when numerous militant organizations sprang into being, the most visible struggle between nationalist and feminist women centered on the legitimacy of suffragists of appealing to the British Parliament, rather than to the Irish population, for their enfranchisement. The divisive question of working within or outside of the British parliamentary system preoccupied nationalists since the Parnellite split of the early 1890s. As we saw in chapter 1, Alice Milligan's debates with James Connolly in the pages of the *Shan Van Vocht* centered on this very problem. A decade later, in 1908, when Constance Markievicz began to write for the advanced nationalist press, suffragists and socialists alike were appealing to Irish readers to advance their political agenda in the British Parliament; both movements generated similar rebukes from abstentionist nationalists, who refused to work within the British parliamentary system. Reading the advanced nationalist press, however, one can observe how the suffrage and nationalist movements monitored one another, criticizing as well as appealing to the other camp so that suffragists would develop a nationalist perspective and nationalists would adopt feminist principles.

Well before the Easter Rising, at a particularly vibrant time for women in Irish politics, when Hanna Sheehy Skeffington and Margaret Cousins were founding the militant Irish Women's Franchise League, Constance Markievicz was endeavoring to bring suffragists and nationalists together. In 1909, the year after she joined Inghinidhe na hÉireann (Daughters of Ireland), Markievicz became involved with its new monthly, *Bean na hÉireann*. Tellingly, her awakening political commitment first found expression in the advanced nationalist press. Later in life, Markievicz noted that she had been introduced to nationalism by reading Arthur Griffith's *Sinn Féin* and W. P. Ryan's *The Irish Peasant*.[11] Throughout her subsequent writings for the nationalist and feminist press, she attempted to enlist her readers in other emancipatory, egalitarian causes as well.

"A Double Battle to Fight": Markievicz's Rhetorical Appeals in *Bean na hÉireann*

In print from November 1908 to February 1911, the penny monthly *Bean na hÉireann* (Woman of Ireland) quickly developed into an important platform for advanced nationalist women seeking a voice in the growing liberation movements of nationalism, feminism, and socialism. In its masthead, the new journal proclaimed its support for "complete separatism; the rising cause of feminism, and the interest of Irishwomen generally." According to Helena Molony, who cofounded and edited *Bean*, Inghinidhe wanted to provide an alternative to Griffith's weeklies, *United Irishman* (1899–1906) and its successor, *Sinn Féin* (1906–14), whose pragmatic nationalism advocated a dual kingdom, rather than an egalitarian republic. As Molony explained, "While we encouraged and carried out the Sinn Féin policy as far as supporting everything Irish . . . and sabotaging and obstructing British Government whenever opportunity offered, we could not see any virtue in joining a mere Repeal Movement, for the original object of Sinn Féin was to restore the Irish Parliament of 1782."[12] *Bean na hÉireann* was to be "a women's paper," Molony emphasized, "advocating militancy, separatism, and feminism."[13] Through her longstanding involvement with trade unionism, it would also offer a stronger analysis of trade unionism than Griffith's nationalist papers, including labor notes and correspondence with James Connolly during his temporary removal to the United States.[14] Although the journal made much of its status as the first and only nationalist newspaper written expressly for women, who also contributed most of its features, as they had in the *Shan Van Vocht*, *Bean na hÉireann* nonetheless found space, despite its modest size, for commentary by male nationalists such as Arthur Griffith (under the pen name "Ier"), James Stephens, and Bulmer Hobson. In keeping with the guidelines adopted at Inghinidhe's first meeting, most of the journal's women writers assumed Celtic personae, though one writer, Sidney Gifford, adopted the persona of a strong Wexford farmer, "John Brennan," in hopes of commanding more respect from her readers.[15]

A central, unresolved question among numerous contributors to *Bean na hÉireann* was how to prioritize the demands of nationalism, feminism, and socialism—Markievicz's "three great movements." Despite its expressed status as "the first and only Irish women's nationalist paper," for example, *Bean* did not support the enfranchisement of women because it could not countenance the suffragist policy of lobbying the British Parliament to that end. Advanced nationalists saw achieving their own Irish government as their primary goal. As Margaret Ward has documented, Inghinidhe's solution was to advocate greater representation of women in the nationalist movement to build up the existing organizations, as well as to enhance women's status in Irish society.[16] Such policies, Markievicz argued, would guarantee that "no one should place sex before nationality or nationality before sex."[17]

If it lacked an explicit commitment to the suffragist cause, *Bean na hÉireann* nonetheless expressed advanced feminist and labor views for its time. Several years before the Irish Women's Franchise League had its own newspaper, *Bean na hÉireann* provided news of the women's movement around the world. Mindful of the growing role of working women in Irish society, it also circulated tips and helpful suggestions for blue-collar, professional, and "independent" women, as well as for single girls.[18] Whereas the literary and advertising content of the *Shan Van Vocht* appealed to male and female readers in the comfortable middle class, *Bean* aimed to provide practical guidance for nationalist women of a broader economic spectrum. Like Delia Larkin's "Women Workers' Column" in the *Irish Worker*, which is studied in chapter 4, *Bean* initially offered sensible advice on dress and domestic topics, but as we will see, *Bean* writers adapted such traditional topics for subversive, revolutionary ends. Its advertisements also moved seamlessly between tradition and modernity, appealing to female readers to purchase Irish-made goods—millinery, jewelry, food—that recalled Ireland's forgotten cultural traditions, even as they assiduously reminded readers that such traditions were actually the latest look for the modern Irish woman.[19]

Despite the monthly's expressed interest in supporting women's independent political and economic responsibilities and opportunities, it found itself the target of long-standing criticism by suffragists, most notably Hanna Sheehy Skeffington, who continually challenged her nationalist sisters to place women's equality at the center of their cultural and political activism. Rebutting Markievicz's blithe optimism, Sheehy Skeffington skeptically challenged women to examine carefully how their male contemporaries treated them in the committee room. Citing examples from the Gaelic League, Sinn Féin, and the Industries revival, Sheehy Skeffington sharply noted that women were recognized not as comrades but rather as mothers and housekeepers, hardly an example of gender equality.[20]

Implicit in nearly every one of Markievicz's columns, features, and letters in *Bean na hÉireann* was her desire to demonstrate that one could indeed yoke the causes of Ireland and of women: "the first step on the road to freedom," Markievicz declared, "is to realize ourselves as Irishwomen, not as Irish or merely as women, but as Irishwomen doubly enslaved and with a double battle to fight."[21] The notion of a "double battle" is consistent with the philosophy of James Connolly, who, back in the 1890s in the *Shan Van Vocht*, was striving to link nationalism and feminism. Published as a chapter in *The Re-Conquest of Ireland* (1915), his essay "Woman" alerted readers to another strategic alliance—between women and workers: "The worker is the slave of capitalist society, the female worker is the slave of that slave."[22]

Whereas the 1916 Proclamation of the Republic announced that Ireland had "organised her manhood" for the insurgent cause, Markievicz's writings focused on conscripting the other half. An analysis of her writings suggests she had three main preoccupations during these years: to enlist women in political activism, to legitimate female militancy, and, implicitly, to unite suffragists and nationalists in a common cause. In the space of some twenty months in 1908–10, Markievicz contributed eighteen articles, features, or letters to *Bean na hÉireann*, under the pen names of "Maca," "Druid of the Fianna," and "Armid," with her gardening columns, which she wrote under as Armith, becoming a cause célèbre.[23] But she chose to make her most explicit call to arms in a lecture, "Women, Ideals, and Nationalism," excerpts of which were published in the November 1909 *Bean*:

> Arm yourselves with weapons to fight your nation's cause. Arm your souls with noble and free ideas. Arm your minds with the histories and memories of your country and her martyrs, her language, and a knowledge of her arts, and her industries. And if in your day the call should come for your body to arm, do not shirk that either.[24]

This lecture, originally delivered to the Students' National Literary Society, an audience Markievicz addressed as "the rising young women of Ireland," most succinctly describes how Markievicz sought to bring together the suffragists and nationalists by supporting women's militancy and by assuming women's intellectual equality. Markievicz implored her female audience to prepare for revolution through physical training, philosophical reflection, and historical and cultural study—a holistic proposition that flies in the face of popular memories of Markievicz as a brash, theatrical aristocrat. In its straightforward appeals, its expectations of women's intellectual and physical stamina, and its overt call to arms, her address also stands in striking contrast both to the pragmatic writings of Arthur Griffith and to the secretive philosophy of the Irish Republican Brotherhood, which kept its methods and its existence out of the public eye.

Hostile critics such as Sean O'Casey and T. J. Smith and sympathetic ones such as Anne Haverty and Margaret Ward have alike suggested that Markievicz's understanding of the national and labor struggle was more emotional than intellectual.[25] "Women, Ideals, and Nationalism" complicates such an assessment. Markievicz prepared the audience for her militant proposal, first, by describing political role models from the past and present: women in Russia and Poland, where they "work as comrades, shoulder to shoulder, with their men"; militant ancestors in Ireland such as Maeve, Fheas, and Macha; members of the Ladies' Land League; women in the United Irishmen Uprising; and female poets and commentators who contributed to the nationalist journal *Nation*.[26] Unlike Milligan's Ascendancy girls or Mary E. L. Butler's nationalist women, Markievicz's representative women found political agency outside the home. She linked the militancy of warrior women, political mavericks, and radical journalists, all activists who stepped outside the private sphere to fight, physically or rhetorically, on behalf of Ireland.

Although most readers of *Bean na hÉireann* would have applauded Markievicz's nationalist call to action, many would have balked at women taking up arms. During a time when even committed nationalists such as Alice Milligan, Anna Johnston, Barry Delaney, Maud Gonne, and Mary Butler described women's political behavior in terms of raising voices or nationalist children, and when feminist activists were largely pacifists, Markievicz challenged both political camps equally. She frankly criticized nationalist women who "have been content to remain quietly at home, and leave all the fighting and striving to the men," and openly rejected "the old idea that a woman can only serve her nation through her home."[27] She also reminded women that if they hoped to be respected as "citizens first, women after," they then needed to find individual ways to advance the cause of Ireland.[28] Drawing on the earlier insights of James Connolly, Markievicz dismissed nationalism that did not promote female equality. She also challenged suffrage societies that failed to link women's freedom with national liberty, proclaiming, "'A Free Ireland with No Sex Disabilities in her Constitution' should be the motto of all Nationalist women."[29] As she rhetorically balanced the competing demands of nationalism and feminism, Markievicz provided concrete examples of ways to meet them. Criticizing two contemporary bills in Parliament—the Liberals' projected Land Tax and the Conservatives' Tariff Reform—while promoting "Voluntary Protection against Foreign goods" (a cornerstone of the Sinn Féin economic platform), Markievicz illustrated how Irish women could "LIVE REALLY IRISH LIVES," not merely by boycotting English goods but also by organizing as women collectively and publicly to ensure the everyday activities of buying Irish goods, dressing in Irish clothes, and eating Irish produce were implemented nationwide.[30]

Markievicz opened another of her editorials for *Bean na hÉireann* by outlining the moral and economic importance of the vote, then listing familiar suffragist complaints about women's second-class status in a country that denied them one of the chief advantages of citizenship:

> Though she must obey the laws and take her share of the expense of government, yet her views are refused the ordinary mode of expression. Though she has to gain her living, and though she finds fierce sex antagonism among her fellow-workers, the weapon that should be hers to use in her own defense in the labour world has been wrested from her grasp, while the men workers unhesitatingly and unscrupulously use the same weapon to turn her out of her employment to make room for themselves or to put such disabilities in her way that her wages are kept down and her employment is jeopardised.[31]

This passage, which reverberates with the brashness of suffragist rhetoric, revealed not only Markievicz's feminism but also her alliance with working women, who paid the heaviest price for being denied the vote. Markievicz's thesis, however, concerned the "more complicated" question of feminist and nationalist relations in a political context where liberty had never been voluntarily granted to the dispossessed. Appropriating the sacred language of Catholicism for two radical political causes, Markievicz argued that gender and nationality are "co-equal and co-existing in one's individuality as indivisible as the three persons of the Trinity." Like the Christian who invokes the example of Christ far more often than that of the Holy Spirit, Markievicz maintained that "no concession . . . given by the British Parliament is worth winning at the expense of [even] a little of [one's] nationality."[32] Although her editorial clearly privileged the nationalist movement over the suffrage campaign, Markievicz's pragmatic advice to women activists also suggests she has learned much about negotiating power among chauvinistic Irish men. Tellingly, Markievicz advises her feminist audience to monitor nationalist women to ensure women's equal participation in the national struggle:

> Force them into public life, make them work for all their country. Force them to serve on all committees and boards to which they are eligible. . . . Insist that when they give their services to collect money for charities, etc., they should be on the committees that have the spending of it. Organise trade unions and get out statistics of women's wages. . . . [33]

Her repeated use of the imperative voice hammers home her steely message. Yet an unusual feature in this disciplined, sharp-toned checklist is Markievicz's strict monitoring of both women's *and* men's behavior in regard to women's activism. Later in the editorial, Markievicz argued that by following her egalitarian-minded advice, women "will teach our men to look upon us as fellow-Irelanders and fellow workers . . . on whose right to citizenship no doubt can be thrown." Throughout Markievicz's career as a dissident journalist, though, she harbored doubts that feminists could transform the nationalist movement; she strongly suspected men might prove recalcitrant students to their feminist teachers. Her lingering doubts turned out to be well founded, as would become plain with the establishment of the Irish Free State in 1922 and of Eire in 1937. In her later pieces for the *Irish Citizen*, the optimism that buoyed her first columns for *Bean na hÉireann* shows signs of sinking, though as we will see, she consistently places blame for disappointing progress at the feet of passive nationalist women.

Allegory as Resistance Literature

Markievicz's best-known contribution to *Bean na hÉireann* was her monthly "Woman with a Garden" column, which ran from February 1909 through March 1910,[34] and especially her slug-crushing advice, highlighted by nearly every writer who has discussed women and Irish nationalism. As Anne Haverty has observed, the "typically outrageous" style is immediately striking, as is her "humorous parodying" of both gardening and nationalist rhetoric.[35] Liz Curtis has noted in passing that the columns provided Markievicz with the "occasional[] opportunity to make a political point."[36] Other critics have focused on the disarming shifts from insurgency to domesticity. Declan Kiberd regrets the "rather strained conflation of violent nationalism with pouting feminine gentility."[37] C. L. Innes, on the other hand, views these "startling" transitions between revolution and roses as evidence of Markievicz's rhetorical entrapment between the nationalist discourse of warriorhood and stereotyped femininity.[38] If one examines the content of her gardening advice in light of the radical message, however, these columns contain the potential to achieve quite the opposite effect. Instead of being trapped by the opposing worlds of male militancy and female domesticity, Markievicz used the garden as a field of multiple political struggles: against the suppression of women *and* the nation.

Of course, the Irish garden has a political history that at once challenges and benefits from its association with the bourgeois private, protected sphere. High walls and crowded shrubs have concealed rebels on the run. Bowers have afforded discreet places for exchanges of information. Freshly tilled flower beds have hidden guns alongside newly planted bulbs. Markievicz's innovation in her *Bean na hÉireann* columns was to reclaim the garden's political potential for both women and nationalists by composing features that allegorically described how readers could resist domesticity *and* imperialism through that most visible icon of the Ascendancy class, the garden.

Markievicz's allegory of the garden would be hard to miss given its ubiquity in nearly every gardening column she wrote. The "tender plants" and "poor wee bulbs" signified nascent nationalism and youthful militancy.[39] Mature blossoms, such as the summer roses, recalled Roisin Dubh and the blood of martyred United Irishmen.[40] Autumn blossoms, like the golden Rubeckia, were emblematized as the vibrant sunburst, a favorite image of Ireland's national aspirations that Markievicz included in the background illustration for *Bean na hÉireann*'s masthead.[41] The garden's enemies—slugs, snails, wasps, flies—were viewed as British soldiers, invaders that destroyed the flowers and fruits of the land.[42] Destructive "forces of the earth," such as heavy frost, cruel blights, bitter gales, and blinding snow, were predictably associated with the British Empire or its colonial presence in Dublin Castle.[43]

Markievicz's allegory of the garden has largely escaped serious critical attention, in no small part because her seemingly facile theater of symbols caused many readers to misunderstand her parodic style. As Barbara Harlow has noted, much of "resistance literature" has been overlooked not only because of its political content but also because it is "radically different from, indeed . . . opposed to, the cult of *bienséances* [aesthetic propriety]."[44] Allegorical writing in Ireland, explains Luke Gibbons, is so tightly woven into the cultural fabric that it can be considered "a part of consciousness itself."[45] The repressive nature of colonialism—codified in the Penal Laws—trained native writers to virtuosic mastery of allegorical expression; many so fully immersed themselves in the imperatives of allegory

Bean na h-Eireann
(THE WOMAN OF IRELAND)

Vol. I. No. 3. Eanair — JANUARY, 1909. Price—One Penny.

To Our Sisters.

The new year is the time for good resolutions and editorial sermons, and a good many pious sentiments and meaningless platitudes are preached from editorial arm chairs at this season. The Bean na h-Eireann does not like sermons. We believe there is in Ireland too much preaching and too little practice. The chief fault we find with men is that they talk very big and do very little, and we would like to foster amongst Irishwomen a desire to work, rather than talk about it in the columns of newspapers.

But because we are at the beginning of another year, it is well that we should and a purer atmosphere. We, Irishwomen, must learn to throw off our present diffidence, and assume our natural position in Irish life, and men will soon have to frankly admit that it is only by working hand in hand that we can hope to **make Ireland free.**

A great many, if not all, the various pressing social problems could be much more effectively dealt with by women than by men. The squalor and misery of the towns, with the poverty and dulness of the rural parts of Ireland, surely need some attention, and we believe women could relieve much of this distressing state of affairs without legislation or any kind of outside help. The grinding poverty of the rural population, and the town-dwellers

3. Masthead of *Bean na hÉireann*, January 1909. Constance Markievicz designed the masthead, drawing on Inghinidhe's banner of the rising sun. Note the influence of the Celtic revival in the lettering and the Tara brooch that adorns the woman. Inghinidhe members such as Gonne and Markievicz were sometimes photographed wearing a similarly styled brooch, designed specifically for Inghinidhe na hÉireann. Reproduced courtesy of the National Library of Ireland.

that it became second nature. Which is why it has "not always been possible to clearly distinguish between what was factual and what was allegorical" in Irish writing.[46] Mary Jean Corbett contends that feminist, materialist, and postcolonial modes of analysis also instruct readers to be alert to the dynamic operations of allegory, "to look for 'hidden' or 'repressed' signs of the cultural and political embedded within representations of the private and domestic, to see them pointing to something outside or beyond the text, to be alert to what their doubleness may conceal or reveal."[47] As a feminist, socialist, and nationalist, Markievicz dedicated her journalistic efforts to enlisting women in all three movements, to teaching her readers how to discover the hidden meanings both in her writings and in their own daily lives. Her use of the home to normalize feminine militancy was not altogether unprecedented either. Writing for the mid-nineteenth-century Young Ireland newspaper *United Irishman*, John Mitchel assured middle-class women that manufacturing bullets was both decorous and domestic: "No lady is too delicate for the culinary preparation of casting bullets. No hand is too white to make up cartridges."[48] Writing fifty years later in this expressly Irish resistant tradition, Constance Markievicz provided readers with a subversive model for rereading a whole body of women's work.

Many of Markievicz's contemporaries simply missed the subversive message of her gardening columns. Most likely responding to the uncanny parallels between Markievicz's parodies of cultivated femininity and brash militancy, on the one hand, and her two principal (and contradictory) personae—the Ascendancy Countess and the Red Revolutionary—on the other, these readers may have viewed Markievicz's "strained conflation" of styles as merely a reflection of her mixed-up theatrical identities. And, truth be told, her lighthearted tone and artless style did indeed mask the artfully subversive, resistant content of her columns. So much so that her enthusiastic pruner whose fingers "itch to hold her knife" provoked only yawns among the censors at Dublin Castle. Yet, even though her work on a woman's home turf may not have spurred her female readers to outright revolution, it gradually drew them out of the garden and into the streets.

During its first months, *Bean na hÉireann* featured traditionally feminine columns such as "Cookery Notes," "Household Hints," and "How Irishwomen Should Dress," many of which focused on womanly topics from an Irish-Irelander point of view. Even here, however, the editor of *Bean* suggested there was no inherent conflict between Irish tradition and international modernity. Indeed, many of the advertising and editorial notices encouraging readers to purchase Irish-made goods, especially millinery, jewelry, and food, insisted on the "modernity" of these items. Markievicz's gardening columns likewise reinterpreted women's traditional domestic activities as modern, political action. When she began her

"Woman with a Garden" column in February 1909, Markievicz appeared to be offering little more than guileless gardening advice about turning "a little sod of dirt" into a flourishing garden. In her introductory column, she conceded that winter seemed "a rather bad time of year to begin. . . . But still much can be done."[49] The double meaning of these seemingly innocuous words became plain, however, in her subsequent columns. Thus, from her first submission, Markievicz was aiming to cultivate not only the dormant Dublin soil but also the dormant nationalism of her female readers, who had little or no experience in public agitation.

Markievicz's first strategy in enlisting women in the cause of Ireland was to use the garden as a forum for nationalist lessons in economics and history. In several early columns she reminded her readers to cultivate native Irish plants, Sinn Féin advice that was both political and practical in the garden.[50] While looking to the gardener's calendar as an occasion for republican history, Markievicz also slipped in tactics for planning an uprising. For example, in May, she recalled the onset of the Wexford Rebellion, and then reminded readers that "hardy annuals may now be picked off" and to "watch for slugs," sound gardening suggestions—and equally sound, though coded, counsel for maintaining a strong army. Her August column began by taking her readers back to the eighteenth-century letters of Lord Edward Fitzgerald, whose initial enthusiasm for and later aversion toward gardening "manage[d] to contain much of his life's history," exposing his alienation from the colonial establishment and his growing militancy as one of the leaders of the United Irishmen. Indeed, Fitzgerald's reversal of attitude about the garden "endowed" Markievicz's own hobby "with a new value—to be yet another link with Ireland's past and Ireland's heroes." Markievicz saw the garden primarily as a measure of revolutionary commitment. It provided her with plentiful occasions for symbolic lessons on the difficulties of defense during war, as when she warns her readers to guard Ireland's still-ripening harvest:

> You must watch your wall fruit trees well for snails and slugs as well as for wasps and flies, and the tender-hearted colleen will

> have to make up her mind which she wishes to preserve—insects or fruit! For both in one garden are impossible.[51]

Markievicz used seasonal plants and the current month to chronicle the experiences of past patriots in colonized countries, drawing on the "calendar of nationalist activity" pioneered by Alice Milligan and Anna Johnston in the *Shan Van Vocht*, and a favorite feature of many advanced nationalist journals. Some columns quickly established a season's link with a revered Irish patriot. September, for example, "is sacred to Robert Emmet," Markievicz claimed.[52] In another column on Emmet, Markievicz remarked on the mnemonic power of scent, as well as Emmet's love of lavender, and observed, "It only requires a breath of lavender-scented air to bring my thoughts back over one hundred years to the Autumn of 1803—the Autumn which Robert Emmet sanctified by a martyr's death." Not only did these aromatic spikes mask the "stuffy atmosphere" of Kilmainhaim Jail, where Emmet was held until his execution; they also hid poison, "a clever and subtle conspiracy to rob [one's captors] of their prize, the rope of its victim."[53]

Markievicz viewed the shifting seasons and natural forces as both a stimulus for Irish popular memory and an allegory for the national struggle. The May garden recalled Ireland's turbulent history of occupation: spring offered "sunshine and promise," but also held the potential for frost and storms that could "leave the garden a tragedy of young growths torn and dead, and rose trees shriveled and broken."[54] In contrast, winter brought cold, which Markievicz associated with the "bitter blight of English rule," but, by causing the "tender plant of nationality" to go dormant, it also allowed her to "recoup[] her vital powers for the struggle that will come." Bulbs planted in the now-frozen January soil prompted Markievicz to remind her readers that Ireland's political dormancy would not last forever:

> Should not Ireland take a lesson from the Snowdrop, and gather her forces together for the supreme effort to gain the

> light? The whole forces of the earth are ranged against the Snowdrop, the whole of the British Empire against Ireland, and if our tiny Snowdrop can prevail and force the pass into life, surely the task is not too great for Ireland.[55]

Although Markievicz here employs a common metaphor of Irish revolutionary rhetoric, her widely circulated assertion that an uprising was as sure to surface as the flowers of spring might well have inspired the nationalist leader Pádraig Pearse to proclaim in 1915:

> Our foes are strong and wise and wary; but strong and wise and wary as they are, they cannot undo the miracles of God who ripens in the hearts of young men the seeds sown by young men of a former generation. And the seeds sown by the young men of '65 and '67 are coming to their miraculous ripening today.[56]

Over the course of its first six months, as *Bean na hÉireann* grew increasingly militant, the light, domestic features gradually disappeared. In September and October 1909, Helena Molony made the journal's case for the legitimacy of physical force in her two-part series "Physical Force."[57] By the first anniversary edition in November 1909, editor Molony acknowledged what was already apparent: the staff had disposed of broad-based, female-oriented journalism to provide needed space for "clear thinking on more important national issues."[58] By retaining "Woman with a Garden," Molony pointedly indicated the political significance and the militant quality of Markievicz's columns, whose focus had already shifted from enlisting women in the Irish nationalist cause to introducing and then normalizing female militancy. Although "arming" women with hoes and rakes hardly sounded revolutionary in the context of the garden, suggesting that they join men in armed insurgency had radical potential. If, as Amy Benton notes, "the readiness to bear arms for the state was the qualification *par excellence* for citizenship," then Markievicz was seeking both to liberate her nation and to ensure equality between the sexes.[59]

Markievicz's gardening columns outlined what women should expect if they wished to be part of the revolution. In October, a chill month that Dublin gardeners dedicated to preparing the soil for the next spring's planting, Markievicz candidly explained that political activism required arduous labor:

> It is our duty to till and to dig and do all that which lies in our power to aid the tender plant of nationality in its struggle for existence, and to protect and arm it in the fight that is before it against the cruel frosts, the cold winds and bitter blight of English rule and occupation that has laid it broken and withered on the ground for so long.[60]

Her gendered language—"to aid" and "to protect" the "tender plant of nationality"—suggested that this was work already familiar to women. Yet her jarring call to "arm it in the fight" against the "bitter blight of English rule and occupation" forced readers once again to face the subversive militancy of her gardening advice. In her infamous June 1909 column about crushing slugs, Markievicz invokes the spirit of the Celtic Twilight in making cheerfully explicit the grisly aspects of war:

> It is very unpleasant work killing slugs and snails, but let us not be daunted. A good nationalist should look upon slugs in a garden much in the same way as she looks on the English in Ireland, and only regret that she cannot crush the Nation's enemies with the same ease that she can the garden's, with just one tread of her fairy foot.[61]

At first glance, Markievicz's gardening advice here resembles the implicitly feminist articles in the *United Irishman* that promoted the "Nationalisation of the Irish homelife," such as Mary E. L. Butler's series "Womanhood and Nationhood" and Maud Gonne's series "Ireland and Her Children," discussed in chapter 2. Yet Markievicz's imaginative zeal in eradicating gardening pests also made more recognizable and less threatening the future likelihood of women engaged in armed conflict, when the sniper's firm, gun-wielding hand might replace the gardener's "dainty foot." Her highly rhetorical discussion of crushing slugs in fact anticipates by several years Pádraig Pearse's militant exhortation: "we must accustom ourselves to the thought of arms, to the sight of arms, to the use of arms."[62]

In her July column, Markievicz again reminded her readers of the sacrifices required for national freedom, invoking July roses then in full bloom for a lyrical, yet realistic account of war:

> On turning the corner to the rose garden a flash of crimson rose leaves arrested me with the vivid shock that comes to one awakened out of a dream, and brought me straight to the reality of July '98. The petals of Roisin Dubh lay as red and as strange then on the green hillsides of Wexford—scattered a crimson shedding over the land from little Arklow to the shores of Lough Foyle, from the sea-bounds of the Atlantic to among the dusty streets of Dublin. . . . [63]

Distancing herself from Pádraig Pearse's death-focused position that "blood is a cleansing and a sanctifying thing, and the nation which regards it as the final horror has lost its manhood,"[64] Markievicz instead views her bloodred rose petals as an image of life: "What our July garden with its roses should remind us is that it is we who must live so that our martyrs' blood shall not have been shed in vain." She seems to suggest that the women of Ireland must preserve their lives because the men would be putting theirs in peril. Indeed, as Amy Benton argues, the Irish republican ethic depended on excluding women from the front lines: Irish militants viewed women as private subjects whom the male citizens must protect.[65] The sole exception were the women of the Irish Citizen Army (in which Markievicz served as a lieutenant second in command during the Easter Rising). Yet Markievicz's advice for eradicating "foreign" pests from the green fields of Ireland openly challenges such exclusionary attitudes. When she instructs her readers, "You must creep about in the dusk, with a lamp, and catch [slugs] in the act; or make traps by placing little heaps of bran near the plants," she is metaphorically describing the quiet, covert activities that women performed during the United Irishmen Uprising of 1798 and the Easter Rising of 1916.[66]

Republican Revival: Markievicz's Historiography in the *Irish Citizen*

Having put down her pen for *Bean na hÉireann* in 1911, Markievicz picked it up again in 1915, this time to address readers of the *Irish Citizen*. Her rhetorical approach had changed strikingly: instead of figurative language and allegory, she used impatient arguments and revisionist history to legitimate female militancy. She was now addressing ardent feminist suffragists, whose campaign, Markievicz later explained, provided her with "my first bite, you may say, at the apple of freedom."[67] Like her sister Eva Gore-Booth, Markievicz had joined the suffrage movement in 1896, and served as president of the Sligo branch of the Irish Women's Suffrage and Local Government Association. Whereas Eva based her activism in Manchester, where she was a leading figure in the English Women's Trade Union movement and tirelessly campaigned for women's political and economic enfranchisement, Markievicz focused her increasingly radical and collaborative activities in Ireland.

During the years 1911–15, Markievicz had lectured for the Socialist Party of Ireland, the Irish Women Workers' Union, and the Irish Women's Franchise League. She had organized mock attacks and defenses with Na Fianna Éireann. And she had served as vice president of Inghinidhe na hÉireann and treasurer of the Irish Citizen Army. Despite her frenetic pace and her involvement with nearly every republican organization of the day, however, Markievicz had also discovered that many male nationalists were uncomfortable standing shoulder to shoulder with a woman. In 1914, for example, Markievicz's Fianna boys had secretly picked up arms at Howth without even consulting her and her sister leaders, let alone inviting them on the mission. Such painful exclusions surely account in part for the tone and message of her *Irish Citizen* writings.

During Irish feminism's first few years, its most devoted champions, the suffragists, had considerable difficulty getting publicity for their cause. Louise Ryan notes that "much of the press boycotted suffrage events and gave the women little or no publicity."[68] In response, the Irish Women's Franchise League (IWFL) established its own journal in 1912. Over the course of its eight years in print, the *Irish Citizen* evolved from a penny weekly to a two-pence monthly. The newspaper supported Irish self-determination; under the editorship of Louie Bennett, general secretary of the Irish Women Workers' Union, it was especially vocal in its support of trade unionism as well. Its writers were unanimously committed to gender equality. Most, as Ryan notes, "considered themselves to be feminists rather than merely suffragists campaigning for votes."[69] Like *Bean na hÉireann*, the *Irish Citizen* wrestled with which cause to put first, feminism or nationalism. From 1914 to 1916, during the formative years of Cumann na mBan, the *Irish Citizen* carefully observed and reported on the organization's success in establishing women's equality and autonomy among militant nationalists. Although politically sympathetic to Cumann na mBan, the IWFL was also its most persistent critic.[70] Like the league, Markievicz expressed concerns about Cumann na mBan, whose primary political ambition seemed simply to support the men, even though by 1915 it was the country's most prominent nationalist organization for women.

In "The Future of Irishwomen," her first contribution to the *Irish Citizen*, Markievicz sought to educate Irish women about their warrior past and to spur them into militant action in the present.[71] She opened by describing what she viewed as a serious contemporary crisis in Ireland: female activists "in danger of being civilised by men out of existence." Recalling the culture of precolonial days, when "ancient Ireland bred warrior women," Markievicz lamented that "that spirit is now only alive in the suffragettes." Like Maud Gonne in her opening lecture for Inghinidhe on the Goddess Brigid, Markievicz viewed the Celtic past as a source of insight and inspiration for the contemporary nationalist women of Ireland. Unlike Gonne, however, who recalled mythic or epic women to galvanize women's cultural activism, Markievicz consistently sought out formidable foremothers to kindle militancy among nationalist women.[72] She studied nationalist history to find examples of everyday women who took up arms; she cited many models of female activism from popular memory. In seeking to recover the political agency in these women's lives, Markievicz also highlighted a telling pattern that would later influence the literary and historical writings about her own life. Markievicz transported her readers to the Land Wars of the 1880s to remind her readers of how an earlier women's mass movement, the Ladies' Land League (1881–82), was suppressed by the men in the Land League because, as John O'Leary later sheepishly admitted, "they were honester and more sincere than the men."[73] Markievicz was far less charitable, asserting that the men had shut down the women's organization because the women had "started to do the militant things that the men only threatened and talked of."[74]

Whereas Markievicz only gently criticized male nationalists who treated women as unequal, and rarely elaborated on the social opprobrium and hostility visited upon militant women, she showed no restraint in attacking the poetics of chauvinistic nationalism. She denounced old ballads and figurative language that objectified women; most especially, she denounced the fruits of such figurative thinking: nationalist organizations that objectified their female participants. In particular, Markievicz disparaged the poet Thomas Moore, whose *Melodies* depicted woman as feeble and passive, "like the lap dog which, when it meets a larger animal, rolls over on its back, turns up its toes, and looks pathetic."[75] In directing her criticism at Moore's sentimental lyrics and, more broadly, at conventional representations of women in the Irish poetic tradition, Markievicz anticipated by some seventy-five years Eavan Boland's critique of Irish nationalist poetry.[76] Her dismissal of ballads that envision a female as "a beautiful houri holding dominion by her careful manipulation of her sex and her good looks" confronted more than the imaginative constructs of poetry. Her biting tone might owe something to her clearly stated view of those members of Cumann na mBan who "demoralise women, set them up in separate camps, and deprive them of all initiative and independence."[77] In her journalism and drama of the 1920s, Markievicz broadened this gender critique of Irish nationalism to include many of the male leaders of the Irish Free State.[78]

At first glance, her withering criticism of Cumann na mBan members, whom she looked upon as camp followers of the Irish Volunteers, seems surprisingly dismissive of the very women she was seeking to enlist, and particularly impolitic, given her past involvement with Inghinidhe na hÉireann and her current position within the leadership of Cumann na mBan. As we will see in chapter 4, however, sharp criticism of fellow activists was not that unusual during the revival, especially among trade union activists. For example, Delia Larkin, the first general secretary of the Irish Women Workers' Union and the editor of the *Irish Worker*'s "Women Workers' Column," routinely berated women workers and the male trade union hierarchy when their vision or action departed from hers. Less routine in her criticism, Markievicz used her columns to single out traditional-minded nationalist women such as Agnes O'Farrelly, Cumann na mBan's first figurehead, who stressed that "each rifle we put in [the Irish Volunteers'] hands will represent to us a bolt fastened behind the door of some Irish home to keep out the hostile stranger."[79] Unlike her earlier columns in *Bean na hÉireann*, which assured readers that men would treat women as comrades if only women demonstrated their leadership, here Markievicz openly opposed O'Farrelly's traditionalist goals of arming men to protect Irish women. Her terse recommendation called for practical, if radical, action: "dress suitably in short skirts and strong boots . . . and buy a revolver."[80]

Markievicz concluded "The Future of Irishwomen" by advising her women readers to "escape from their domestic ruts, their feminine pens" by actively assuming responsibilities in what Markievicz suggested was imminent war.[81] Just two months later, she committed herself to a feminist recovery project on the women of the United Irishmen Uprising of 1798. From November 6 to December 4, 1915, the *Irish Citizen* published her five-part series "The Women of '98."[82] In contrast to "The Future of Irishwomen," which impatiently outlined nationalist women's shortcomings, Markievicz's historical series on the women of '98 employed a more mindful tactic, one that, like her gardening columns, provided women with multiple models for political activism. In it she displays her dedication to narrating women's place in the revolution and inspiring her audience to action, as well as to legitimating her own seemingly anomalous militancy as a leader of the Fianna, a soldier in the Irish Citizen Army, and later a sharpshooter in the Easter Rising. Undertaken only months before the Rising of 1916, her recovery project represented an important intervention in Ireland's evolving narrative of national identity. Such "myths of foundation," Amy Benton argues, are especially significant for women, for "it is in that myth that women are often deleted from history, and the peculiar 'warrior' qualities of men are elevated to heroic status. . . . It is in this telling of national myth that the political authority of women has so often been expunged."[83] Implicitly understanding Walter Benjamin's insight that "every image of the past . . . not recognized by the present as one of its own concerns threatens to disappear irretrievably,"[84] Markievicz used the example of past republican women not only to ensure the continuance of present Irish nationalism, but also to safeguard women's future rights.

In her romances across the border, Alice Milligan imagined intrepid, eighteenth-century Ascendancy girls willing to mold luxury items into tools of national resistance. As we have seen in chapter 1, Milligan's stories helped her contemporary middle-class readers contemplate the myriad ways they could fight for Ireland, even from their comfortable, well-appointed homes. For her part, Markievicz found feminist and nationalist inspiration in the tales of 1798. In the first installment of her series "The Women of '98," she asserted the political urgency of learning about the many roles women played in the United Irishmen Uprising of 1798, given the "utter indifference to the struggle" among her contemporaries and the considerable difficulty in tracing the women's stories.[85] Markievicz faults the Penal Laws, even though most had been repealed by the 1790s or were simply not enforced, for the silencing of women's nationalist history: "it was considered a crime to love your county, and anyone daring to teach her history, and tell of the bravery of her patriots was punished with the 'utmost rigor of the law.' "[86] But she leaves unspoken a more likely explanation for nationalist women's "hidden history": the very gender norms that worked to dismiss her athletic, feminine militancy as aberrant. Gleaning memoirs, letters, even old ballads, Markievicz relates stories of women who chose a variety of roles, from heroic activists such as Molly Weston,

Mary Doyle, Mary McCracken, and Betsy Grey to "timid" sorts who served as messengers, nursed the wounded, and provided safe havens for fugitives. Constructing a body of Irish women's republican history, Markievicz's mini-biographies of Irish women wrest iconic events such as 1798 out of what Adrienne Rich has described as the "book of myths / in which / our names do not appear."[87]

Although many of the women in "The Women of '98," could be described as aggressively militant, they were, like Milligan's heroines, armed with the tools of domestic life. Molly Weston raced on horseback and faced the insurgents "with no weapon but a riding whip [and] led the patriots to the charge." Mary Doyle, "armed with a billhook," used it for the grisly and dangerous task of cutting ammunition belts off the enemy's dead and wounded. Susey Toole, a woman who, like Markievicz, was endowed with theatrical flair and impressive endurance, employed her gifts for the revolution: disguising herself as a peasant baker, she "tramped the country gathering information and sending the enemy on the wrong scent."[88] Markievicz also recounted smaller acts of courage and commitment. She told the story of Biddy Magee, a "mere child of twelve and of nervous, timid temperament," whose patriotism "gave her courage" to travel the countryside in the dead of night to warn her rebel comrades that British soldiers were coming.[89] She also told about female messengers such as Betty Palmer, who carried rebel intelligence to some of the United Irishmen leaders, such as Thomas Long, Frederick Hervey, Edward Fitzgerald, and Thomas Russell. Woven into every account was the implication that activism took many forms and relied on different talents. It would be hard for Markievicz's female nationalist audience to read this series without finding at least one model whom they could strive to emulate.

A recurrent theme in "The Women of '98" was what to wear in the revolution. In one installment, Markievicz described a "mysterious woman" who rode with the French army, "dressed in a green habit, with the tricolour and red plume in her hat."[90] She also recalled Molly Weston, who also "dressed in a green habit with the United Irishmen's cockade in her hat."[91] Such details about clothing suggest that Markievicz's own Easter Rising uniform, a green Irish Citizen Army coat and a hat with the ostrich

4. Constance Markievicz, posing with gun (Keogh Brothers), the National Library of Ireland. This photograph of her cloaked and striking a militant pose was a frequently circulated image of Markievicz. Reproduced courtesy of the National Library of Ireland.

plume feather, was selected not merely to express her "theatrical flair," as many commentators have asserted, but also to establish a connection with earlier militant women fighting for Ireland. Her focus on clothing, moreover, recalls Douglas Hyde's intimate link between clothing and language, wherein Irish tweeds, like the Gaelic language, were promoted to signal Irish national identity. More radical than Hyde's Celticism, though, Markievicz's emphasis on symbolic dress shares a closer bond with the "transgressive costume drama" of agrarian militants such as the Mummers and Strawboys of pre-Famine Ireland, whose disguised identity assisted their guerrilla activities.[92]

Like the Mummers and Strawboys, Markievicz focused her militant performances on the ambiguities of gender: some of the best-known photographs of her (enlarged and on display at places as diverse as Kilmainham Gaol, the National Museum, and Strokestown Famine Museum) feature her in cloaked attire with a pistol in her hand. In many of Markievicz's most evocative poses—her portraits with a handgun, her tableau as an armor-clad Joan of Arc clasping a sword—the costumes and props she chooses seem especially chosen to obscure the feminine body and to play up the agency of masculine combativeness, creating the impression that Markievicz felt the need to cloak her natural shape in order to enhance her militant, nationalist energy. The question of radical dress would preoccupy her to the end of her life. Markievicz would return to this question of clothing and politics when she penned her republican New Woman melodrama *Broken Dreams*, which was posthumously produced in 1927.[93]

Conclusions: Popular Memory and the Militant New Woman

Undoubtedly, Markievicz's militancy has had lasting consequences for both scholarly and popular accounts of her life. Her chroniclers, from the hostile Sean O'Casey to the bemused D. J. Smith, have described her with outrage or smirks, unleashing a catalogue of complaints. She was a play actor, and, worse, a scene-stealer. She was inauthentically Irish, unconvincingly socialist, and unthinkingly militant. She took to political organi-

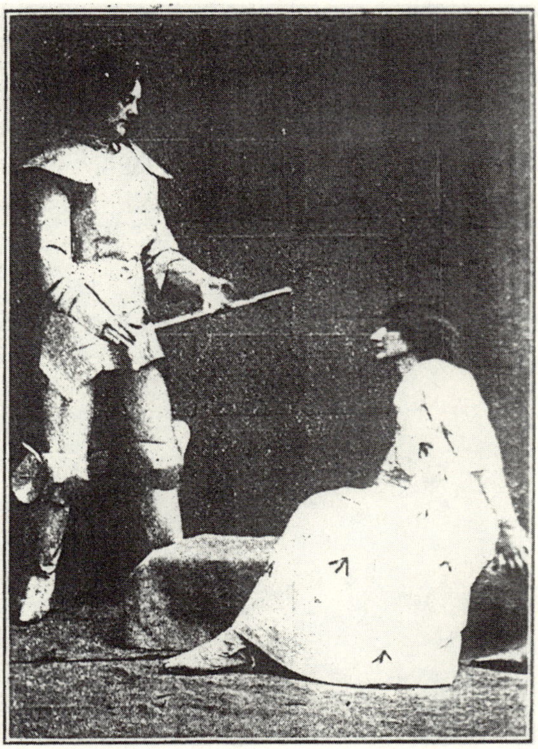

5. Constance Markievicz, posing as Joan of Arc at the Irish Women's Franchise League Daffodil Fête, a two-day cultural festival held in March of 1914. Reproduced courtesy of the National Library of Ireland.

zations "like a child to a toy."[94] Many men, the chroniclers felt sure, "laughed at her sometimes."[95] Yet Markievicz also represented a threat: she was a fury, a harpy, a shrill voice in the cacophony of revolution. Her journalism helps balance these portraits. However negatively Markievicz's redefinition of the militant New Woman may have affected her literary and popular reputation, it established a clear precedent for the armed New Woman, not only for herself, a woman who had already dismissed the cultural and class expectations into which she was born, but also for other women desiring a role but unsure of what part to play. Her writings for the nationalist and feminist press shed light on her part in the long, unacknowledged tradition of Irish women writing in an expressly nationalist, militant tradition. This buried, often-forgotten, yet enduring tradition, in turn, shows Markievicz to be, not a singular activist who countenanced the notion of her exceptionality, but rather part of a collective movement going back centuries, and reaching forward decades to contemporary female mavericks such as Bernadette Devlin McAliskey and Mary Robinson.[96] And however slightly Markievicz's allegories and feminist mini-biographies may have affected public opinion on the legitimacy of female militancy, they nonetheless help us understand her committed desire to establish parts for women in the battles against national, gender, and class oppression of her day and days to come.

4

The Art of Contention

Delia Larkin, Augusta Gregory, and the Workers of Ireland

More than any event before it, the Lockout of 1913 galvanized and transformed the lives of Dublin's workers. As one city historian notes,

> 1913 was the *annus terribilis* of the Dublin working class. Before it ended, a bewildering variety of strikes, often with no obvious relation to one another, rocked the port and city of Dublin in a manner characterized by the Lord Mayor as tantamount to "civil war."[1]

Political controversies, from petty to grand, consumed writers and workers, connoisseurs and critics, amateur players and establishment playwrights. Dubliners of all walks of life clashed over different ideals for the future of Ireland.

A relatively small controversy over theater rights and socialist activism pitted artists against women workers. Its beginning in late spring 1914, in the wake of the devastating lockout and just months before the outbreak of World War I, was visible only in the small print and occasional notices of the trade union weekly *Irish Worker.* Readers were alerted to an English tour of the Irish Workers' Dramatic Society, led by Delia Larkin, the sister of trade union leader Jim Larkin. This small group of working-class amateur actors left Dublin in May 1914 to perform two Irish plays, Augusta

Gregory's *The Workhouse Ward* (1908) and William Boyle's *The Building Fund* (1906), in order to raise funds for those impoverished during the Dublin Lockout and to set up a workers' cooperative upon their return. The group raised little money, however, and was threatened with legal action by Gregory over using her play without permission. Though neither Delia Larkin nor Augusta Gregory left a written record, the pages of *Irish Worker* provide us with a clear account of a dispute that engaged gender, class, and culture in the wake of Dublin's greatest labor struggle of the early twentieth century.[2]

This chapter focuses on Delia Larkin's "unauthorized" dramatization of Augusta Gregory's play during the Larkin company's 1914 tour of England. The controversy not only reveals how Gregory and Larkin wrestled over political ideals and cultural capital; it also raises the question of the place of art in the material and political lives of Irish workers during the revival. Reading Larkin's trade union journalism in the *Irish Worker* against Gregory's literary-nationalist dramaturgy on behalf of the Abbey Theatre, the chapter aims to uncover the extent to which the issues of labor and art complemented one another during the years 1913–14.

Although Delia Larkin's columns in the *Irish Worker* and Gregory's play *The Workhouse Ward* have thematically much in common, comparing how each woman adapted the rhetoric of contention provides us an instructive lesson in the divergent results that can arise when women engage in a language of critique. Whereas there are many accounts of the life and work of Lady Gregory (1852–1932), little is known of Delia Larkin (1878–1949), the sister of formidable labor leader Big Jim Larkin. This chapter aims to make visible the cultural and socialist program of a little-known worker, Delia Larkin, while reassessing the political project of Augusta Gregory's drama. Gregory's *The Workhouse Ward,* a comedy in which two men battle over "whose version of truth will have the stronger claim,"[3] presents us with an apt setting in which to understand Gregory's and Larkin's dispute about cultural ownership and the right of workers, be they Abbey Players or Liberty Hall amateurs, to represent Ireland and its future. *The Workhouse Ward* derives its energy and humor from the interminable squabbling of two workhouse invalids, whose misery has less to do with their penurious surroundings than with "the misfortune [of having] a bad next door neighbour that was yourself."[4] Bedridden with painful rheumatism and unable to leave each other's company, Michael Miskell and Mike McInerney vigorously joust over every detail in their hostile past. Yet when Mike McInerney's sister unexpectedly arrives, offering to share her "wide lovely" cottage by the sea with him—but only him—Mike chooses to stay in the workhouse with his contentious companion, so as to continue "fighting and scolding and attacking one another" for all the days of their lives.

The play teaches a wry lesson about Irish national sensibilities, for these two squabbling antagonists prove there is nothing that produces greater pleasure than a good fight. Small wonder that Larkin and her theater company used the play to communicate the emotional tenor of Irish trade unionism and Irish cultural nationalism to audiences abroad.

1913: Annus Pugnax

At the turn of the century, Ireland's faded capital, which had never experienced industrialization, housed a disproportionate number of casual laborers subsisting on meager wages in "horrific" conditions.[5] The city could claim the dubious distinction of having the worst urban adult mortality rate in the British Isles; indeed, Dublin's 1911 death rate matched that of Calcutta.[6]

By the summer of 1913, after two years of dynamic union mobilizing by Jim Larkin, who taught workers the bargaining power of the sympathy strike, Dublin employers mobilized as well. In an attempt to crush Larkin's powerful Irish Transport and General Workers' Union (ITGWU) and the newly established Irish Women Workers' Union (IWWU), they demanded that every worker sign a promise never to join a Larkin union or resign from the union if already a member. Led by William Martin Murphy, Dublin's principal employers effectively declared war on organized labor. When union members refused to comply, they were locked out of their jobs. In graphic detail, the weekly trade union newspaper *Irish Worker* covered the intimidation, starvation, and strife of the seven-month

Dublin Lockout, one of the most protracted labor disputes in Ireland's history. Three thousand workers and families were fed by the IWWU, which provided its members victimization pay while vociferously supporting the right of all workers to unionize.

Also in 1913, as the British government prepared to bring the Home Rule Bill before the House of Commons for the third time, Ulster-based Unionists and Dublin-based nationalists established ideologically opposed, unofficial armies—the Ulster Volunteer Force and the Irish Volunteers—in anticipation of Ireland's political separation from the British Empire. Meanwhile, the Irish Citizen Army began drilling irregular units of workers to underline the physical potency of the trade union movement. Women also joined the competing militant organizations, which prompted a wrenching debate among female activists in the feminist, nationalist, and trade unionist movements, and forced women such as Constance Markievicz to clarify publicly their priorities in working for more than one emancipation movement at the same time.[7]

Although artists such as William Butler Yeats and George Russell (AE) made common cause to support the workers' strike, the years 1913–14 were contentious for intellectual and artistic workers as well. Augusta Gregory's art aficionado nephew Hugh Lane had struggled for a decade to convince the the Dublin Corporation to fund construction of a new municipal gallery of modern art. To that end, he had provisionally bequeathed thirty-nine of his paintings to the proposed gallery. When the corporation balked at the cost of the gallery, doubting the quality of Lane's paintings and speculating on his likely profit from the arrangement, Lane threatened to take back his bequest.[8] On the eve of the lockout, September 9, 1913, the Dublin Corporation voted to reject the plan, prompting Lane to withdraw his paintings and Yeats to write one of his greatest polemics, the masterful lyric poem "September 1913." The gallery campaign never died, however, and was the subject of further controversy when Lane drowned in the sinking of the *Lusitania*, torpedoed off the coast of Cork in 1915. Just days before his departure, he had drafted an unwitnessed codicil to his will that bequeathed his entire collection of paintings to Dublin.

Because of the close ties between Hugh Lane and Augusta Gregory, the gallery campaign also affected the Abbey Theatre, which was having financial and artistic difficulties of its own. Abbey directors Gregory and Yeats found themselves mired in controversy over what to do with the Guarantee Fund, the money raised by the Abbey for the failed campaign. The Abbey had suffered a weak year, especially in the London season. Discontented over poor pay, and having returned from a contentious tour in the United States during the fall and winter of 1912–13, in which a New York audience rushed the stage and Philadelphia police arrested the actors for the immoral content of *Playboy of the Western World*,[9] the Abbey Players sued to have the fund transferred to the theater's coffers. Thus conflict was rampant in 1913–14, not only between employees and workers, Unionist and nationalist volunteers, but also between directors and actors; it spread to Catholic clergy and Catholic strikers, to feminists, socialists, and nationalists generally, who each saw their movement in acute crisis during this momentous time.

Delia Larkin and the Irish Women Workers' Union

An instrumental trade union activist during the height of the Dublin labor crisis of 1913, and one whose feisty personality and temperament were clearly a match for the pugnacious Dubliners of that time, Delia Larkin is today little remembered, even in social and economic histories of early-twentieth-century Ireland.[10] In part, this is because she so often toiled in the shadow of her charismatic brother, Jim Larkin. In 1911, two years after Jim had founded the Irish Transport and General Workers' Union, Delia moved from her native Liverpool to Dublin, expressly for the purpose of helping her brother found the Irish Women Workers' Union in September of that year. Though a newcomer, she proved to be a surprisingly effective union organizer, recruiting some 1,000 members within her first month as the IWWU's first general secretary.[11] By the end of the year, 3,000 women had signed up; within two years, Larkin had increased union membership to 14,000.[12] In 1912, she was elected to represent women workers of Dublin on the Irish Trades Board. Although she earned the heartfelt respect of the working class for her dedicated management of the soup kitchen in Liberty Hall during the Lockout of 1913, that fall, she would incur the wrath of both the Catholic Church and nationalists such as Arthur Griffith and Maud Gonne for one of her many miscalculations about the sectarian sentiments surrounding her. To ensure that Dublin's most impoverished children were housed and fed, she attempted to send them to Protestant England for a temporary stay. The "kiddie transport" debacle might have taught her about the limits to making alliances with other social and political movements, but as we will see, it did not.[13]

A committed suffragist and amateur actress, Delia Larkin also engaged in political and cultural work in her own right, quite apart from collaboration with her brother. She spoke out repeatedly to demand inclusion of female suffrage in the proposed Home Rule Bill, while attempting to set up worker cooperatives for women recently unemployed due to the lockout. Like her sister activists in Inghinidhe na hÉireann (by 1913, a defunct organization), Delia Larkin also linked political and cultural affairs by organizing the ITGWU's social program, founding the Irish Workers' Choir in 1912 and arranging dance, drama, and Gaelic-language classes in Liberty Hall.[14] Her efforts in this regard reflect Larkin's social idealism, shared by her brother and by Inghinidhe na hÉireann's founder, Maud Gonne. Perhaps her most ambitious cultural project, the Irish Workers' Dramatic Society was founded in 1912; by the end of the lockout, with morale low, funds scarce, and the organization in considerable disarray, Delia Larkin took the Irish Workers' Dramatic Society on tour to England to give performances in aid of her cooperative scheme. Although the company aroused interest in the cause of labor, they raised little money.[15] Denied permission by Augusta Gregory, they were also prevented from performing her play in Manchester and London. In Gregory's carefully considered words, the production "was likely to do injury to the Abbey Theatre players and any injury to them would be an injury to the Dublin Workers."[16]

Upon her return to Ireland, Larkin posted advertisements in the *Irish Worker* for the "Irish Women Workers' Co-operative Society" to be based in Liberty Hall, which, however, never came into being because of her increasingly strained relationship with many in the union leadership. By the time Delia Larkin left Dublin in 1915 to find work in London, an influential, charismatic replacement, James Connolly, stepped in to supervise the production of performances by the Irish Workers' Dramatic Society; the company put on monthly plays from September 1915 through April 1916.[17] When she returned to Ireland again in 1918, Larkin discovered that the place was "changed, changed utterly": she was rebuffed from membership in the very union she had helped to found.[18]

Contentious Labor of Women in the *Irish Worker*

Delia Larkin moved to Dublin during a period of chronic unemployment and nascent union activism. Unlike Belfast, where the linen industry employed two to three times as many female as male workers,[19] Dublin afforded female workers very few industrial jobs at this time. As a result of the extreme shortage of work, Dublin employers could demand long hours for meager wages. According to Delia Larkin's figures, working-class women earned, on average, a weekly income ranging from 2 shillings 6 pence to 6 shillings a week in 1912.[20] By comparison, Dublin's higher-paid male workers earned more than 20 shillings a week, although many families subsisted on less than 15.[21] Trade unionists in Dublin, moreover, showed little sympathy for those they considered "cheap laborers," individuals who might undercut trade union rates.[22] Whereas Mary Galway had founded a women's union among Belfast textile workers in the 1890s, unskilled female workers in Dublin did not organize until the founding of the Irish Women Workers' Union in 1911. The first call for formal recruitment appeared on the pages of the August 19, 1911 issue of the *Irish Worker*. The timing was excellent, for within three days of this call, 3,000 women at Jacob's Biscuit factory withdrew their labor in pursuit of a pay claim, and the IWWU got its start.[23] One of the union's most significant achievements remained, in true Larkin fashion, organizing disparate groups of unskilled laborers, such as laundry workers, rosary bead makers, mill laborers, and even domestic help, who, because of their isolation and comparative youth, were notoriously difficult to unionize.[24]

After serving as a correspondent for the *Irish Worker* over the summer of 1911, in August, Delia Larkin assumed responsibility for editing the weekly "Women Workers' Column," which, thanks to the remarkable success of her brother's paper, could claim an unusually large Dublin readership. Within a month of its establishment in June 1911, the one-penny weekly *Irish Worker* had sold 26,000 copies and, by September, nearly 100,000 copies all told. Though its readership was far larger, a primitive printing facility limited the *Irish Worker*'s weekly press run to 20,000 copies, compared to a monthly press run of some 8,000 copies for Arthur Griffith's newspaper *Sinn Féin* at the same time.[25] The *Irish Worker* served as an effective transmitter of the flamboyant, confrontational style of both Jim and Delia Larkin, mixing sensationalist rhetoric and socialist theory, while shaming and ridiculing bosses who "sweated" (overworked and underpaid) their workers. Irish trade union news was stamped with the Larkin brand: editor Jim Larkin's name appeared prominently not only on the masthead but also on the middle of the second page, where the thrifty one-penny price was listed next to the subscription information. The paper specialized in exposing unjust and unsafe working conditions and enjoining workers to unify and organize, as Constance Markievicz urged, "into an army of fighters."[26] The *Irish Worker* directly rebuked the middle-class-oriented, employer-identified *Irish Independent*, owned by William Martin Murphy, and advocated a militant nationalism, thus competing with the comparatively staid nationalism of Griffith's *Sinn Féin*. According to Seamus Cody: "The newspaper increased the identification of Labour and Larkinism in the public eye and thus effectively isolated the conservatives in the Dublin labour movement."[27]

The Irish Women Workers' Union began recruiting members under the auspices of the Irish Transport and General Workers' Union, recognizing Jim Larkin as its president and using rooms at the ITGWU headquarters in Liberty Hall rent-free. Delia Larkin displayed her own talents and singular vision as an organizer of female labor, both in her union leadership and in her columns for the *Irish Worker*. The "Women Workers' Column" appeared prominently every week on the far left of the second page. In keeping with many advanced nationalist journals, Larkin's weekly column served as a forum of exchange and debate, affording other writers a space in which to elaborate on women's particular challenges and priori-

2 The Irish Worker.

WOMEN WORKERS' COLUMN.

TRAM-CAR POLITENESS.

When a working man or woman commits a breach of good manners they are at once dubbed unmannerly boors. But the well-dressed, idle class can commit as many breaches as they like with impunity. One only has to enter a tram-car to meet with unlimited rudeness. Women in this respect are greatest offenders. On entering a tram-car one afternoon of this week, which was occupied solely by women, the following incident occurred. On either side of the car there was room for one more passenger. As a new passenger I patiently waited for a few seconds for those occupying the seats to sit closer together. They made no attempt to do so, whereupon I sat down in the small space unoccupied; still these women made no attempt to move until the conductor ordered them to go closer together, which left comfortable space for all passengers. Not content with the uncalled for rudeness they had displayed they thought it best to continue it. After the conductor had issued his order, and I had procured comfortable seating-room, the women coolly and insolently stared at the new passenger, with expressions of disdain on their faces. Surely every passenger has a right to a seat in a tram-car when a seat is available. All those women in the car were well-dressed, and would undoubtedly style themselves "ladies." It is to be hoped that this class of tram-car passengers will alter their attitude and their manners.—VICTUS.

THE SERVANT QUESTION.

This question has been and is a much talked of and badly abused one. There is a great deal to be said for both sides, but the bulk of the grievances undoubtedly lies with the servants. It is not my intention to deal with the domestic servant class as a whole at the present time, but with a certain section of them—the badly treated, hardly-used general servant. With very few exceptions, the lot of the general servant is a sad one; in fact the term "household drudge" would be a much more appropriate name. The classing of this section as general servants gives some idea of the work they are required to do. Their duties begin in the early hours of the morning, and only end at a late hour at night. As a rule they are required to be able to understand something of the art of cooking; must wash and undertake the principal cleaning of a house. Now, these duties would be quite hard enough if performed with the help and under the control of a competent, kind-hearted house-wife. But as a rule the persons who are in a position to be able to employ a general servant belong to the class who term themselves the 'middle class,' and look upon domestic work as an indignity, and the poor creature who is so unfortunate as to be general servant in such an establishment is deserving of the greatest pity. It is no exaggeration to say that her work is never done, and to get a few hours off one evening in the week is more a trial than a pleasure. Then as regards the food supplied to these servants, this is another of their many grievances. It would be greatly to the advantages of the mistresses if they considered the servants more and fed them in a proper manner, not leave them as many do to dine on the scraps and leavings o' the family. How can any girl do efficient work, or take an interest in her surroundings, when the body is badly nourished. It is no uncommon thing for a mistress to cater for and buy in food for the household, quite disregarding the fact that while the servant is in her household; she is a member of it, and has every right to be considered. It is quite a humane act, without doubt, for a mistress to get a servant to cook a dinner that is just sufficient to satisfy the members of the family. Is it any wonder that we find that girls will go and work in the factories instead of going as a domestic servant? The dearth of good general servants is due to the manner in which they are treated by the mistresses. Of course, there are exceptions to every rule, and some mistresses do treat their servants humanely, and the result is that these housekeepers are considered in a kindly way by the servants, and the household work is done in a satisfactory manner. Again, there is the question of evenings off. This is another of the drawbacks to girls going into domestic service. They find that by going to work in the factories they are at liberty in the evenings. Certainly the factories are not havens of kindness and easy work, but for the few hours of liberty that they enjoy in the evenings they put up with the slave-driving of the managers of the factories. Now, would it not be better both for householders who are in the position to employ a general servant and for girls who are desirous of becoming general servants (but who object and rightly, to the long hours, insufficient food supplied, and the curtailing of liberty) to come to a better understanding with each other?

It only requires a little more consideration for the health and welfare of the servant, and a certain amount of tolerance towards their demand for more freedom.

D. L.

All classes of Women Workers are eligible to join THE IRISH WOMEN WORKERS UNION. Entrance fee, sixpence; Contribution, twopence per week.

All communications for this column must be addressed to—

"D. L.,"
The Women-workers' Column,
THE IRISH WORKER,
10 Beresford Place, Dublin.

Irish-Ireland Notes.

IN GAELIC FIELDS.

By "Observer."

SOCIALIST PARTY OF IRELAND.

"An injury to One is the concern of All."

—THE—

Irish Worker

AND PEOPLE'S ADVOCATE.

Edited by JIM LARKIN.

THE IRISH WORKER will be published weekly—price One Penny—and may be had of any newsagent. Ask for it and see that you get it.

All communications, whether relating to literary or business matters, to be addressed to the Editor, 10 Beresford Place, Dublin. Telephone 3421.

Subscription 6s. 6d. per year; 3s. 3d. for six months, payable in advance.

We do not publish or take notice of anonymous contributions.

DUBLIN, SATURDAY, NOV. 11TH, 1911.

OUR PREDICTIONS.

We have been justified in our predictions. We opined that the result of the cogitations of the Party who call themselves the Irish Party (who should be properly styled as the Irish Farmers' and Employers' Party) has resulted in the base betrayal of the claims of the workers of Ireland to the same benefits under the new Insurance Act as the English, Scotch and Welsh workers are to enjoy. Why, …

WEXFORD LOCK-OUT.

(From our own Correspondent).

6. "Women Workers' Column." Delia Larkin began this column, which appeared on the second page of each issue of the *Irish Worker*, on August 12, 1911. Reproduced courtesy of the National Library of Ireland.

ties in trade unionism. Most guest columnists contributed pseudonymously, choosing names that revealed their occupation ("Shellback," a name for a veteran sailor), their religion ("Fortescues," a family that refused to support Henry VIII's abolition of the Catholic Church in England) or trade unionist perspective ("anti-sweater," a worker who actively resists employer attempts to overwork and underpay employees). Because no records of the IWWU exist before 1918, Larkin's "Women Workers' Column" provides us with precious documentary evidence of the prevailing concerns within the union leadership during its formative years;[28] it is particularly valuable to feminist and labor historians today as an archive of multiple trade unionist voices.

Delia Larkin outlined her aims in editing the "Women Workers' Column" in the inaugural August 12 column:

> (I) The house: hints on how to keep it clean and lessen labour; (II) The home and its comforts; (III) Cookery hints; (IV) Dress and dress reform; (V) Women Workers grievances; (VI) Then a little article on women, their mission and work in the world, will be acceptable either in prose or verse. Now there is plenty of brains among the women-workers and here is a splendid opportunity for using those brains, so send along anything you think will benefit the cause of labour, lighten the burden of the toiler, or help build an Irish-Ireland.[29]

From the outset, Larkin viewed her primary goals as reforming the home, the workplace, and working-class leisure activities. And, as her rhetorical understatement "a little article on women . . . will be acceptable" implies, Larkin was capable of grim irony in subjugating feminine consciousness raising to columns on women's duties within the home. Her attitudes about the social, economic, and political roles of women were well in keeping with English trade union journalism, which based its support of women's enfranchisement on the differences between the sexes.[30] Delia Larkin approvingly endorsed a married woman's place within the home, just as she accepted the placement of the "Women Workers' Column" on the newspaper's second page, and her brother's position as president of the IWWU. Just as Alice Milligan's romances in the *Shan Van Vocht* simultaneously advocated politically subversive yet socially conventional roles for women in the national struggle, Delia Larkin's trade union columns agitated for economic justice for women in the workplace while insisting on married women's primary duties in the home, although this suffragist union organizer displayed little interest in reforming woman's social role as wife, mother, and housekeeper. In her December columns from 1911 and 1912, for example, she provided space for others to share "useful hints" for cooking the Christmas feast, though she never felt moved to share her own domestic pearls of wisdom.[31]

In some of her columns, it is hard to tell whether Larkin is writing for or against women workers. One column exemplifies the seemingly contradictory aims of her journalism. Taking to task a popular media onslaught on "women who drink," for example, Larkin shifted the spotlight from working-class women's putative moral failings to the social circumstances that prompt both men and women to drink. In a column dedicated to discussing the living conditions of working women, however, she proves most devoted to improving those for men:

> Although condemning the women who have allowed themselves to become slaves to the drink mania, and saddling them with the awful results which arise from their indulgences, still there is some excuse for them, when one knows the awful conditions under which the majority of these women live. . . .
>
> [But] what a crime this system of married women going out to work is. It is a crime against the woman herself, against the husband, and against the children. This cause has a bad effect on the whole community of workers; it keeps women's wages at a starvation rate, men's wages low, and is the means of making drunkards of both men and women.
>
> The woman goes out to work the same as the husband and works as many hours. [There] is no home life for them, and no meals are prepared. . . . A married woman's duty is not to help the sweater and publican but to look after her home and those

> who live there. This can only be done when the men's wages are of such a standard as will enable them to live in decent houses and provide in a right manner for their wives and children.[32]

This column seems to shift alarmingly between two different impulses. Though Larkin begins by analyzing the living conditions that prompt the working class to abuse drink, in an abrupt switch, she then caustically appropriates the upper-class critique of working women's behavior (drinking as a "crime") to another context, the economic system that requires married women to work. By labeling married women's public labor as a "crime," Larkin bases her radical call for improved working conditions on a woman's social duties to husband and home. Such a view of working-class women may not be so very different from comments made by James Connolly, who also highlighted the challenges of married women who are denied "a rest from outside labour" because of their "double domestic toil."[33] Indeed, in trying to assist women in making domestic labor less onerous, many of the "Women Workers' " columns tacitly acknowledge the need to help women who shoulder this double burden.

Yet, in focusing her critique on raising male wages, Larkin neglects the very girls and women she was seeking to organize in her union. She turns her back, in this column at least, on the insights of the critical thinker Friedrich Engels, who pointed out in 1884 that "the emancipation of woman will only be possible when women are enabled to take part in production on a large, social scale, and when domestic duties require their attention only to a minor degree."[34]

Delia Larkin's ambivalence to married women workers has an interesting corollary in the nostalgic masthead image displayed each week on page one of the *Irish Worker*, where a toga-clad man labors at an anvil and a classically draped woman operates her spinning wheel. As a nationalist-socialist emblem, the spinning wheel signals the value of women's economic contributions in preindustrial, precolonial Ireland. Such nostalgic symbolism, as we have seen in previous chapters, was widespread among Irish-Irelanders, who selectively cherished cultural and social practices in Ireland's past in an effort to discount the modernizing influence of the col-

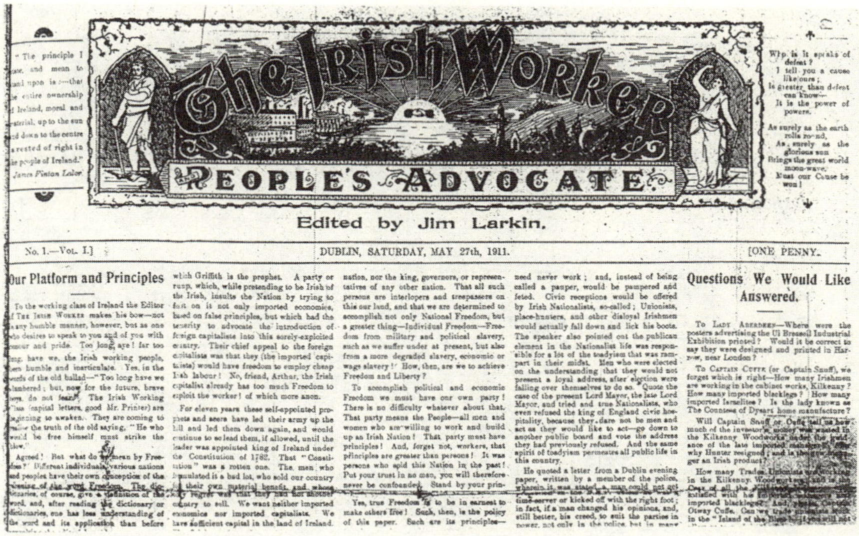

The Irish Worker

People's Advocate

Edited by Jim Larkin.

No. 1.—Vol. I.] DUBLIN, SATURDAY, MAY 27th, 1911. [ONE PENNY.

Our Platform and Principles

Questions We Would Like Answered.

7. Masthead of *Irish Worker,* May 27, 1911. The classical figures of male and female workers of this masthead, used for only the first few months the *Irish Worker* was in print, sharply contrast with the industrial and agricultural landscapes. Note that the advanced nationalist image of the sunrise is here connected with the workers' handshake. Reproduced courtesy of the National Library of Ireland.

onizer, Great Britain. Yet this imagery, like Larkin's diatribe against working wives, seems to be based on the same wistful premise that anti-suffrage commentators adopt in decrying the impact of public women on the putative harmony of the home. Her radical argument on behalf of male workers is also mollified when placed beside de Valera's 1937 constitution, which similarly professed to recognize the common good of "woman within the home" but in effect extended no new economic opportunities for working-class men, and indeed barred married women from any gainful employment at all.[35]

In another column dedicated to reforming women's behavior outside the home, Larkin focused on women's education. Her emphasis on "practical" domestic skills over "decorous" facility in academic fields just opening up to women provides another example of Larkin's alliance with

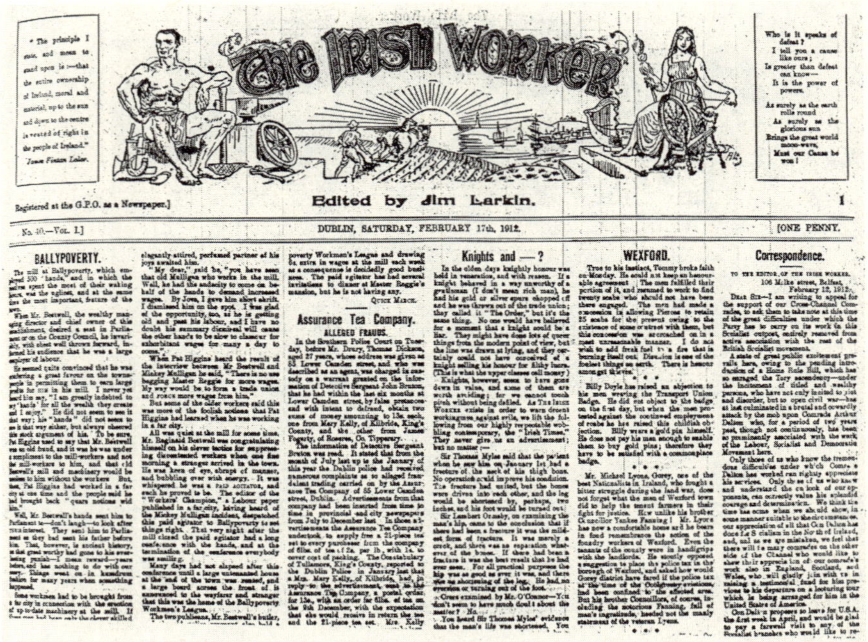

The Irish Worker

Edited by Jim Larkin.

Registered at the G.P.O. as a Newspaper.]

No. 40.—Vol. I.] DUBLIN, SATURDAY, FEBRUARY 17th, 1912. [ONE PENNY.

BALLYPOVERTY.

Assurance Tea Company.

Knights and — ?

WEXFORD.

Correspondence.

8. Masthead of *Irish Worker*, February 17, 1912. The revised, less cluttered masthead enlarges the images of the male and female workers and returns them to a specifically Irish peasant landscape. Note that the smoking factories, the newspaper's motto, "The People's Advocate," and the workers' handshake have all been removed. Reproduced courtesy of the National Library of Ireland.

"womanly woman" proponents such as nationalist Mary E. L. Butler, whose writings proposed that women could best contribute to the nation by remaining at home. First endorsing the sentiments of a practical-minded educator of females, who laments that women can now maintain "a first-class knowledge of English, French, and German and a total unfamiliarity with the ingredients of vegetable soup," Larkin then underscores the middle-class male complaint where "the teaching leans too much to the artistic and literary side and too little to the homely and practical."[36] Though, as we will see, Larkin cajoled her working-class readers to join language classes, singing schools, and amateur theatrical productions, this column indicates that, for her, such cultural enrichment should only be enjoyed by women once they had dispatched with their duties at home.

Larkin's other writings, as well as her political and cultural activism on behalf of women workers, tell a broader, more complicated story than these two early columns suggest, however. During her three-year stint as editor of the "Women Workers' Column," Delia Larkin covered a range of issues, from lessening the drudgery of domestic chores to entrenched labor battles such as the strikes at Jacob's Biscuit factory and the Pembroke Laundry, or the Savoy Café lockout. In her inaugural column in the *Irish Worker,* for example, she injected a feminist perspective into her brother's socialist philosophy, so prominently proclaimed on the masthead: "An injury to one is the concern of all."

> The women of Ireland are as awake as the men, they are weary of being white slaves who pass their lives away toiling to fill the pockets of the unscrupulous employers, receiving for their labours not sufficient to enable them to exist. The wages and conditions of the working women in the city of Dublin are a rebuke to any country. . . . We do not want a certain few to be doing well, we want all women workers to at least be in a position to procure the ordinary necessaries of life.[37]

Larkin's feminist rhetoric resembles that of militant suffragists, who were also actively writing, meeting, and giving speeches to advance their political agenda of universal suffrage. Not long after Larkin made this pronouncement, James Connolly pointed out the logic of feminism and trade unionism echoing the style and substance of each other's movement; this "awakening amongst women" in the feminist and trade unionist fields was "synchronized" by the shared "realization . . . that modern society was founded upon force and injustice."[38]

Whereas female contemporaries such as Alice Milligan and Maud Gonne overlooked or ignored differences of money, religion, philosophy, or social status in their collaborations with other women, Delia Larkin persistently highlighted the differences among women workers in her efforts to rally them to join her union. In one particularly perceptive column on "Women and Dress," for example, Larkin explored how working-class clothing functions as a "badge of servitude." In response to "the latest craze" in the newspapers to "attack" working girls' dress, Larkin aggressively analyzed how upper-class objections and expectations operated to "perpetuat[e] a state of serfdom" in the working class. In the domestic servant's life, Larkin explained, the crisp, white cap and apron "stamp" the working girl "with the badge of servitude," as the clothes serve no utilitarian purpose; they provide no assistance in a domestic servant's many, varied tasks. To the upper-class ladies who cluck over the modern mill girl who discards her peasant shawl and clogs for more urban fare such as a jacket and hat, Larkin sneeringly alerts her readers to the class-based double standard inflicted by what she labels "the idle, selfish woman who revels in luxury of every description" while declaiming working women cannot enjoy the same freedoms: "It is not sufficient that these working women should be wage slaves, but it is now advocated that their garb should proclaim them as such."[39]

As often as Larkin offered analysis and heated commentary in defense of the working girl, so often would she write like a gumshoe reporter, continually "making searching investigations" about the laborious toil of pensionless and aging workers at Goulding's Manure Manufacture, of sexual harassment endured by young female workers, or of cruel, uncharitable treatment toward servants in the house of the Reverend Mr. Good. Whether documenting the unsanitary working conditions in Thompson's Confectionery or in the Keogh Sack Factory, Larkin shed harsh light on the bare facts: long hours, dangerous labor, unscrupulous overseers, all at less than one-third of a man's wages. Like Maud Gonne, whose sympathetic presence in the homes of famine-ravaged peasants elicited unforgettable stories of maternal suffering and loss, Delia Larkin provided a safe space—her column and her offices in Liberty Hall—for workers to report abuses against them. As she assiduously gathered stories of the "tyrannical foreman," the "sordid employer," and the "fraudulent Sergeant-Major," she also, like Gonne, disseminated these anecdotes to a wider newspaper-reading audience in hopes of politically unifying workers to demand better terms for all. In a constant refrain, she told her women readers: "As individuals, we are entirely at the mercy of mean, unscrupulous employers, but as an organized body we are powerful, helpful to ourselves, and all other workers."[40]

As part of her effort to upbraid employers and to demand better working conditions for women, Larkin repeatedly solicited information from her readers about working conditions in every facet of women workers' lives, insisting that such information could be powerful ammunition in negotiating on behalf of Dublin workers. Larkin's sharp, ironic tone made itself heard in occasional pieces outside the confines of the "Women Workers' Column." For example, one savagely parodic column, "Irvin's Paper Sorters—Vacancy for Female Slave," used the occasion of a female worker's dismissal to drum up business for Larkin's union:

> Woman worker dismissed last Friday, September 29, 1911, for daring to have an independent wish. Age 24 years, wages 2s. 6d. per week. I am quite sure there was a tremendous rush for the above vacancy, but trust there was no one seriously hurt in trying to procure it. If anyone can solve the problem of how this dismissed employee existed on the enormous amount of (to make it appear more) we will say thirty pence per week, I would be glad of the information.[41]

Here Larkin uses irony to arouse a sense of solidarity among working girls. Although such news could be interpreted as a lesson in the perils of workers "daring to have an independent wish," Larkin's ironic voice refuses such a reading, going on to sympathetically label wage negotiations as "daring" and aimed at worker "independence."

Whereas the above "ad" aimed to publicize intolerable conditions for women workers, Delia Larkin would often use her column to publicize new benefits and to chide her female readers for their reluctance to organize and resist the wretched working conditions under which they were suffering. Adopting a tone that recalls Constance Markievicz's toward the domesticated members of Cumann na mBan, Larkin belittled and scolded her fellow women for their "appalling want of common sense and reason . . . owing to the lack of interest they take in their own welfare by not becoming members of the Women's Organization."[42] Whereas Markievicz, at least in her earlier pronouncements, maintained a buoyant optimism that women would make the right choices, Delia Larkin would often voice her frustrations and bitter disappointments when women workers lacked the sufficient courage to claim trade union membership.

Relishing her role as the artful contender, Larkin saved her most scathing criticism for those "in the family." After a Labor Day demonstration in 1913, the first time that the IWWU had participated in such an event, Larkin took pains to berate her trade union sisters who left her standing nearly alone:

> But what of the poor, weak, backboneless creatures, members of the Women's Union—yes, some of them members since it first started—who tried to hide themselves among the crowd of onlookers as the procession passed by? For such woman and girls we express our pity and contempt—pity for their ignorant weakness and contempt for their narrow-mindedness, which prevented them from coming into the ranks of their co-workers.[43]

Though she focused her attacks on bourgeois women, as we have seen above, Larkin consistently reserved her sharpest scorn for those closest to the cause. The very audience she sought to cultivate she often spotlighted as the direst "cause of their conditions": for refusing to report unjust working conditions; for indifferently accepting substandard wages; for devaluing women's work; and for maintaining social and occupational barriers between women workers. "The greatest drawback we have" in correcting gender inequalities in the workplace, Larkin declaimed, is "the women themselves, who, although they know they are being sweated and robbed, still do not give us the assistance they ought by reporting at once any employer who deals unjustly."[44]

Such tough love did not endear her to the movement. Her raw expressions of frustration, irritation, and bewilderment clearly reflected the difficulties of organizing the disparate parts of Dublin's female working class under the broad banner of "women workers." As Robin Miller Jacoby has pointed out in her study of British and American women's trade unions of the same period, organizing women workers entailed dealing with a number of intractable factors: the comparative youth of female workers, the typically short length of their employment, the widely different types of jobs they held, the rigidly defined positions for females, the significant wage disparity between women's and men's work, the structure of the labor movement, and the common expectation (certainly shared by Delia Larkin) that women's public employment would be only temporary.[45] Falling membership numbers in IWWU, which dropped to 700 by the summer of 1913, may in part have prompted Delia Larkin's sneering tone, just as her aggressive rhetoric may have prompted many girls and women to let their membership lapse.[46]

Yet, in spite of her contentiousness, Larkin managed to achieve concrete results both for the trade union movement and working-class cultural development. Even as her union dwindled in size, she succeeded in two small, if symbolic, strikes—at the Keogh Sack Factory and the Pembroke Laundry in 1912.[47] She was also elected to represent her union at three successive annual conferences of the Irish Trade Union Congress.[48] Laboring women—and men—joined her Workers' Choir, language classes, and dramatic productions. In fact, she managed to persuade dramatist and actor A. Patrick Wilson to direct the Irish Workers' Dramatic Society's first four one-act plays.[49] Her rhetorical style called to mind her charismatic brother, a brilliant speaker who mesmerized Dublin crowds even as he bullied and berated them for their failings.[50] "Jim Larkin's methods," Keir Hardie later explained, "are not those of the rose leaf or the kid glove."[51] But her brother's aggressive, confrontational rhetoric attracted readers and engendered larger union membership, and even though he was reputed to have "more enemies than any other man in this country," he managed both to ally workers and hold fast to his leadership, despite heaping thick abuses on workers.[52]

In contrast, Delia Larkin's abrasive, assertive style ended up alienating even her political allies. By September of 1915, a confrontation with trade unionists at Liberty Hall over the use of a piano caused the entire ITGWU committee to resign en masse rather than challenge Jim Larkin over his combative sister.[53] It is hard not to conclude that Delia Larkin's rhetorical failures were an object lesson for female writers who violated gender norms during the revival. Delia frequently experienced social opprobrium for the very behavior that Jim exhibited to rousing applause. In writing for Ireland's advanced nationalist press, Alice Milligan, Maud Gonne, and Constance Markievicz implicitly understood that, to preserve a readership and stimulate change or action, women writers could only manipulate, adapt, and transform existing genres (such as romances, allegorical dramas, and gardening columns). Delia Larkin, instead, opted to match the brashly masculine style of her brother, and was consequently punished for her efforts.

Yet, however ill suited Delia Larkin's derisive style proved even for the notoriously pugnacious Dubliners, her choice of staging Gregory's play *The Workhouse Ward* on her drama company's English tour is telling on two counts. First, it suggests that Larkin might have found a far better outlet for her derision in staging male rancor than in voicing female ire. As we will see in *The Workhouse Ward*, many of Larkin's Irish contemporaries viewed contention, if expressed by males, as pleasurable rather than punishing. Second, her choice suggests that she might have understood how scolding paupers in the rural west could provide political commentary about women workers in the urban east as well. Gregory's life and the very language of the play give us ample reason to see her two feuding but inseparable male characters as workers whose artful labor is "the talk" of a quarrelsome past and a contentious future, who are united in hardship, but bonded in the spirit of "the two of us together it's not likely . . . we would fail."[54]

Reassessing Gregory as a Republican Workers' Dramatist

Lady Gregory can now claim a central creative role in the Irish literary renaissance, but she remains even today, in the minds of too many critics, the "bored widow," the "frail old lady," the "Big House aristocrat," the "indispensable mediator," the "dutiful Dowager," the "Abbey Theatre director," the "Victorian matriarch," the "maternal mentor," or the "passive vessel." Although, as Lucy McDiarmid and Maureen Waters aptly observe, "any Lady Gregory is someone's construction,"[55] the Irish literary canon has often asked that we read her within the context of high art, in particular, her drama, rather than within the more complicated context of her diverse writings, in particular, her early folklore and later republican journalism. Moreover, Augusta Gregory has for too long been considered beside men such as her husband, Sir William Gregory, and the poet William Butler Yeats, rather than beside activist women such as Delia Larkin, Maud Gonne, and Constance Markievicz. In keeping with the ongoing project of feminist reappraisal,[56] this chapter nonetheless recognizes the delicate challenge of separating Gregory from Yeats's representations and myths because "cultural nationalism grew and thrived in collectivities."[57] Following the lead of McDiarmid and Waters, I will consider Gregory, not only as a nationalist, a Fenian, an anti-imperialist, and a feminist, but also in light of the workers and peasants on whose backs her material and literary demesne were built.

Like many of her finest dramatic characters, Gregory maintained divided loyalties that reveal marked political and aesthetic growth over her lifetime. She was, for example, born into wealth: her family, the Persses, was among the few to benefit financially from the Famine.[58] By the time her husband, Sir William Gregory, died in 1892, however, she found her Coole Park estate encumbered by debt and she faced the necessity to retrench.[59] Moreover, her Protestant Ascendancy class was under siege on two fronts: from the rising Irish Catholic nationalists, who succeeded in increasing taxes on Big House owners and decreasing their tenants' rents, and from members of a new English capitalist elite, who were, in the words of Declan Kiberd, "by no means certain that the occupants of draughty, decaying mansions in windswept Irish landscapes really counted as 'top drawer.' "[60]

Like Delia Larkin, Augusta Gregory evinced a fierce loyalty to home throughout her life, though what "home" meant and for whom it was preserved varied considerably in her writings. Gregory's divided feelings over home were shared by another Ascendancy nationalist, Alice Milligan, who, during the *Shan Van Vocht* years, never fully reconciled her loyalty to her nationalist politics with that to her privileged upper-class background. Milligan could not countenance dismantling the privileges of her class; Gregory, for her part, dedicated enormous creative energies to managing the legacies of powerful, wealthy Ascendancy men, such as her husband, Sir William, her son, Robert, and her nephew, Hugh Lane. Yet she also concentrated a large proportion of her artistically productive years to creating, running, and maintaining Ireland's National Theatre. Indeed, it was Gregory who fiercely protected the Abbey during the worst of its political and financial troubles, and then nurtured the company back to health. Out of upper-class duty to her son, she scrimped and often starved herself to remove the estate's debt, yet she acknowledged relief in 1921 at the prospect of selling Coole Park, which would spare her the "anxieties and loneliness" of "having my last years cumbered with thoughts of management and money."[61] Seven years later, when her daughter-in-law, Margaret, finally did sell the estate, Augusta's republican sympathies and Ascendancy sentiment tumbled over one another: "Coole no longer ours," she wrote in her journal. "But the days of landed property have passed. It is better so. Yet I wish some one of our blood would after my death care enough for what has been a home for so long, to keep it open."[62] Such divided loyalties seem less at odds when placed in the context of Ascendancy writers such as Milligan and of Gregory's enduring pursuit of protecting, preserving, and recording the culture of home.

Indeed, Gregory cloaked some of her most radical political commentary in matronly concern for domestic peace. Where Milligan sternly counseled her readers in the *Shan Van Vocht* against insurgency, for fear of the sectarian bloodshed that would ensue, Gregory's painful, daily observations of colonial brutality in her home county of Galway prompted her, in the 1920s, to a committed sympathy for the tactics of the IRA. During some of the worst outrages of violence inflicted by the Black and Tans during the War of Independence (1919–21), Gregory anonymously published a series of her diary entries in the English liberal journal *Nation*.[63] Revealing herself only as "a distinguished writer and landlord," she proceeded to enumerate the savage reprisals visited upon the modest homes and cottages nestled in a "quiet part of Ireland, not dominated by the Extremists."[64] In each of her five weekly postings, Gregory established a case for republican resistance by appealing to middle-class values such as the sanctity of the home and motherhood. Ever careful to foster a fair, unbiased stance in these reports, she relays her stories as the Lady of the House sharing in the gossip of her neighborhood. This intelligence, however, conveys unspeakable horrors: the stories of house burnings, drunken looting, robbery, sexual humiliation, torture, rape, and murder must be represented anonymously by citing initials rather than names. Such scrupulous anonymity tacitly conveys the vulnerability of both her neighbors and herself as spokesperson for the community.

"Straddling the hyphen"[65] of her Anglo-Irish identity, Gregory frequently compared the dazed helplessness of her neighbors to that of Belgian refugees during World War I, a comparison that would resound with readers of the British press who had been inundated with war atrocity stories such as the sinking of the *Lusitania* and the execution of nurse Edith Cavell.[66] She reserved her most partisan remarks, however, for rebutting the fundamental English misunderstandings of Irish resolve. Sharply responding to a *Punch* cartoon lampooning "The Irish Volunteer Army," Gregory disclosed her unambiguous sympathy for IRA leader Terence MacSwiney, who at the time of his death through hunger strike in 1920 was Lord Mayor of Cork: "I felt the Lord Mayor had not given his life in vain if even to contradict that [cartoon], for his portrait also must be in some of this week's papers. It is, they say, in all the American ones."[67]

Yeats solidified Augusta Gregory's reputation by always addressing her as "Lady Gregory," a name that not only defined their mentor-artist relationship, but also reinforced her role as patron rather than cocreator of the Irish National Theatre.[68] In opposition to Yeats's portrait of a nurturing aristocrat, Sean O'Casey warmly described a woman with "lofty humility" who, like O'Casey, resisted class expectations to be a writer. "You had to fight against your birth into position & comfort," he recalled in a letter to Gregory, "as others had to fight against their birth into hardship & poverty, & it is as difficult to come out of one as it is to come out of the other."[69]

Increasingly, we learn from her journals, Gregory viewed herself as a worker strongly sympathetic to the cause of labor. At Constance Markievicz's death in 1927, she admitted that, though she had never countenanced Markievicz's militancy, she had nonetheless admired her commitment to her homeland. Recalling an evening encounter with Markievicz on the tram a decade earlier, when both were "tired and jaded" from Abbey rehearsing and Fianna drilling, Gregory remembered: "I felt drawn to her. There was something gallant about her. We were each working for what we believed would help Ireland."[70] Not long after this entry, in 1928, she enthused about George Bernard Shaw's socialism, in part because she saw her past efforts as a playwright and Abbey manager, as well as her present toil of preparing her papers for publication, as hard labor indeed: "G.B.S.'s socialism leads one on. . . . Being a worker myself my withers are unwrung, but it would be hard to get the wasters into the traces."[71] Shaw apparently agreed with her assessment, affectionately naming her, in 1910, "charwoman of the Abbey."[72] Elsewhere in her journal, Gregory recalled a supportive exchange with Jim Larkin when his workers expressed interest in performing her play, *The Rising of the Moon*. When Sean O'Casey requested permission to perform the play in Queen's Theatre, writing on behalf of Larkin, who hoped "to show the work of an Abbey playwright to many who have never been inside the Abbey theatre," Gregory replied, "I am giving leave—my heart goes out more to workers than to idlers."[73] We know, moreover, that this reciprocal respect was not merely a one-time occurrence, for in the 1920s and 1930s, Jim Larkin regularly encouraged trade unionists to visit the Abbey whenever they could afford to.[74]

If Gregory later gave permission for workers to perform her plays and indeed often described herself as sympathetic to the cause of labor, why did she refuse permission to Delia Larkin and the Irish Workers' Dramatic Society in May 1914, a time when Irish workers were in particular distress? A likely answer is her own financial and proprietary distress over the

Abbey: her struggle to keep the theater solvent and independent was especially challenging at this time; without the donation of monies from the Abbey's 1912–13 tour to the United States, the Hugh Lane gallery campaign would have completely collapsed.[75] In *Seventy Years*, Gregory marveled at how much energy she had squandered during the years before the Easter Rising on endless squabbles and anxious worries about money to keep the Abbey afloat, "endless affairs that almost crushed out all other interests."[76] In her journals, Gregory kept meticulous record of funds needed and small earnings received, taking delight in the smallest of triumphs: £2 18s. 50d. earned by Abbey actors in a performance on the deck of a steamship en route to the United States in 1913; £35 from *Golden Book* magazine for a reprint of *The Workhouse Ward*; £8 6d. for a single performance in London.[77] Fretting like a scrimper on a budget—like the very women workers that Larkin was striving to assist—Gregory took great pride when her creations brought income to the Abbey, at one point admitting: "I think of that fourteenth verse of Proverbs xxxi sometimes applied to me . . . : She is like the merchants' ships: she bringeth her food from afar."[78] Gregory's dispute with Delia Larkin would thus appear to be less over who could represent Ireland than who should profit from such labors.

The Workhouse Ward as Social(ist) Commentary

Augusta Gregory's popular one-act comedy *The Workhouse Ward* (1908) is, then, in many ways an apt play to present quarrels about class and kinship. The play is set in a poorhouse ward in Cloon, a borderland between counties that, Ann Saddlemyer has suggested, makes it "the boundless country of comedy," a specific place and a netherworld that opens up the possibility of allegory.[79] On the feast of Galway native, Saint Colman, a day before the Ides of March, we meet two crusty, quarreling neighbors more alike than they will admit. Even their interchangeable names, Michael Miskell and Mike McInerney, suggest they are cut from the same cloth, though each spars to prove his differences in familial achievements or personal suffering because of that "bad neighbor that was yourself."[80] When

Mike McInerney tells his ward mate, Michael Miskell, "to open me to analyse me you would know what sort of a pain and a soreness I have in my heart and in my chest," we realize that he is not merely seeking to establish a one-upmanship of woe.[81] In offering up an allegorical description of Ireland before the Rising of 1916, a time of quarrels and contentions over the path to national independence, he is expressing the theme of the play. Mike's comment, placed next to Delia Larkin's bitter rebuke of women workers who hid in the crowd, reveals that at the core of all these disputes between nationalists was the desire for workers, women, activists, and artists to be seen as sharing a common goal—"working for Ireland"—though this unifying aim was expressed in many ways.

Gregory reserved this portrait of a divided Ireland for some of her most lasting theatrical efforts. In *Kincora,* Gregory's tragedy about the conflict between service and rebellion, one character presciently warns:

> Those who serve Ireland take for their lot lasting battles—lasting quarrels. . . . Those who would be most their friends, turn to be most their enemies, till the heart grows dry with bitterness; dry as the heads of the mountains under the summer heat.[82]

The Workhouse Ward dramatizes the plight of two men who pursue "lasting quarrels": neighbors animated by and unified in their devotion to seemingly endless and superficial disputes over a lifetime of oppositions. But the quarrels of Mike and Michael generate an effusive outpouring of words rather than arid acrimony. And though one of them must confront a symbolic filial betrayal, the play's comic, companionable outcome belies its Ides of March setting. Bickering over every point, from who is a worse "cheater and schemer" to whose pig or dog is more "wicked and well ringed" to the other, the men must agree on Miskell's point: "Isn't it a bad story for me to be wearing out my days beside you the same as a spancelled goat?"[83] Herein lies the play's central paradox: like the goat who grazes best when tethered to its pasture, the men express their greatest gift, linguistic mastery, when trapped together in their ward beds.

Each man views himself as an object of pity, given the "chains" that bind them both, to "a man that is ransacking his mind for lies."[84] But the play suggests that dedicating one's life to lies hardly constitutes a "bad story." "Lying, the telling of beautiful untrue things," Oscar Wilde reminds us with his characteristic flair for inversion, "is the proper aim of Art."[85] In defiance of Keats's "solid stolid" Grecian urn, Wilde maintains that "those who do not love Beauty more than Truth never know the inmost shrine of Art."[86] This love of lying, Terry Eagleton tells us, or what he calls "blarney," is an axiomatic feature of the Irish. In his irreverent mock-tourist guide, *The Truth about the Irish,* Eagleton traces the origin of "blarney" to the Elizabethan colonization of the island, when Irish chieftains were compelled to swear an oath of loyalty to Elizabeth and instead used their gifts of speech to "bamboozl[e] their British masters": the Earl of Blarney "gave such a florid speech that nobody could tell whether he was submitting or rebelling."[87] If Michael Miskell and Mike McInerney cannot give up what Miskell calls "your lies and your chat and your arguing and your contrary ways," they are simply demonstrating themselves to be characteristically anticolonial Irish kind of men. Indeed, as McDiarmid and Waters note, the men's battle of the wits draws on the pattern of bardic "contention" seen in Gaelic tradition, most notably in *Cúirt an Mheán-Oíche (The Midnight Court)* by Brian Merriman.[88]

Reading Miskell and McInerney's irascible bickering against Delia Larkin's rancorous barbs clarifies one reason that Gregory's literary effort was a rhetorical success in conveying contention, whereas Larkin's journalism was not. In her *Nation* columns and her comedy of wits, Augusta Gregory alternately veils her identity or bamboozles her listeners. Her writing placates rather than threatens; her staged contention entertains rather than attacks. Yet, even though Gregory successfully worked within the patriarchal, colonial order, her writing, fund-raising, and organizing efforts often actively resisted the British Empire.[89] James Pethica argues that this dual pursuit of "pragmatic and visionary modes of nation building" was a hallmark of every element of Gregory's cultural nationalism.[90] Her pragmatic choices in *The Workhouse Ward*—to express rancor as comedy, to set her peasant realism in Galway rather than the streets of Dublin—in no way diminish either the hidden idealism of the play or its celebration of working men's wit and sharp tongues.

Perhaps *The Workhouse Ward*'s most valuable connection to Larkin's trade union journalism is its knowing portrait of how contentious rhetoric cannot thrive in isolation. For, even though Miskell and McInerney claim their dearest wish is to be rid of each other, we recognize that this is precisely what they cannot abide. As each takes his turn in describing the vastness of space that should divide their existence, what each in fact craves is the chance, as Miskell clamors, to "have everything to say":

> Mike McInerney: And I say, and I would kiss the book on it, I to have one request only to be granted, and I leaving it in my will, it is what I would request, nine furrows of the field, nine ridges of the hills, nine waves of the ocean to be put between your grave and my own grave the time we will be laid in the ground!
>
> Michael Miskell: Amen to that! Nine ridges, is it? No, but let the whole ridge of the world separate us till the Day of Judgment! I would not be laid anear you at the Seven Churches, I to get Ireland without a divide!
>
> Mike: And amen after that again! I'd sooner than ten pounds in my hand, I to know that my shadow and my ghost will not be knocking about with your shadow and your ghost, and the both of us waiting our time. I'd sooner be delayed in Purgatory! Now, have you anything to say?
>
> Michael: I have everything to say, if I had but the time to say it![91]

In this comic, beautifully cadenced exchange, rife with hyperbole, the men aptly embody the art of contention, saving their greatest eloquence and imagination for the inimical adversary who has heard it all before. For men barely on speaking terms, their fondest wish is to rebuff "Ireland without a divide" by dedicating a lifetime to arguments that get better every day. Christopher Murray sees Miskell's final declaration, "I have everything to say," as the central theme of both Gregory's oeuvre and twentieth-century Irish drama.[92] Augusta Gregory's words urgently voice an important refrain that runs through all of Larkin's trade union journalism, and indeed the journalism of many women writers of advanced nationalism—the need to have a say in Irish affairs, to be heard and recognized. Although Larkin violated the norms of gendered behavior in her columns for the *Irish Worker*, she certainly shared a key quality with Gregory's pugnacious paupers: like any good polemicist, she seemed most happy in the midst of a fight; even her writing seems more relaxed when she has reason to be least content.

Augusta Gregory self-effacingly claims that all of her drama might be considered "mere talk"; in her autobiography *Seventy Years* she insists that an "education in talking"—conversation, debate, and repartee—was her main training for playwriting: "For what is the substance of drama but conversation clipped and arranged?"[93] Her emphasis on dialogue, deliberation, and debate is a fundamental feature of the literary revival years, when arguments about the nation and its political and cultural future were most intense. For Gregory, her background and her literary interests produced divided loyalties—her Ascendancy background and republican sympathies, her insider privilege and her outsider gender. Such complex political considerations are suggestive of why the question of the nation (which was in 1908, when she composed the play, still an "imagined community") is often staged in divided or mirror characters. As Anne Fogarty explains, Gregory insistently tests the "belief system of nationalism" in her plays through representing instability and disharmony among locals: her "skeptical vision" of political ideologies such as nationalism or trade unionism owed much to Gregory's own divided position.[94] Thus, whereas Larkin scolded and sneered at workers out of her desire to unify them, Gregory staged rancor to test the limits of unifying itself.

A key element in Gregory's artful staging of contention is her sympathetic portrayal of the contenders. For example, nowhere do we appreciate the battling neighbors so well as when they are threatened with separation from one another. When McInerney's widowed, bourgeois sister Honor Donohoe arrives, in hopes of persuading him to return and brighten the "lonesomeness" of her manless home, we witness the depths of sacrifice one man will endure in order to "have his say." As she describes her comfortable cottage, the sweet grass, and the plenty of her table, the audience can see McInerney hungering and straining to get out of the workhouse: within moments, his sister's humble cottage on the sea has transformed in his mind into the horn of plenty and Tir na nOg:

> Every good thing! The goat and the kid are there, the sheep and the lamb are there, the cow does be running and she coming to be milked! Ploughing and seed sowing, blossom at Christmas time, the cuckoo speaking through the dark days of the year. . . ! Wheat high in hedges, no talk about the rent! Salmon in the rivers as plenty as turf! Spending and getting and nothing scarce! Sport and pleasure, and music on the strings! Age will go from me and I will be young again. Geese and turkeys for the hundreds and drink for the whole world![95]

McInerney's baroque catalogue of pleasures invites an ironic reading: just as we know that frost-burned plants will not blossom anew in December, so, too, we can be sure that any "spending and getting" by McInerney will be infrequent indeed on his sister's close watch. A sister who priggishly sniffs, "It is no credit to me a brother of my own to be in this place," seems an unlikely candidate for funding her brother's magnanimous wish, "drink for the whole world."

Whereas the ironically named "Honor Donohoe" proves small-minded and selfish, her seemingly petty brother turns out to be the one with a heart of gold. Within moments of recognizing the loneliness and suffering that will remain with his old rival if he departs, McInerney's conscience troubles him. When Miskell poignantly discloses what we could see from the start: "All that I am craving is the talk,"[96] Mike chooses to remain in the spare and shivering poorhouse rather than depart from his aggressively combative companionship with Michael. Like Delia Larkin's inaugural column in the *Irish Worker*, which rejected prosperity for only "a certain few," McInerney's choice represents solidarity and companionship, even if it is quarrelsome and contentious.

In her introduction, Gregory was the first to suggest that the play might be read as symbolizing the divisiveness of pre-independence Ireland: "I sometimes think the two scolding paupers are a symbol of ourselves in Ireland—'It is better to be quarrelling than to be lonesome.' "[97] Michael MacLiammoir has called *The Workhouse Ward* "that most subtly national and topical of one-act plays."[98] Although I, too, find the play allegorical, I would suggest that the scolding paupers might be read most particularly in light of working-class struggles over "having their say" in the future of Ireland. Like the later rebels of the Easter Rising, who, as Kiberd quipped, "Wilde-like, opt[ed] to invest their genius in their life and only their talent in their work,"[99] the scolding paupers are best understood in terms of their triumphant failures. For even though the men failed to break free from poverty and the workhouse, they will have each other to sharpen their tongues for a life dedicated to perfecting the art of "having everything to say."

Conclusions: Art and Ardor for Contention

It would seem that Augusta Gregory's efforts on behalf of the Abbey Theatre and Delia Larkin's aspirations for women workers complemented rather than competed against each other. As one writer to the *Irish Worker* emphasized, Larkin's two great gifts to Dublin laborers—union organizing and cultural programming—were both "genuinely effective civilising and humanising" endeavors. Gregory likewise explained her contributions as playwright and manager in terms of nurturing both Abbey Players and Irish workers.[100] Although Larkin and Gregory came from widely different backgrounds and employed dissimilar techniques in their writing about contention, they were equally dedicated to a common ideal: to advance the cause of Irish culture and Irish workers.

Both women, as we have seen, gravitated to contention: Delia Larkin in her personal style, Augusta Gregory in the central theme of her drama. Although Delia Larkin's art of contention put off her fellow women workers and alienated her own union's leadership, her style was never far from the popular, entertaining squabbles between Miskell and McInerney. Ironically, then, Gregory's work on behalf of the Abbey, and notably her great comedy of contention, *The Workhouse Ward,* represented the character and content of trade unionism, even though she refused in 1914 to let the trade union movement profit from such political drama.

5

Suffrage on the Barricades

Motherhood and Militancy in the Irish Citizen

In the final two years before the Easter Rising of 1916, activist women in Ireland faced a host of challenges, from the fights for suffrage and for trade union representation to world war and nationalist conflict. As we have seen in previous chapters, women working in the political and cultural movements of the Irish revival were hardly unified, either in theory or in practice. Their attitudes ranged across a broad ideological spectrum, from the feminine Ascendancy nationalism of Alice Milligan, to the collaborative nationalism of Maud Gonne, to the feminist nationalist trade unionism of Delia Larkin, to the militant socialist republicanism of Constance Markievicz. Many of these women continued to polish and refine their points of debate and disagreement. In the years 1914–16, however, Ireland's great champions of feminism, the suffragists, would shift the focus of their movement, to reconsider a subject that had preoccupied Irish nationalists for decades—motherhood and nationhood, and what these meant to each other. By this time, feminists had developed a variety of theories and practices with regard to the emancipation of both women and Ireland. Although the suffrage movement could not of course fully resolve wartime disagreements over the meaning of Mother Ireland and motherhood, its most discerning theorists, this chapter will argue, consistently embraced the ideal of feminist activism inextricably bound up with nationalism and socialism—the other two "great movements" of the day.

We have seen how the fluid, public dialogue of the advanced nationalist press, in which editors, commentators, and readers could speak and respond, made it a unique cultural and communication forum for debates about woman's place in Ireland. Writers for the premier weekly suffragist newspaper, the *Irish Citizen,* were strongly committed to that journal's role as a debating platform and took advantage of it to great effect. Anticipating the 1916 Proclamation of the Republic, which declared that Mother Ireland "cherish[ed] all the children of the nation equally," the *Irish Citizen* cherished a wide diversity of political and cultural opinion during some of the most tumultuous times in Ireland's transition from colonization to independence.

This final chapter focuses on an exemplary debate that took place on the pages of the *Irish Citizen* during the crisis years 1914–15. The outbreak of World War I prompted Irish feminists to clarify woman's role in a pan-European conflict, even as it forced them to work their way through a whole range of previously suppressed debates, between constitutionalists and separatists, pacifists and militarists, internationalists, whose allegiance lay with an imagined community of transnational feminists, and nationalists, whose allegiance lay with an independent Irish state. This particular debate, which played out in a series of editorials, letters to the editor, and a New Woman play in the *Irish Citizen,* included feminists holding Unionist, nationalist, constitutionalist, and militant viewpoints. Most significant was how these women grappled with the meaning of an iconic institution—motherhood—in the context of war. Reexamining their debate helps clarify how Irish feminism on the eve of the Easter Rising was a much more conflicted, heterogeneous, and multifaceted movement than previously acknowledged.

Motherhood offered suffragists an opportunity, in the words of Adrienne Rich, to "revive and renew all other institutions."[1] This feminist debate reveals how the institution and icon of motherhood became caught up in the discourse about suffrage and war, how strands of Irish feminism accommodated other social movements seeking gender equality in support of the national struggle.[2] Critics have often noted how both feminism and nationalism can become embroiled in the struggle between tradition and modernity, between Enlightenment reasoning and atavistic, tribal im-

THE IRISH

CITIZEN

Printed in Ireland on Irish Paper.

For Men and Women Equally
The Rights of Citizenship;
From Men and Women Equally
The Duties of Citizenship.

Weekly One Penny. Annual Subscription 6s. 6d. post free.

Vol. 1. JUNE 15th, 1912. No. 4.

"UNITED IRISHWOMEN."

NATIONALIST AND UNIONIST, MILITANT AND NON-MILITANT.

Chairman and Delegates at Historic Mass Meeting.

Dr. Mary Strangman, T.C. (Waterford). Mrs. Gibson (Limerick). Mrs. Sheehy-Skeffington, M.A. (Dublin). Senator Mary Hayden, M.A. (Chairman). Mrs. Cousins, Mus.Bac. (Dublin). Miss Geraldine Lennox (London). Mrs. Chambers (Belfast).

[Reproduced from "The Weekly Irish Times" by kind permission of the Editor].

Advertising the Mass Meeting: A Proof of Earnestness.

UNANIMOUS DEMAND FOR POLITICAL FREEDOM.

WHAT IS THE GOVERNMENT'S ANSWER?

9. Front page of *Irish Citizen,* June 15, 1912. In the wake of the Home Rule Bill deliberations, Irish suffragists organized as "United Irishwomen" to show solidarity in expressing the "unanimous demand" for woman suffrage. Reproduced courtesy of the National Library of Ireland.

pulses.[3] Reading the suffragist debate about the meaning of motherhood in the context of competing nationalisms—traditional and feminist—thus proves an excellent way to understand many of the outgrowths and ideological fissures of Irish feminism that exist to this day.

The Irish Suffrage Movement: Feminism Colored Green

As we have seen in previous chapters, and as many have noted, political, social, and economic challenges converged in the years leading up to the Easter Rising, and to Ireland's becoming a modern free state. But the distinct rhythm, cadence, and pace of the "three great movements" of these years—nationalism, feminism, and socialism—have often been overlooked.[4] The Irish suffrage movement began in 1876 with less than fifty members. During its most contentious years, from the rise of militancy in 1912 to the outbreak of World War I in 1914, its membership grew to more than 3,000, and the movement began to flex its muscles. Suffragists attracted a larger audience when some activists broke glass, experienced imprisonment, and discovered the weapons of heckling and hunger strikes. At the height of the suffrage movement in 1914, there were over twenty different societies organized under the umbrella of the Irish Women's Suffrage Federation (IWSF). Dominating the suffragist activities of these years, despite its small numbers, was the militant Irish Women's Franchise League (IWFL), founded in 1908 by Margaret Cousins and Hanna Sheehy Skeffington.

In his study of suffragists across the British Empire, Ian Christopher Fletcher observes that "women's suffrage movements have always been bound up with national projects, yet bound together by transnational linkages."[5] This was nowhere truer, nor more damaging, than for Ireland's suffrage movement. Irish militant suffragists, in their early years of organizing, frequently collaborated with the British suffrage movement, traveling to London to march and to petition Parliament. Over the course of their militant campaign, thirteen members of the Irish Women's Franchise League served prison sentences in England.[6] The leader of the British Women's Social and Political Union (WSPU), Emmeline

Pankhurst (known most often as "Mrs. Pankhurst"), and her daughter Christabel each traveled and toured major Irish towns in 1910 in an effort to establish Irish affiliates of the WSPU.[7]

The alliance between the Irish and British suffrage movements was to be short-lived, however, as Irish suffragists soon came to resent the overbearing, self-interested style of certain members of the WSPU.[8] Even in the brief, harmonious period of collaboration, Irish suffragists took especial care to highlight their separate national identity when traveling and protesting in England. In public marches, they wore green dresses, rather than the customary white, raised aloft Irish flags rather than suffrage banners, and frequently walked alongside Irish pipers.[9]

The intensified contest over Irish Home Rule during the spring of 1912 ultimately took the greatest toll on Irish suffragists bent on transnational alliances. In the House of Commons debate over the Conciliation Bill, members of Parliament overwhelmingly rejected the compromise proposal on women's enfranchisement. When the British government advanced its Home Rule Bill for Ireland, it did so without any provision for enfranchising Irish women.[10] British socialist MP Philip Snowden promoted an amendment to clause 9 of the Home Rule Bill that would enfranchise 100,000 Irish women who had the necessary property qualification, only to have it soundly defeated.[11] In pitting supporters of Irish Home Rule against supporters of women's suffrage, the parliamentary contest alienated Irish suffragists from their British feminist sisters and placed intense pressure on the Irish suffrage movement, which fissured into Unionist and nationalist organizations when activists could not agree on which issue to place first. Even among nationalist suffragists, membership divided over how to promote national independence, whether through the conciliatory, legislative methods of the Irish Parliamentary Party or through the radical, militant methods of Sinn Féin and Cumann na mBan.

Dialogue in the *Irish Citizen*

The brief transnational alliance between Irish and British militant suffragists would leave a lasting legacy in the *Irish Citizen*. When, in 1912, Francis Sheehy Skeffington convinced the Irish Women's Franchise League to establish an independent Irish suffragist journal to "keep the British and Irish suffrage movements distinct and carry on propaganda along our own lines," the British Women's Social and Political Union smuggled £260 to Margaret Cousins as venture capital to start the weekly newspaper.[12] From its first issue on May 25, 1912, the eight-page, one-penny weekly *Irish Citizen* announced its impeccable advanced nationalist credentials on the masthead: "Printed in Ireland on Irish Paper" (see illustration above), a Sinn Féin slogan first promoted by Arthur Griffith's *United Irishman* in 1899.

The *Irish Citizen*'s motto declared its gender-inclusive attitude about Irish nationalism: "For Men and Women Equally the Rights of Citizenship; From Men and Women Equally the Duties of Citizenship." Although men were excluded from membership in the league itself, the IWFL welcomed Francis Sheehy Skeffington (1878–1916) and James Cousins (1873–1956), husbands of IWFL founders Hanna Sheehy Skeffington (1877–1946) and Margaret Cousins (1878–1954), to serve as joint editors of the journal during its early years, uniquely reversing the gender norms of the time for men's and women's political work. Rather than expecting women to work and write on behalf of their political movement while remaining at home (as Mary E. L. Butler encouraged them to do a decade earlier in the *United Irishman*), the *Citizen* called on activist women to fully assume their public responsibilities as citizens, that is, not only to write for the new journal, but also to deliver speeches, heckle politicians, march at demonstrations, and, if necessary, throw stones and break politicians' windows.

On the other hand, men who wished to join the suffragist cause were encouraged to contribute as supportive spouses and as anonymous editors and writers. For the first four years of its existence, three men had primary editorial duties for the *Irish Citizen*. James Cousins and Francis Sheehy Skeffington shared responsibilities until the Cousinses departed for India in 1913, whereupon Francis assumed full control. On the rare occasions when he was away from Dublin, Maurice Wilkins produced the newspaper, with the assistance of Mary Bourke-Dowling and Marion Duggan.

After her husband was murdered during the Easter Rising of 1916, Hanna Sheehy Skeffington took over editorial duties, depending on Louie Bennett (1870–1956) to oversee the production while she went on an extended trip to the United States from December 1916 to June 1918 to publicize the brutality visited on Irish rebels and her pacifist husband, arrested and summarily shot by a British soldier for attempting to stop looters. In its final year, 1920, Louie Bennett assumed full editorial and financial responsibility for the *Irish Citizen*, consulting with Hanna Sheehy Skeffington even when the two women differed over the extent to which the journal should serve as an organ of the Irish Women Workers' Union.[13]

In its inaugural issue of May 25, 1912, the *Irish Citizen*'s main editorial announced the journal's "immediate objectives":

> (a) to form a means of communication between Irish Suffrage Societies and their members; (b) to provide a reliable source of publicity for suffrage activities in Ireland untainted by party bias; (c) to provide a means of cheap and effective propaganda amongst those ignorant of the principles underlying the movement by the publication of articles dealing with all its bearings.[14]

That said, the *Citizen* revealed, from the outset, a keen interest in promoting genuinely open dialogue about what its editors viewed as the most pressing topics of the day. At least four editorials in 1913 alone mocked the putative freedom of the press, notably in its biased coverage of suffragist events.[15]

Taking as its mission "to publish what the other papers will not print" and "to expose the suppressions and misrepresentations of the daily Press," the *Irish Citizen* fostered debate, dissent, and discussion on all matters pertinent to the suffrage fight. Indeed, it became the leading voice of Irish feminism in its most heterogeneous sense at a time when political leaders such as Arthur Griffith, John Redmond, and Éamon de Valera were notoriously reluctant to support female equality publicly. Like many advanced nationalist papers of the time, the *Citizen* regularly featured excerpts from other publications, both sympathetic (the *Woman's Journal*, Fabian Society printings, the *Christian Science Monitor*) and notoriously hostile (the *Irish Times*). It also printed long-running disputes, often filling an entire page each week for several weeks, over key questions such as militancy versus pacifism and the competing demands of nationalism and suffrage.

During its formative years, Francis Sheehy Skeffington quietly and surely shaped the direction of the *Irish Citizen*. A lover of debate and a devoted champion of equality, he declined to publicly claim his critical role as editor. In a letter to suffragist Charlotte Payne-Townsend, the wife of George Bernard Shaw, Francis maintained, "I personally write very little, merely keeping [the journal] going as a medium of expression for Irish women suffragists."[16] Such a remark was clearly disingenuous. Francis's background as an experienced freelance journalist and his characteristic relish for lively repartee are apparent in every issue he produced. Indeed, the years 1913–16, when he had full editorial control, remain the most interesting period in the *Citizen*'s history, during which it served as a welcoming forum for divergent viewpoints, with lively, impassioned, and often witty debates every week. His choice to remain anonymous was well within the venerable tradition of anonymity in radical, republican publications. He may also have chosen anonymity as a man working for the cause of women. Or perhaps he may have wished to conceal the extensiveness of his contributions to the journal and thus to promote the impression of multiple voices in the movement, a technique used by other advanced nationalist writers, such as Arthur Griffith and William Rooney back at the turn of the century in the *United Irishman*.[17]

That the *Irish Citizen* sold only 3,000 copies per issue in 1912 reflects the suffragists' comparatively small audience.[18] Delia Larkin's *Irish Worker* and Arthur Griffith's *Sinn Féin*, by contrast, sold 20,000 and 8,000 copies per issue, respectively, in the same year. Like the *Shan Van Vocht*, the *Citizen* exercised influence through its selective, global readership. It frequently printed excerpts of letters from readers living in Seattle or the Falkland Islands, who appreciated updates on the Irish suffrage movement, enjoying them "as one does a fresh breeze after being pent in a stuffy room."[19] It also proved quick to call attention to the difficulties in distributing its issues to a wider audience. In one letter to the editor, Rosamund Jacob, a republican feminist who frequently wrote in the advanced nationalist press, alerted readers to a disappointing experience she had at a Carnegie Free Library in Tramore, County Waterford. When Jacob asked whether she might leave a few copies of the *Irish Citizen* in the ladies' reading room, she was told that the library committee, comprised solely of men, declined her request. Taking care to emphasize that the library's hostility to feminism did not extend to radical journalism, Jacob added: "*Irish Freedom* [the organ of the Irish Republican Brotherhood] is allowed at the Free Library."[20]

The *Irish Citizen* also worked assiduously to train its readership in writing as political activism. For example, one editorial in the spring of 1913 called suffragists' attention to the educational potential afforded in the correspondence columns of newspapers:

> Frequently we hear from suffragists, either in letters or in conversation, expressions of indignation at some peculiarly gross misrepresentation, some characteristic instance of anti-feminist prejudice, some startling examples of man-made laws and man-ruled society, which has met their eye in the daily Press. Usually the *Irish Citizen* is asked to take up and expose the matter. That is one of the things the *Irish Citizen* exists for, and we are always glad to do whatever we can in this direction. But we should like to point out that readers can do much themselves to rectify these misrepresentations and to call public attention to these grievances.[21]

Not only did it encourage its readers to speak out in other journals; the *Citizen* also was unusually open to publishing its own readers' criticisms. In May 1914, in the heat of the suffragist debate over the impending war, for example, it published another letter to the editor by Rosamund Jacob, in which she meticulously identified the many logical fallacies in the *Citizen*'s relentless attacks on Cumann na mBan, notably in its characterizing Cumann members as "slave women." She closed, however, by acknowledging the journal's long-standing strength as an open forum: "The *Irish Citizen* sets a badly needed example to most journals in being always ready to publish criticisms of its own policy."[22] Indeed, it demonstrated an uncommon willingness to promote among its readers the fine art of talking back, even to its own editor.

Although the *Irish Citizen* was never suppressed, as many other advanced nationalist journals were under the Defense of the Realm Act of 1914,[23] rising wartime costs forced Francis Sheehy Skeffington to scale back from weekly to monthly publication in the spring of 1916; in the January and February issues of that year, editorials announced the establishment of a shilling fund to support the journal during "these tough times."[24] After the murder of Francis Sheehy Skeffington during the Easter Rising, the *Citizen* temporarily suspended publication, issuing a "Memoriam" special in July of 1916 and several more bimonthly issues for the duration of the year. Over the course of the next three years, Hanna Sheehy Skeffington, then Louie Bennett assumed editorial duties for an ever-slimmer publication (two and a half to four pages in each issue) until the journal's press was smashed by the Black and Tans in 1920 and it was forced to close its doors.

Contentious Militancy: Maternal Rhetoric, 1912–14

The *Irish Citizen* emerged during a particularly contentious period in the suffrage movement. In 1912, feminists began to quarrel over the militancy of Irish Women's Franchise League members who, during the summer months, first began to throw stones, break glass, and experience imprisonment for their militant activism. Because the mainstream press either maligned or ignored such behavior, the *Citizen* provided ample space on its pages for writers to debate the legitimacy and efficacy of militant means to achieve political ends. A key component in this debate was the icon of motherhood, which suffragists had deployed in vastly different ways outside the context of militancy to advance particular notions of femininity. One writer advocated woman's place on local boards to ensure that the mother's interests in the home were adequately represented; another railed against the inequities of the father's versus the mother's rights with regard to children born outside of wedlock.[25] The *Citizen* featured a serialized editorial on "the biological aspects of feminism," refuting essentialist notions of maternity and advocating "the abolition of an old idea of motherhood"; a letter to the editor admonished readers that "we are apt to forget, when speaking and writing about man-made laws, man's attitude, man's ideas and ideals, man's honour, etc., etc., that men are very largely what their mothers make them."[26] Though few consciously acknowledged it, Irish suffragists were in effect arguing over two competing genealogies of feminine political activism: they were wrestling over whether they spoke as tradition-bound mothers or as modern-living daughters in the style of Inghinidhe na hÉireann.

The *Irish Citizen* provided space for a serialized, three-month discussion on militancy and motherhood by Lillian Suffern and Marion Duggan. Both commentators were well known to *Citizen* readers. As one of the *Citizen*'s most prolific contributors,[27] Duggan employed her legal mind and schooling to write about the suffrage movement, morality, the Irish theater, and the courts. She openly opposed militant tactics, maintaining that the true split between suffragists was between "high franchise suffragists" (who supported the franchise for middle-class women only) and "universalist suffragists" (who insisted on achieving the franchise for all women).[28] A member of the Irish Women's Reform League, the Irish Women Workers' Union, and the Labour Party, Duggan often wrote in support of enfranchising all women who met a minimum age requirement of thirty.

The debate over militancy and motherhood began with "Two Roads to Liberty," in which Duggan outlined what she saw as the key differences between peaceful and militant suffragist tactics.[29] In the *Citizen*'s next issue, Lillian Suffern, a middle-class, Unionist member of the militant Irish Women's Franchise League, aggressively rebutted Duggan's characterization of militants as impractical attention seekers bent on martyrdom. Arguing that a militant woman is instead an "exceedingly practical woman, who knows well what she is doing and why she does it," Suffern invoked the motto of the militant, British-based Women's Social and Political

Union: "The militants' object, as defined by their leader Mrs. Pankhurst, is 'that children should be better born, into better conditions.' " The "fighting spirit" of a militant woman differed little from a mother's "instinctive fighting for the future" or when "its young are in danger," Suffern claimed,[30] eager to underscore the middle-class respectability of militancy.

This dependence on traditional gender norms had its limits, however, as Suffern's next installment demonstrated. A woman who turned her back on her duties as wife and mother had no role in the revolution. Singling out the U.S. feminist Charlotte Perkins Gilman, who divorced her husband and relinquished custody of her child to her husband and his second wife, Suffern maintained that those who "so little understood the true meaning of marriage and of motherhood . . . cannot be a leader, in any true sense of the word, in the woman's movement, since women's one great work and supreme duty must always be that of motherhood." Though she was careful to praise Gilman's "constructive genius" and originality, Suffern insisted that "it is by their fruits that all principles must be judged; the life they produce is their test."[31]

Marion Duggan, and numerous others who wrote in response, took Suffern to task for her militant essentialist view of motherhood. Duggan sought to relocate motherhood in the nonviolent camp by rejecting Suffern's insinuation that "only militants are animated by mother instinct," noting how deplorably "anti" (that is, anti-suffrage) her reasoning revealed itself to be. At the same time, Duggan rejected the idea that "only those women who have missed 'motherhood'—real or collective—could want a career." She implicitly dismissed Suffern's severe judgment of Charlotte Perkins Gilman by suggesting that many militants would come up wanting if judged by the same standard as that imposed upon Gilman: militant "enthusiasts do not show to any advantage over all other women. . . . Their lives do not always justify their theories."[32]

As a peaceful, constitutionalist suffragist, Louie Bennett opposed war and militancy of every kind, yet supported pacifism on precisely the same essentialist or biologically determinist grounds that Suffern supported militancy. Founder of the Irish Women's Reform League and the Irish Women's Suffrage Federation, Bennett maintained that "because woman's truest instinct was towards life," suffragists should eschew violence.[33] Elsewhere, she also maintained that both militant activism and support for the war—like Irish nationalism and British patriotism—were barriers to "that spirit of international fraternity and goodwill without which peace is impossible."[34]

Shared Rebellions: Republicanism as a Feminist Example

Whereas Suffern, Duggan, and Bennett established the foundations for their militancy *and* pacifism in woman's natural life force, other suffragists, such as Meg Connery and Hanna and Francis Sheehy Skeffington, drew on the example of Irish republicanism to explain their commitment to women's equality. A prominent member of the Irish Women's Franchise League, Meg Connery justified her radical activism, such as throwing rocks and breaking MPs' windows, as an intrinsic part of her feminism, a commitment that had its foundation in Irish national resistance:

> I had to choose between being a slave or a rebel; I have chosen to be a rebel. I refuse to wear my chains passively. I broke windows as an unmistakable token of my revolt.[35]

Though she was a university-educated middle-class lady, Connery here pointedly rejects Suffern's equating militancy with respectability. Instead, she argues that a woman awakened to her gender subordination differs little from a slave who recognizes the injustice and inhumanity of her servitude, that the free woman's civic disobedience is as morally necessary as a slave's violent revolt from the plantation. Connery's equating her own symbolic rebellion with another long-lived, transnational liberation movement, abolitionism, effectively raised the moral stakes in the militant debate. In labeling her activism as a "rebel" act, though, she was also clearly reminding her audience of the venerable tradition of "legitimate violence" by Irish patriots since the Plantation of Ireland in the seventeenth century.

Like Meg Connery, Hanna Sheehy Skeffington linked her militant feminism to a lifelong commitment to the principled activism of Irish republicanism:

> I have always realized the potency of the dock. Thoreau says somewhere that the time may arise when the prison may be the only place of honour left to an honest man. Many a brave Irishman has proved the truth of that axiom; it is now time for Irishwomen to realize citizenship by becoming criminals.[36]

Thus a critical component of the suffragist activism of both Connery and Sheehy Skeffington was its relationship to another liberation movement, which offered them theoretical and practical insights into how to practice feminism in Ireland. When questioning the respectability of pacifism, Sheehy Skeffington liked to compare her outlaw experiences in jail to upstanding middle-class accomplishments such as attending university or becoming a nun:

> Michael Davitt used to say that jail had been his only University. He certainly learned there more of life and philosophy than many an M.A. in his academic career. . . . One wonders when the authorities will realize that prison for politicals is no deterrent. They enter novices, to emerge consecrated and vowed to the cause in whose service they have graduated.[37]

Hanna Sheehy Skeffington traces her genealogy of feminist activism to the working-class Fenian Michael Davitt (1846–1906), a committed republican who helped organize and later defend the Ladies' Land League in the 1880s. As the founder of the Women's Graduate Association, Hanna Sheehy Skeffington had, by 1912, discarded the middle-class credentials of her university education for the more radical credentials of imprisonment.

In his captions, illustrations, photo galleries, editorials, and drama, Francis Sheehy Skeffington also attempted to normalize suffragist militancy by locating the suffrage movement in relation to militant republicanism. In 1912, as suffragist militancy was inaugurated in Ireland, the

Irish Citizen published a series of subversive curricula vitae of militant suffragists. In the wake of a trial of IWFL members accused of breaking glass, the front page featured a prominent picture of Hanna Sheehy Skeffington. Underneath the picture, a narrative situated her rebel activism alongside her family's impeccable background as venerable republicans well familiar with the inside of a jail:

> Mrs. Sheehy Skeffington is the eldest daughter of Mr. David Sheehy, M.P., who was six times imprisoned for political offences in connection with the agrarian and Home Rule agitations. Her uncle, Father Eugene Sheehy, was the first priest imprisoned as a "suspect" for Forster. She graduated with distinction in the Royal University, winning Scholarship, 1897; Honours B.A., 1899; M.A. with First Class Honours and Special Prize, 1902. Member of Committee, Irish Association of Women Graduates. One of the founders of the I.W.F.L., 1908; Chairman of Committee, 1911. With Miss Hilda Webb, heckled Mr. Birrell at Greystones, Oct., 1910. Heckled Sir Edward Carson, Dec., 1910. Went on deputations to Mr. Redmond, Dec., 1908; July, 1910; Jan., 1911, and April, 1912. Took part in Poster Parade, Home Rule Sunday, and in deputation to National convention.[38]

In this most subversive of curricula vitae, the *Irish Citizen* placed university honors on the same plane as heckling Irish MPs and marching for woman's suffrage. Wryly questioning the prestige garnered from inherited wealth, academic achievement, and patrilineage, this caption suggested that activism and prison sentences constituted the greatest legacy that Hanna Sheehy Skeffington could have received. As Sheehy Skeffington and other women accumulated further prison sentences, the *Irish Citizen* continued to publish such subversive vitae, returning again and again to the critical association between militant feminists and nationalists.[39]

In the midst of heated exchanges over motherhood and militancy in the *Irish Citizen*, Francis Sheehy Skeffington wrote a one-act play on this very theme. *The Prodigal Daughter* (1914), which further developed Meg

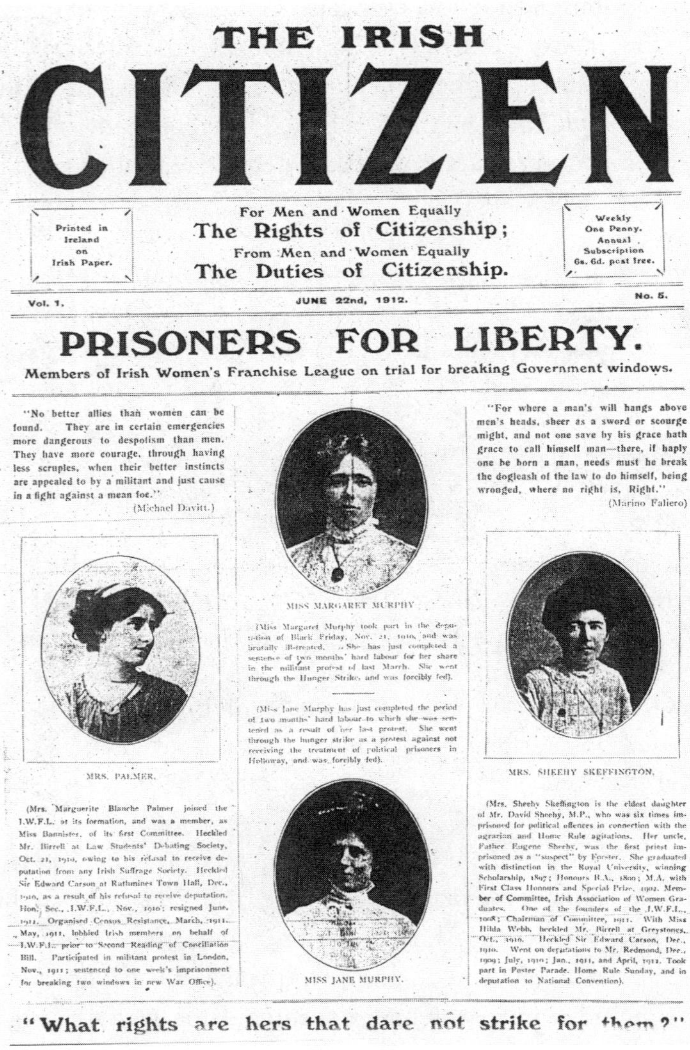

THE IRISH
CITIZEN

Printed in Ireland on Irish Paper.

For Men and Women Equally
The Rights of Citizenship;
From Men and Women Equally
The Duties of Citizenship.

Weekly One Penny. Annual Subscription 6s. 6d. post free.

Vol. 1. JUNE 22nd, 1912. No. 5.

PRISONERS FOR LIBERTY.

Members of Irish Women's Franchise League on trial for breaking Government windows.

"No better allies than women can be found. They are in certain emergencies more dangerous to despotism than men. They have more courage, through having less scruples, when their better instincts are appealed to by a militant and just cause in a fight against a mean foe."
(Michael Davitt.)

"For where a man's will hangs above men's heads, sheer as a sword or scourge might, and not one save by his grace hath grace to call himself man—there, if haply one be born a man, needs must he break the dogleash of the law to do himself, being wronged, where no right is, Right."
(Marino Faliero)

MRS. PALMER.

(Mrs. Marguerite Blanche Palmer joined the I.W.F.L. at its formation, and was a member, as Miss Bannister, of its first Committee. Heckled Mr. Birrell at Law Students' Debating Society, Oct. 21, 1910, owing to his refusal to receive deputation from any Irish Suffrage Society. Heckled Sir Edward Carson at Rathmines Town Hall, Dec., 1910, as a result of his refusal to receive deputation. Hon. Sec., I.W.F.L., Nov., 1910; resigned June, 1911. Organised Census Resistance, March, 1911. May, 1911, lobbied Irish members on behalf of I.W.F.L. prior to Second Reading of Conciliation Bill. Participated in militant protest in London, Nov., 1911; sentenced to one week's imprisonment for breaking two windows in new War Office).

MISS MARGARET MURPHY

(Miss Margaret Murphy took part in the deputation of Black Friday, Nov. 21, 1910, and was brutally ill-treated. She has just completed a sentence of two months' hard labour for her share in the militant protest of last March. She went through the Hunger Strike, and was forcibly fed).

(Miss Jane Murphy has just completed the period of two months' hard labour to which she was sentenced as a result of her last protest. She went through the hunger strike as a protest against not receiving the treatment of political prisoners in Holloway, and was forcibly fed).

MISS JANE MURPHY.

MRS. SHEEHY SKEFFINGTON.

(Mrs. Sheehy Skeffington is the eldest daughter of Mr. David Sheehy, M.P., who was six times imprisoned for political offences in connection with the agrarian and Home Rule agitations. Her uncle, Father Eugene Sheehy, was the first priest imprisoned as a "suspect" by Forster. She graduated with distinction in the Royal University, winning Scholarship, 1897; Honours B.A., 1899; M.A. with First Class Honours and Special Prize, 1902. Member of Committee, Irish Association of Women Graduates. One of the founders of the I.W.F.L., 1908; Chairman of Committee, 1911. With Miss Hilda Webb, heckled Mr. Birrell at Greystones, Oct., 1910. Heckled Sir Edward Carson, Dec., 1910. Went on deputations to Mr. Redmond, Dec., 1909; July, 1910; Jan., 1911, and April, 1912. Took part in Poster Parade, Home Rule Sunday, and in deputation to National Convention).

"What rights are hers that dare not strike for them?"

10. Front page of the *Irish Citizen*, June 22, 1912. Like the *United Irishman*, the *Irish Citizen* initially adopted a spare style, though later issues often used photographs as well as editorial cartoons to capture readers' attention. With flattering, framed photographs and appreciative captions such as these, the *Irish Citizen* publicized imprisonment and also normalized militant feminist activism. Reproduced courtesy of the National Library of Ireland.

Connery's and Hanna Sheehy Skeffington's association of suffragist militancy with republicanism,[40] owes a quiet debt to Maud Gonne's *Dawn* (1904) in focusing on the political potency of a daughter who suffers for a larger political goal. Building on the proto-feminism of Gonne's play, whose mother and daughter inspire men to fight, Francis Sheehy Skeffington's suffragist drama centers on the physical and intellectual agency of an unmarried modern woman. Perhaps the most telling detail in the play is its effortless repudiation of the old symbolic order: maternal authority is swept aside by the modern daughter, whose university education prompts her to renounce the conventional social values of her staid mother.

The context of the play's original production sheds light on why Sheehy Skeffington would cast a daughter—and a militant republican suffragist, at that—as the lead in his play. He wrote the play for the IWFL's Daffodil Fête, a two-day cultural festival held in March of 1914 that drew its energy and excitement from a new generation of emancipated women. The Daffodil Fête showcased the diverse talents of Irish suffragists. In addition to viewing dramatic performances, attendees could watch suffragist competitions, hear their feminist fortunes told, and listen to an all-woman orchestra. The highlight of the festival was suffragist drama, which included many of the same political performances and *tableaux vivants* that Inghinidhe na hÉireann inaugurated over a decade earlier. Some of the key performances—Constance Markievicz and Kathleen Houston dramatizing Joan of Arc in battle or about to be martyred, Muriel MacDonagh as the warrior queen Maeve, Sidney Gifford as a tortured Anne Devlin—impressed upon the audience a highly valiant image of militant nationalist femininity.[41] Margaret Ward notes that, for these two days, suffragists put aside their political and strategic differences to enjoy the common cause of feminist festivities. Based on the content of the final dramatic productions, with their militant, republican subtext, though, it seems unlikely that Unionist suffragists would have felt fully welcomed at the party.[42] Sheehy Skeffington's play, as the opening performance, served to entice audiences to settle in for the militant tableaux that followed, and it stays true to the Daffodil Fête's theme of valiant militancy. The play's emphasis on the tradition of Irish republicanism, rather than on religious history or epic sagas, served to validate his suffragist heroine's principled activism.

The Prodigal Daughter deviates sharply from the parable that inspires its title. A comedy of manners, the play aims chiefly at provoking intellectual laughter over the battle of wits between the rational suffragist Lily Considine and her stolid shopkeeping family. It also rejects the allegory of Christ's parable; where the prodigal son finally comes to realize the love of an all-forgiving Father, the prodigal daughter is the only one equipped to model and to instruct others in the values of respect and equality. Even the protagonist's name, Lily (a visual and cultural emblem evoking the Virgin Mother and the martyred Christ), signals a symbolic transformation, from maternal selflessness and male martyrdom to feminist political engagement.

As the play opens, the Considine family is nervously preparing for Lily's return home from prison, where she has been confined for "suffragettin'." Mrs. Considine, a plump, respectable, middle-class lady, and her starchy eldest daughter, Maggie, now prosperously married to the town's doctor, fret over how Lily's activism is "makin' a show of yourself here—and ruinin' all belonging to you into the bargain."[43] When they try to shame Lily into settling down with a man or entering a nunnery, they discover that Lily's resolve is far more tenacious than their own. Unfurling a tricolor with the words "Votes for Women" emblazoned on the front, Lily shares her fondest ambition: to convert the citizens of her hometown to the suffrage cause.

A visual reminder that she supports both an independent Irish republic and equal rights for women, her flag prompts Lily's father, Michael, to say that just because she supports Ireland's independence is no guarantee her hometown will also support the emancipation of her sex. When Michael observes, "Sure she'd be laughed out of the town," Lily responds, in a manner reminiscent of Grania in Alice Milligan's *Last Feast of the Fianna*, "It'll take a lot more than laughter to put me down, father." Soon, father, priest, and daughter battle over the competing demands of Home Rule and Votes for Women. When Father O'Sullivan, the parish priest, argues that nationalist militancy is "a sacred motive for the cause of the whole country," Lily raises the moral stakes: "This fight is for a still more sacred motive—for the sake of half the human race."[44]

Despite Lily's words, the playwright is far less interested in the transnational solidarity of feminists than in trans-movement alliances between feminism and republicanism. When the doctor primly reminds Lily he's never been in jail, Michael replies, "No, you never had the spunk," before disclosing his proud past, a jail term served at Kilmainham for his "fighting spirit." Even Lily's mother, a pompous keeper of the family lore, will not be left out of this recovery of her own family's republican past:

> 'Deed an' it isn't the Considines that have all the fightin' spirit! Wasn't your uncle Thomas, that stood for Tommy here, out in '67? And wasn't my father, the Lord be merciful to him, out in '48? An' wasn't my great-grandfather's brother shot in '98?[45]

Applauding her family for passing on the inheritance of "fighting blood," Lily points out that her feminist activism owes its vibrancy to her republican forebears. Like the playwright, however, Lily refrains from forcing the point: "You know, you needn't say you agree with me—just ask [others] to listen to me and give me a fair hearing."[46] The play established the rationality of feminist militancy by personifying it in the reasonable, eminently agreeable Lily Considine. Lily's most persuasive argument—both for her family and for the audience of suffragists watching the production—surely lies in her upbeat equation of two social movements invested in equal rights.

As a New Woman play, *The Prodigal Daughter* challenges its audience to canvass republicans, rather than the middle class, in seeking support for women's suffrage, although more often New Woman drama draws an intrinsic connection between the enfranchisement of women and the needs of the working class. Thus, in *Mrs. Warren's Profession* (1894), George Bernard Shaw provides a cautionary portrait of gender emancipation severed from socialist insight. Vivvie Warren's focused mathematical training at Cambridge's Newnham has ill equipped her to understand the pressing needs of working women. Though a wiz in mathematics, she cannot comprehend the economic circumstances that force working-class girls, like her mother, to become prostitutes. As Shaw makes clear, however, Vivvie's deficiencies in comprehension are not so different from those of her scrappy mother; neither woman considers the ethical limitations of capitalism to provide women with broader economic choices.[47] In Elizabeth Robins's *Votes for Women!* (1909), the materialist analysis and rhetorical sophistication of a female Cockney speaker make this working-class woman the most persuasive in a long list of polished, prepared orators addressing the crowds at Trafalgar Square. Yet, in one important respect, all three New Woman protagonists—Lily in *Prodigal Daughter,* Vivvie in *Mrs. Warren's Profession,* and Vida in *Votes for Women!*—display a similar vision of a new world order where daughters turn their backs on mothers and motherhood. Indeed, Robins's Vida reverses the direction of Suffern's and Duggan's logic by explaining that childlessness is the responsible choice for women living in a profoundly unjust society: "Since men alone have tried and failed to make a decent world for the little children to live in—it's as well some of us are childless."[48] In *Prodigal Daughter,* Lily shares a similar viewpoint, though she chooses a Catholic model of female chastity. Like an evangelizing nun, Lily dedicates herself to the "higher cause" of votes for women.

Even among feminists and nationalists, *The Prodigal Daughter* had its critics. A reviewer for the *Irish Citizen,* which would publish the play in its November 7, 1914, issue, found it altogether implausible that the mainstream objections of her middle-class family to militancy could be "bowled over like ninepins" by Lily's arguments.[49] A commentator in the IRB-affiliated *Spark* took umbrage at Lily's blithe dismissal of Mass as mere "idling at home."[50]

Feminists who wrote in every week to contribute to this ongoing debate over militancy do not appear to have influenced entrenched thinkers in the opposing camp. Yet the very fact that the debate occupied so many pages in the *Irish Citizen* is telling in itself when one considers how divisive militancy was at the time. Cliona Murphy explains that when a suffrage conference was being planned for 1913, the organizers deliberately took militancy off the agenda, despite the topic's obvious relevance to their intended discussions, presumably to avoid further divisions at the time.[51]

The battle over which was the more appropriate expression for suffragist activism—militancy or constitutionalism—prompted feminists to ask themselves other divisive questions. Were they rebels or respectable citizens? Nationalists or internationalists? Did they favor sexual equality or sexual difference? Were they individualists or essentialists?

Suffrage on the Barricades, Act Two: War, Maternity, and Militancy

The *Irish Citizen* became even more committed to publicizing dissent and disagreement when Britain entered the war. Whereas most advanced nationalist periodicals reacted to the news with surprise, with few antiwar perspectives published at all, the *Irish Citizen* provided precious space to writers whose perspectives were excluded from the mainstream press because of their antiwar stance.[52] Across the Irish Sea, British suffragists also initially disagreed on the proper response to the pan-European hostilities. Some leaders, such as Emmeline Pethick-Lawrence of the Women's Social and Political Union, Nina Boyle of the Women's Freedom League, and Sylvia Pankhurst of the East End Federation (and daughter of Emmeline Pankhurst), refused to end their suffragist activities on the socialist or constitutionalist ground that, as political outsiders, women had nothing to do with the war.[53] On the other hand, Great Britain's preeminent suffragist organization, the Women's Social and Political Union, prominently closed shop, rechristening *Votes for Women Britannia* and redirecting the energies of its members to the war effort. By September 1914, Christabel Pankhurst had published *The War*, her first recruiting speech for "the preservation of the Empire" in pamphlet form.[54]

For Irish suffragists and militant nationalists, however, the outbreak of war crystallized how divided the movements were, from each other and within themselves. Whereas the Easter Rising healed divisions between feminists and nationalists as women took up arms, braved bullets to deliver food and supplies, and shared cells at Holloway and Kilmainham Gaols, the Great War, by awakening Irish feminists to the myth of international solidarity among women, gave rise to new divisions within their ranks.

Some organizations, such as the Munster Suffrage Society, actually split apart and then folded over the leadership's desire to fund ambulance relief services on the war front.[55]

The wartime divisions among suffragists affected the language of motherhood in new and troubling ways. As a "British" conflict, World War I forced many Irish writers to retire the Mother Ireland trope. Though denied the rhetoric of romantic Irish nationalism, many could not, however, resist reclaiming the institution of motherhood for both tradition *and* modernity. In her study *Of Woman Born,* Adrienne Rich observes that the institution of motherhood "is more fundamental than tribalism or nationalism."[56] Irish suffragists attached different histories and ideologies to it, depending on how they related feminism to nationalism, internationalism, and socialism. Some suffragist writings employed a maternalist perspective to argue that the experience of motherhood afforded women political viewpoints. Like current feminist scholarship on motherhood,[57] suffragist writings during World War I were often divided over the meaning of motherhood and the political viewpoints it might dictate, in part because here was where social attitudes about women were most acutely strained.[58] Indeed, throughout the suffrage campaign—both in Great Britain and in Ireland—writers for and against woman's suffrage battled repeatedly over definitions of normative and deviant femininity.

For Irish feminists, the symbolic role of motherhood has always had a marked ideological subtext because of the Catholic Church and Irish nationalism, both of which frequently espouse prescriptive ideals of what constitutes feminine identity and behavior. Mother Ireland, for example, is a ubiquitous nationalist image of suffering or self-sacrificing femininity, tracing its roots to the goddess of the land, particularly the triadic female deity Eriu, Fodla, and Banbha. The maternal goddess was also appropriated and altered by the Catholic Church in its cult of the Virgin Mary. In its emphasis on Mary's "sinless" fertility, however, the church sent an unrealistic message to women: be fruitful but do not enjoy becoming so. Irish feminists at the turn of the century, moreover, had to contend with the middle-class Victorian cult of domesticity and the idealization of maternity, most famously captured in Coventry Patmore's *Angel in the House,* but quite similarly deployed by Irish women writers such as journalist Nora Tynan O'Mahony, in her adulation of the domestic Dublin angel, "The Mother."[59]

A frequent contributor to the *Irish Monthly*, O'Mahony exemplifies the complicated, changing role of women in the Irish press at the beginning of the twentieth century. She wrote character sketches and Celticist essays, such as "Ancient Civic Processions" and "Elysian Fields"; she celebrated the bucolic pleasures of Ireland through walking tours of County Clare. She also sternly defended the well-established if threatened doctrine of separate spheres for men and women by valorizing "the holy and beautiful attributes of Motherhood."[60] Lamenting the "hysterical shriekings of the suffragette sisterhood," which brought with them "gradual distortions" in woman's nature, O'Mahony advanced a familiar anti-suffrage argument: by clamoring for the vote, women forfeit their "royal prerogative as undisputed mistress and queen of the home."[61] O'Mahony's language tells us as much about her views on colonialism and labor as it does about her views on women. Notwithstanding her rosy-hued, upper-middle-class vision of a mother's life of ease, her contrasting scenes—the cacophony of democracy versus the serenity of monarchy—reveal how easily motherhood can absorb a broad range of ideologies while simultaneously registering the anxieties of an age.

Although O'Mahony's portrait of motherhood can hardly be distinguished from Patmore's domestic angel, other contemporary writers in the advanced nationalist press sought to paint the domestic Irish mother in broad strokes of green. Whereas Maud Gonne, in the 1890s, wrote stirringly about the harsh reality of impoverished Irish mothers in "Famine Queen," George Russell (AE) extolled the domestic Irish woman as part of the redemptive rural civilization of his philosophy in the *Irish Homestead*.[62] Unlike O'Mahony, however, Russell and other contributors to the *Irish Homestead* (the weekly organ of the Irish Agricultural Organisation Society) who wrote about the United Irishwomen movement viewed the domestic sphere as a means by which women could establish authority in the public realm. Moreover, in contrast with the later veneration of Irish Catholic motherhood enshrined in article 41, clause 2 of the 1937 constitution, Russell's domestic vision for rural Irish women primarily focused on their role as workers on family farms or in rural businesses, rather than as housewives and mothers.[63]

"Like Sheep Astray": Motherhood in the Context of War

As we have seen in the debate over suffragist militancy, Irish suffragists writing in the *Irish Citizen* after the start of World War I could not agree on the value of motherhood. When Britain joined the growing coalition against "Prussianism" in the summer of 1914, the old suffrage debates over militancy and motherhood were restyled as a battle over war, which was labeled "militarism." As the Women's Social and Political Union and its once-respected leader Christabel Pankhurst were drawn into the battle, one contributor to the *Irish Citizen* maintained that both those who approve or damn the war have a right to their opinions: "Neither of them cease thereby from being suffragists!"[64] Yet Louie Bennett, writing to Hanna Sheehy Skeffington during the same period, lamented that the war revealed the Irish suffrage movement's want of a unifying theory regarding gender in the discourse of nationalism. With the exception of the Irish Women's Franchise League, Bennett complained, feminists were "like sheep astray, and I suppose when the necessity of knitting socks is over—the order will be—bear sons. And those of us who can't will feel we had better get out of the way as quickly as we can."[65] Bennett's remark reveals precisely how marginalizing maternal appeals could become in a time of crisis. Of course, not all suffragist writers weighing in on the war were merely bleating. And even when Irish suffragists sometimes went astray, their contradictions and contentions are a valuable testament to how feminism, like nationalism, ever oscillates between tradition and modernity.[66]

Although the majority of suffragists in all thirty-two counties of Ireland became active in relief work, a vocal minority—the IWFL—continued to press for "suffrage first, above all else." Stridently refusing to follow the example of Britain's WSPU, the *Irish Citizen* printed posters proclaiming, "Votes for Women Now! Damn Your War!" Yet even the IWFL membership could hardly ignore the war altogether. Indeed, for well over a year, editorials, letters, and follow-up comments in the *Irish Citizen* debated whether suffragists should support or oppose the war, and on what constituted appropriate avenues to do so. Given the paucity of such discussion in the mainstream and advanced nationalist press of the time, reading this debate in the *Irish Citizen* is especially valuable today for understanding how Irish feminists sought to gain control over their lives and to foster alliances with other political and social movements of the day.

The suffragists' debates about war allow us to see precisely how "images of the maternal shape and are in turn reshaped by cultural practices."[67] Motherhood often functioned as a free-floating signifier, attaching itself to a wide range of ideologies in the war years.[68] British suffragists invoked motherhood to promote unity among women, to create a sense of stability, and to maintain a shared experience during a time of anxiety and social change.[69] Irish suffragists invoked motherhood for many of the same reasons, though, more often, how they did depended on what David Lloyd, in a different context, has called their "conjectural relation" to other social movements, such as Irish or British nationalism or internationalism.[70] Indeed, the most pressing issue before Irish feminists was their capacity to forge alliances with other national or international movements.[71] Irish suffragist writings thus help us better understand both the explicit political claims of Irish feminists and the political disagreements among Irish nationalists over the emergent Ireland's march toward modernity.[72]

Irish feminists, many of whom were also active in the nationalist and trade unionist movements, frequently referred to tradition and modernity in their arguments about motherhood and war. Like many of the writers for *Bean na hÉireann*, suffragist commentators did not necessarily find Irish tradition and international modernity antithetical: many advertisers and editorial writers held that Irish-made goods, such as millinery and jewelry, could both evoke the Irish past and set new fashion trends. Not surprisingly, Irish feminist pronouncements on motherhood and war moved between three primary responses—pro-war, peaceful antiwar, and militant antiwar—that revealed how readily traditional and modern practices intermingled.[73]

A key advocate of suffragist militancy, Lillian Suffern also revealed her Unionist convictions when she began to write in support of the war effort. Appealing to tradition—as well as to British wartime propaganda—to explain her militant pro-war stance, Suffern reminded readers that all democracies have war at their foundation, and that even heaven has witnessed ferocious battle.[74] She then expounded on why women, and especially mothers, should support the war: "This closeness to the vital forces of creation," she wrote, qualified women for suffragist militancy—as well as wartime relief—because mothers, above all others, understand and embrace cultural expectations of feminine self-sacrifice:

> To give yourself in work for the future, as a mother gives herself for her child, is indeed to "hitch your wagon to a star," and to have the universe itself work for you! For you are then in line with it, its forces flow through you, and use you, and to live or die is gain.[75]

For Suffern, both motherhood and political activism demand selfless deference to the demands of "work for the future," although, in her vision, neither entails much agency for women. Rather, Suffern's mothers exert influence chiefly by submitting to the forces of the universe, not by controlling them. Another pro-militarist suffragist, Violet Crichton, used similar language of maternal self-abnegation to expound on her Unionist convictions and to chide the nationalist Irish Women's Franchise League for refusing to support "their" British nation in crisis:

> It is surely possible to remain true, in the highest sense, to the suffrage cause, and yet realize the supreme moment that has come to our national life, calling for extreme effort and exceptional sacrifices on the part of every individual. . . .[76]

Crichton's letter reveals how her idea of nationality (British rather than Irish) and her definition of femininity (essentialist rather than individualist) shape her militarist views. Tellingly, her nationalist appeal is remarkably similar to that of Irish nationalists, who called on women to subordinate their suffrage demands to the "higher calling" of national politics, whether that meant Home Rule or Revolution.

Whereas Suffern and Crichton supported war out of Unionist convictions, another prominent writer, Margaret Cousins, cofounder of the IWFL, developed a theory of strategic militarism: war was to be allowed if it advanced the suffrage cause. Drawing on the underlying philosophy of the *Irish Citizen*, expressed on its masthead as "For Men and Women Equally the Rights of Citizenship; From Men and Women Equally the Duties of Citizenship," Cousins skirted the question of the war's legitimacy altogether. Instead, she wryly proposed: "The endowment of motherhood, Government pensions equal to full pay, and votes for women, should be claimed by women as compensation for what they have lost through the war."[77] Other columns in the *Citizen* used a similar tactic. In response to Lord Charles Beresford's proposal to enfranchise all soldiers, one unsigned editorial bitterly proposed: "If every soldier is to vote as a matter of course, then so should every soldier's mother—every woman who has risked her life to produce that cannon fodder which, on militarist principles, is all that henceforth is to count as of value to the State."[78]

Many suffragist contributors to the *Irish Citizen*, both militant and constitutionalist, nationalist and internationalist, drew on biological determinism to bolster their pacifism: war was incompatible with a woman's mothering instincts. But where Suffern and Crichton used motherhood to legitimate the war effort, these pacifist writers argued for what feminist theorist Sara Ruddick has called "maternal resistance," namely, that "*preservation*, *growth*, and *social acceptability* constitute maternal work."[79] For example, the nonviolent constitutionalist feminist Louie Bennett wrote that "women were more sympathetic to internationalism than men because of the bonds created by the special function of motherhood." If "some women support the war," she surmised, "they were merely victims of patriarchal oppression which suppressed their natural tendencies."[80]

Although the militant pro-war stance of Suffern and Crichton was shared by most Irish suffragists at this time,[81] militant opposition to the war, a platform of the IWFL, received a great deal of attention as well, thanks largely to Francis and Hanna Sheehy Skeffington and the *Irish Citizen.* One antiwar contributor to the *Citizen,* Margaret McCoubrey, a socialist member of the militant Belfast Irish Women's Suffrage Society, continued to press for suffragist activism even though she lived in Unionist-dominated Northern Ireland. McCoubrey argued that her status as a mother sharpened her ability to recognize the true human dimension of war:

> Women, looking down on the battlefield, would not see, as men, "there lie so many Germans, so many British, so many French;" instead, they would see "so many mothers' sons! All our service of motherhood gone to naught."[82]

Living in Ulster, a province whose population expressed sharply divergent national aspirations, McCoubrey may have found it politic to focus on women's supposedly shared concerns, rather than on nationalism, a strategy that follows Milligan and Johnston's unifying efforts in the *Shan Van Vocht.* Whereas Milligan, in particular, glossed over the class differences of nationalists and women, McCoubrey infuses her ideal mother with a socialist valuation of domestic labor. Whereas "so many mothers' sons!" expresses McCoubrey's essentialist view of woman's interpretive strategies—women, unlike men, view human beings always within the context of the immediate family—"all our service of motherhood gone to naught" expresses her socialist view of motherhood as professional domestic labor. Her comparison of childbirth to undervalued and underpaid efforts depreciates motherhood, domestic labor, and childbirth alike. Just as Suffern's and Crichton's earlier accounts displace mothers in their emphasis on maternal self-sacrifice, McCoubrey's account of "so many mothers' sons" effectively empties motherhood of social status through its focus on children.

A small faction of suffragists made the case for their militant antiwar stance by renouncing the traditional veneration of motherhood. Like McCoubrey, Meg Connery expressed her "passionate revolt against waste, degradation and wholesale sacrifice of humanity in the interests of material things."[83] Yet, instead of finding common cause as a mother, Connery—a committed rebel—defended her antimilitarist stance by rejecting woman's primary function as a nurturing, procreative female. Linking the war's "wholesale sacrifice of humanity" to the "militarist" ideal of woman as mothers, Connery sharply criticized how that ideal reduced woman to "simply a breeding machine, a thing of sex, the female of the species, strictly limited to one sphere of activity—the purely animal function of reproduction."[84]

Francis Sheehy Skeffington radically extended Connery's line of reasoning: if women were no longer slaves to reproduction, the world would not need war to keep the population in check. In "War and Feminism," Sheehy Skeffington provocatively claimed that "war is necessarily bound up with the destruction of feminism [and that] feminism is necessarily bound up with the abolition of war."[85] Like Connery, he supported his thesis with illustrations of evolution and natural selection. Although humans were at the top of the Great Chain of Being, their numbers were kept in check only by famine, pestilence, and war. Thanks to the advances in agriculture and medicine, they would overpopulate the earth without the intervention of war, infanticide, or "artificial restrictions" such as birth control. Raising moral objections to all three, Sheehy Skeffington posited a natural means of population control, the emancipation of women. If women would "cease to be 'an appendage of the uterus,' " then humanity would have little use for the devastating, however naturally necessary, function of war:

> Woman must count in and for herself, as a human being, with the human rights of an individual. Woman's vital energy, hitherto dammed up into one channel—that of reproduction—will be spread over all the fields of constructive human thought and action. And automatically, by the quiet action of the conservative processes of nature, the amount of woman's vital energy available for reproduction will diminish.[86]

With this line of creative, if unscientific, reasoning, Francis Sheehy Skeffington posited that feminism functioned as the best, most effective form of birth control. If women bore fewer children because of a natural refocusing of their "vital energy," then the need for war would vanish. For all of his fighting feminist instincts, though, Sheehy Skeffington assumed, as many Victorian antifeminists did, that woman could not simultaneously sustain a developing brain and a childbearing uterus.

While many of the key suffragist writers in the *Irish Citizen* battled over the meaning of motherhood in the context of war, Hanna Sheehy Skeffington—perhaps the most skilled, persistent, and eloquent advocate for suffragist militancy and republicanism—directly repudiated motherhood in her commentary on war. In her strongest-worded editorial, "The Duty of Suffragettes," Hanna expounded on her "suffrage first, above all else" imperative. She began by embracing McCoubrey's premise of woman's shared experience during wartime; like both McCoubrey and Connery, she rejected war as a waste of maternal labor:

> The women of Europe, whose motherlands are engaged in strife, are all alike in their voteless condition. Like us, they have to pay the price none the less to the uttermost farthing. They have to deliver up the sons they bore in agony to a bloody death in a quarrel of which they know not the why or wherefore. . . . [87]

As the editorial developed, however, Hanna illustrated the blind spots in viewing war through a mother's eyes. Rejecting government demands and pro-war feminist appeals "to roll up the map of suffrage with the map of Europe," she brusquely outlined the fate of suffragists who used national crisis as a reason to resume their traditional role as mother:

> Here is a list compiled from the daily Press of things that we may do to show "we are not unworthy of our soldier brothers". We are to knit "soft woolen comforters" for the departing soldiers, to replenish their cigarette-cases from our pin money, to

> see to food supplies at home, so that no unseemly riots take place among the starving poor to disturb the progress of affairs, to accompany the troops as Red Cross nurses, helping to patch up the shattered victims of machine-guns and torpedoes. . . . Some of these tasks are noble, some ignoble, but all end for suffragists in a cul-de-sac. When the war is over we shall be gently but firmly put back in our place once more—on our pedestals.[88]

Rather than return to second-class status in society, as nurturing nurse or comforting mother, Hanna Sheehy Skeffington advised women to press for lasting equality. Emphasizing that "it is not for us to mitigate by one iota the horrors of war," she declared that women must reject their internalized function in society to mollify, sustain, and tend to others. Lest her readers miss her militant antiwar position, she closed her commentary by proclaiming the real battle before Irish feminists: "Our guns must be directed, not against the Germans (from whom, by the way, we have much to learn), but against our common enemy, the warmongering politicians, the pledge-breaking Government, now so sentimental over the wrongs of oppressed nationalities. . ."[89]

Implicit in this editorial, as well as her actions as a heckler, stone thrower, and hunger striker, was a defiant refusal to mother at all. Whereas other feminists attempted to demonstrate the respectability of suffragist mitiancy,[90] Hanna Sheehy Skeffington seemed to relish, instead, what she called "an element of unwomanly selfishness in the idea of women fighting for themselves," though she often wrote to justify why a university-educated nationalist would employ such "unwomanly" tactics as the stone and the shillelagh.[91] Using her voice as a weapon and her strong arms to throw rocks, Hanna was three times imprisoned for such militant behavior. Her strongest refusal to mother took place in jail, when she went on a hunger strike to achieve her political goals. As Jane Marcus has argued, because women are the "quintessential nurturer," "the tactic [of hunger strike] was a symbolic refusal of motherhood."[92] Indeed, Hanna's numerous writings, captions, and editorials in the *Irish Citizen* celebrated and repeatedly underscored her political credentials by reminding readers of her commitments as a thrice-imprisoned and hunger-striking activist.[93]

Yet she was quick to indicate the republican precedent that trained her in feminist militancy. In the *Irish Review*, in fact, she pointed out that Irish men have long benefited from Irish women's acts of rebellion: "At the siege of Limerick the women gathered aprons and stockings full of shards, glass and flints, which they hurled upon the Willamettes; in Land League times 'Temporary stone-throwers' became proverbial." Republican history, she went on, teaches that men's complaints about female militancy owe much to the cause over which the battle is fought: "the stone and the shillelagh need no apologia: they have an honored place in the armory of argument. So, too, men applaud the stone-thrower as long as the missile is flung for them and not at them."[94]

Conclusions: Rhetorical Burdens of Motherhood

Ann Daly has remarked that "more than anyone else, politicians understand the expediency of idealizing the mother."[95] Not surprisingly, Irish suffragists—unelectable and without parliamentary clout—proved eager and ready to reshape the meaning of maternity to suit their various ideological positions at the beginning of World War I. As we have seen, however, the icon of motherhood proved a burdensome weapon, and not only because of its association with demanding nationalist icons such as Mother Ireland or Britannia. The choice of most effective rhetorical strategy had important repercussions, as the Irish Republican Brotherhood, the Irish Volunteers, Cumann na mBan, and the Irish Citizen Army clashed and merged to deliver forth the still-imagined Irish nation.

Like feminism and nationalism, motherhood betrayed its ever-shifting capacity to embody revolutionary ideologies or dominant values, to justify resisting domination or propping up the governing elite.[96] During World War I, peaceful constitutionalists such as Louie Bennett and Margaret McCoubrey used the discourse on motherhood to broaden the appeal of internationalist feminism. In later years, human rights activists—"The

Mothers," Irish political dissidents who formed the Irish Women's Prisoners' Defence League in the 1920s and 1930s, the Argentinean protest group Las Madres de la Plaza de Mayo in the 1970s, the Green Belt movement in Kenya, and the Women Strike for Peace in the United States—employed a similar strategy.[97] Yet even as women skillfully deployed maternity to broach the boundaries between private and public and to turn the state's proclaimed sanctity of motherhood against it, by invoking motherhood, they also marginalized their claims to political independence. As "unmanageable revolutionaries," Meg Connery, Francis and Hanna Sheehy Skeffington were consistently skepticial about drawing on the ethos of motherhood, preferring to foster alliances with the republican movement instead. Such a strategic choice positioned them to participate more centrally in debates about women and the nation in the coming years. Yet, ironically, in the decades after 1921, the voices of these and other dissident women were silenced by the now partially independent Irish Free State, which worked assiduously, through both rhetoric and legislation, to restrict women to the home, as wives and mothers—and to suppress their role as authors of the revolution.[98]

Coda

> Ireland, Mother Ireland, with your freedom-loving sons,
> Did your daughters run and hide at the sound of guns?
> Or did they have some part in the fight?
> And why does everybody try to keep them out of sight?[1]

In the last two decades, a small, determined group of Irish historians have made it possible for us to respond to the questioning voice of this feminist republican ballad.[2] We now know that Irish women did assume many roles in Ireland's battles for independence. During Ireland's revolutionary years, from the Rising of 1916 through the War of Independence (1919–21) and Civil War (1922–23), women shouldered many of the same responsibilities as Ireland's "freedom-loving sons." Some women, such as Mary Childers and Mary Spring-Rice, smuggled guns; some, such as Constance Markievicz and Margaret Skinnider, saw action as sharpshooters. Other women, such as Kathleen Clarke and Hanna Sheehy Skeffington, were entrusted with running the Irish Republican Brotherhood or the Civil Provisional Government. Still others helped run the secret courts, delivered military dispatches, gathered intelligence, and served in the illegal Dáil Éireann (Irish Parliament).

During the Easter Rising, according to the estimates of Ruth Taillon and Sineád McCoole, women made up some 10 percent of the 1,600–2,500 Irish activists who mobilized during the insurrection.[3] Perhaps 60 percent of these women were members of Cumann na mBan, and performed work as couriers, intelligence gatherers, nurses, first-aid providers, and cooks; the remaining 40 percent were members of the Irish Citizen Army (ICA) and served shoulder to shoulder with men as soldiers, medics, and intelligence officers. As ICA member Helena Molony later impatiently explained, women's roles were as diverse as men's:

> I feel they might as well ask me what did the tall fair haired men do in the wars and what did small dark men do. My answer in both cases is the same: they did what came to their hands to do—day to day, and whatever they were capable of by aptitude or training.[4]

That the women in the army did "whatever they were capable of by aptitude or training" was due in no small part to the lessons given them by the women of the advanced nationalist press. Alice Milligan's romances, Maud Gonne's collaborations, Constance Markievicz's gardening columns, Delia Larkin's and Augusta Gregory's rhetorical contentions, Francis and Hanna Sheehy Skeffington's editorial debates each, in a slightly different fashion, taught Irish readers that women had many creative, and sometimes combative, contributions to make to Ireland's future.

If Irish women assumed many of the same tasks as male activists in the Rising of 1916, albeit in smaller numbers, why are their stories still so seldom heard? The answer to this and the final question posed in Brian Moore's song—"Why does everybody try to keep them out of sight?"—is complicated. Female revolutionaries who actively involved themselves in the Easter Rising, the War of Independence, and the Civil War have not, of course, been completely forgotten. Their stories, however, fit uneasily in the well-established nationalist narratives that prescribe woman as symbol, icon, or emblem of the nation. As a result, activist women's contributions linger on, Lisa Weihman suggests, as "a repressed memory" in the national subconscious.[5]

One notable, irrepressible exception is Constance Markievicz, a woman whose performative militancy was critiqued years before her untimely death in 1927. On the occasion of the unveiling of a bust of Markievicz in Saint Stephen's Green in 1932, Hanna Sheehy Skeffington alerted her audience to the way that popular histories and national commemorations often transform women such as Markievicz into "chocolate box heroines": "Monuments to the dead," Sheehy Skeffington warned, "are often misused—sometimes, no doubt, unconsciously—by the living to misinterpret what those whose memorial is unveiled truly stood for."[6] Perhaps one of the most glaring misinterpretations of Markievicz is the notion of her exceptionality. To situate her stone likeness alone on a pedestal in Saint Stephen's Green is also to suggest, wrongly, that that were no other women like her, striving, fighting, and rebelling for national independence, economic justice, and gender equality.

There are many other reasons why Irish women's contributions as writers and activists have been lost or forgotten by the literary historians and historiographers of Ireland. As the introduction to this study has indicated, a range of influential, self-interested individuals, from Matthew Arnold to William Butler Yeats, erected a formidable wall that separated "great literature" from the "scribblings of the masses." This imposing barrier effectively ensured that popular forms of writing, such as Irish women's journalism, would be forgotten. Margaret Ward has detected a similar effect in Irish historiography, where, over the course of the last eighty years, women's contributions to Irish independence have been increasingly demoted to the footnotes of studies by revisionist historians eager to underscore their scholarly objectivity and critical distance from nationalism.[7]

In fact, Yeats's influential elegy "Easter 1916" enacts precisely what later revisionist historians have accomplished in diminishing, then ignoring women's roles in the revolution. Feminist critics have persuasively explored the poem's concise criticism of feminine activism: the coded critique of suffrage in Markievicz's "shrill" voice, the pat assessment of her socialist commitment as "ignorant good will."[8] Less often remarked is how the poem's development, from the second stanza to the last, quietly but surely edits women out of this national lyric of remembrance. For, although Yeats dedicates six lines to Markievicz (albeit to judge her inappropriate activism), in the end, he substitutes the name of James Connolly, her male mentor, for Markievicz when he arrives at his memorable (and oft-memorized) conclusion:

> MacDonagh and MacBride
> And Connolly and Pearse[9]

The very nature of Irish women's activism, especially during wartime, also contributed to the relative invisibility of revolutionary women in Irish history. Because women's activism most often depended on secrecy or disguise, there were few, if any, witnesses to recognize and record their contributions to the revolution.[10] When Maeve Cavanagh, who carried military dispatches to Waterford during Holy Week and the first days of the Easter Rising, dressed as a lady to travel undetected, her disguise fooled more than British soldiers and the Royal Irish Constabulary.[11] In a comment that applies as much to Cavanagh as to the female soldiers in the Flying Columns to which she refers, Constance Markievicz remarked, "It says a great deal for their cleverness that so few of them were ever caught, and many of the best girls were never even suspected."[12] In response to the paucity of documentation about her sister rebels in Cumann na mBan and the Irish Citizen Army, Markievicz dedicated considerable energies in the 1920s composing plays, giving speeches, and writing for nationalist journals to establish a public record of Irish women's activism.[13]

In the years and decades to follow Ireland's battle for independence, both men and women involved in the struggle have sometimes deliberately, sometimes inadvertently, facilitated a national amnesia about women's contributions to the national struggle. As noted in the conclusion to chapter 5, a significant proportion of the women who mobilized during the Rising of 1916, War of Independence, and Civil War were silenced during the early Irish Free State years because of their intractable republicanism.[14] Yet women have also played a part in downplaying their own work. In her account of the Easter Rising, "Women in the Fight," Constance Markievicz prefaces her remarks with the apology that she can "only give . . . a little account" because her activities "were confined to a very limited area."[15] So, too, Maud Gonne—another woman better remembered for her self-aggrandizing behavior—modestly admits in her autobiography, *A Servant of the Queen,* that her political arena was only "the small corners of the battlefield."[16] For many more Irish women, especially those with far less confidence and far more modesty than Markievicz and Gonne, their family and friends heard merely fragments and snatches, or simply nothing, about these women's historic, if unseemly, experiences as rebels, prisoners, and soldiers.[17]

Although the women of *Women, Press, and Politics* stood out for their capacity to speak and write dynamically on the subjects of nationalism, feminism, and trade unionism, the crisis of the Easter Rising, during which the journals of the advanced nationalist press briefly ceased publication, temporarily silenced even their unfaltering voices. They registered multiple responses to the war at home. Those directly involved or drawn into the conflict—such as Constance Markievicz and Hanna Sheehy Skeffington—had less recourse and less inclination to take to their typewriters, preoccupied as they were with the absorbing tasks of warfare (Markievicz) or of supplying and feeding the insurgents (Sheehy Skeffington). In the weeks and months that followed the surrender on April 29, 1916, Markievicz's and Sheehy Skeffington's lives were irreparably undone: they lost comrades and loved ones to British reprisals. For her role as second in command of the Irish Citizen Army in Saint Stephen's Green, Markievicz was sentenced to death, although her sentence was first commuted to life in prison, then vacated altogether in the General Amnesty of 1917. Sheehy Skeffington, in turn, secretly traveled to the United States to plead the republican cause before President Wilson and to press for justice in the murder of her pacifist husband, Francis. Even while in prison, on the run, or traveling incognita, however, Markievicz and Sheehy Skeffington repeatedly took to their pens, writing for and editing journals, composing speeches, letters, and diary entries that documented their wartime experiences.

Others women writers studied here, such as Milligan, Gonne, Gregory, and Larkin, were out of the country or far removed from the action. For Alice Milligan, the Rising of 1916, and the subsequent news of the executions, added politically charged agony to her own personal grief in nursing three of her closest family members—her sister, Charlotte Milligan-Fox, through her illness, and both of her parents until their deaths. She knew nothing about the planning for the Easter Rising, consumed as she was with her family's needs and her own grief. Yet 1916 marked a turning point in Milligan's literary productions and political activism. After the death of her parents, Milligan's life became that of a dependent sister; her wide-ranging work was considered, by family members, to be an eccentric, doddering hobby that could be set down at a moment's notice for the more pressing concerns of tending to her brothers and their families. As she disclosed in a letter to Sineád de Valera, "Since the opening of 1919, I have been more or less a prisoner, entirely secluded by circumstances amongst relatives entirely opposed to the Republican cause."[18]

Though Maud Gonne did not suffer the deprivations of economic dependence, family circumstances also caused her to be out of Ireland during the Easter Rising. In the wake of her failed marriage to John MacBride in 1903, Gonne fought a lengthy battle in court for legal divorce and sole custody of her son Seán; because her marriage separation verdict was valid only in France and because she refused to share custody with a man she considered abusive, she lived for the next decade in France, together with her daughter, Iseult, and her son, Seán. Although she would make occasional visits to Ireland, notably to support the launch of Inghinidhe's *Bean na hÉireann* and to support relief efforts, such as the School Meals Campaign and the feeding and clothing of destitute children during the Lockout of 1913, she largely refrained from political activity to avoid dissension among nationalists. Upon hearing news of the Easter Rising and of her estranged husband's execution, however, Gonne embarked on a difficult, time-consuming effort to return to Ireland. Because of family illness, world war, and her own reputation as a dangerous subversive, her arrival was delayed for a year and a half. Soon afterward, she was imprisoned in Holloway Gaol under suspicion of being party to a pro-German plot; she shared a cell with Constance Markievicz, Hanna Sheehy Skeffington, and Kathleen Clarke. In the years to follow, Gonne continued to write for the advanced nationalist press and to fight for the Irish Free State's prisoners, effectively returning to the same amnesty campaign that, a half century earlier, had drawn her into nationalist politics.

Lady Gregory, at home in Coole in County Galway, felt as distant from the action in Dublin as Gonne did in France. Whereas Milligan in London and Gonne in France gleaned information from news reports and the letters of friends, Gregory relied on local gossip. Though much of what she heard later proved to be untrue—as she judiciously underscores in editing her diary—she nonetheless found "what a stimulant it is to conversation, getting all one's news from word of mouth and none by letters or telegrams or newspapers." Forced from the sanctuary of her demesne, swapping stories and accumulating a repository of reflections and speculations, Gregory discovered how this "mere talk" brought her closer both to her community and to an appreciation of "the leaders who had some ideal."[19] In the years to follow, Gregory's grief at the loss of her only son, who fought for the British Empire in World War I, and her anxious experiences during the reprisals of the Black and Tans during the War of Independence, pushed her beyond mere support of those fighting for "intellectual freedom" to become a dramatist and anonymous journalist working to prepare Ireland for its political and cultural independence from Britain.

Delia Larkin's experiences and reaction to the Easter Rising are perhaps the most difficult to trace among those women we have studied here. The strain of the Dublin Lockout, the departure to the United States of her brother Jim, and the tensions in Liberty Hall surrounding her militant behavior prompted her to return to England in 1915. Living in London rather than her native Liverpool during the war, she found employment as a nurse. Though she returned to Dublin again after the war, she was never welcomed back into the women's union she helped organize, although she continued in her own way to contribute to the cause of labor, editing a short-lived trade union journal, the *Red Hand,* in the early 1920s.

The women writers of advanced nationalism, who actively maneuvered around, revised, and sometimes rejected their appointed roles as passive embodiments or modest maidens, have been largely forgotten or overlooked in Irish history and literature. As we have seen, they left behind intricate textual legacies that challenge many of the standard narratives of Ireland's literary and political revival. Although the authoritative study of the Rising of 1916 has yet to be written,[20] the Bureau of Military History Archives, locked away in eighty-three steel boxes for the last fifty years in Dublin's Cathal Brugha Barracks and only opened to the public in 2003, contain 149 statements by women involved in the Rising of 1916 and the War of Independence.[21] Tracing the contentious history of these statements, Diarmaid Ferriter comments on the wealth of information they bring to social historians,[22] and, it should be said, to literary historians and feminist critics as well. Moreover, significant collections of original documents possessed by or concerning prominent republican women—notably Helena Molony and Kathleen Clarke—will provide historians and biographers with indispensable material for a whole new body of scholarship on women, cultural nationalism, and republicanism.

Scholars of the cultural revival, however, need only open the pages of the advanced nationalist press to discover the wealth of information and the range of artistry produced and published daily, weekly, and monthly by a talented cadre of writers, many of whom were women. Widely available at research libraries in Ireland, the United Kingdom, and the United States and increasingly affordable for university libraries to obtain on microfilm, journals such as the *United Irishman* or the *Irish Citizen* deserve broader dissemination among those seeking to understand the Irish revival. The editorials, polemics, poems, and plays in these journals—and the vibrant, wide-ranging array of men and women who wrote them—need to be studied for their innovations and transformations in thinking about nation, gender, and class during this exceptional era.

Notes

◆

Bibliography

◆

Index

Notes

Introduction

1. Constance Markievicz, *Women, Ideals, and the Nation* (Dublin: Inghinidhe na hÉireann, 1909), 16.

2. For background about the advanced nationalist press and the Irish-Ireland movement, see Virginia Glandon, *Arthur Griffith and the Advanced-Nationalist Press, 1900–1922* (New York: Peter Lang, 1985), 1–27.

3. Glandon, *Griffith*, 5; Ben Novick, *Conceiving Revolution: Irish Nationalist Propaganda During the First World War* (Dublin: Four Courts Press, 2001), 29.

4. See "Mary" of the *Nation*'s appeal for such a project to be undertaken in the *Nation*, Oct. 31, 1846, as quoted in Antoinette Quinn, "Ireland / Herland: Women and Literary Nationalism, 1845–1916," in *Field Day Anthology of Irish Writing*, ed. Angela Bourke et al. (Cork: Cork Univ. Press, 2002), 5:889.

5. Few substantial literary studies have concentrated on the role of Irish nationalist periodicals in shaping and assessing an expressly female literary tradition of patriotic expression. Noteworthy feminist reappraisals of the revival that consider journalism include C. L. Innes, *Woman and Nation in Irish Literature and Society, 1880–1935* (Athens: Univ. of Georgia Press, 1993); Declan Kiberd, *Inventing Ireland* (Cambridge, Mass.: Harvard Univ. Press, 1995); and Marjorie Howes, *Yeats's Nations: Gender, Class and Irishness* (Cambridge: Cambridge Univ. Press, 1996). Such feminist analyses were indebted to the path-breaking scholarship of historian Margaret Ward. See esp. Margaret Ward, *Unmanageable Revolutionaries: Women and Irish Nationalism* (1983; reprint, London: Pluto, 1989) and *In Their Own Voice: Woman and Irish Nationalism* (Dublin: Attic Press, 1995).

6. For recent criticism on Alice Milligan, all of which labors to rescue her from the dustbin of literary history, see Catherine Morris, "From the Margins: Alice Milligan and the Irish Cultural Revival, 1888–1905" (Ph.D. diss., Univ. of Aberdeen, 1999); Richard Harp, "The *Shan Van Vocht* (Belfast, 1896–1899) and Irish Nationalism," *Éire/Ireland* 24

(1989): 42–52; Carl Racine, "Alice Milligan and Irish Nationalism," *Harvard Library Bulletin* 3, no. 1 (1992): 47–52; and Virginia Crossman, "The *Shan Van Vocht:* Women, Republicanism, and the Commemoration of the 1798 Rebellion," *Eighteenth Century Life. Ireland, 1798–1998: From Revolution to Revisionism and Beyond* 22, no. 3 (1998): 128–39, ed. Robert P. Maccubbin.

7. Anne K. Mellor, *Mothers of the Nation: Women's Political Writing in England* (Bloomington: Indiana Univ. Press, 2000), 6; Margaret Beetham, *A Magazine of Her Own? Domesticity and Desire in the Women's Magazine 1800–1914* (London: Routledge, 1996), 13.

8. Marie-Louise Legg, *Newspapers and Nationalism: The Irish Provincial Press, 1850–1892* (Dublin: Four Courts Press, 1998), 475.

9. Maria DiBattista and Lucy McDiarmid, eds., *High and Low Moderns: Literature and Culture, 1889–1939* (New York: Oxford Univ. Press, 1996), 15.

10. Laurel Brake, *Subjugated Knowledges: Journalism, Gender and Literature in the Nineteenth Century* (New York: New York Univ. Press, 1994), xii.

11. Yug Mohit Chaudhry, *Yeats, the Irish Literary Revival and the Politics of Print* (Cork: Cork Univ. Press, 2001), 38–39.

12. Matthew Arnold, "Up to Easter," in *Complete Prose Works of Matthew Arnold,* ed. R. H. Super (Ann Arbor: Univ. of Michigan Press, 1970–77), 11:190–209. First published in *Nineteenth Century* 21 (1887): 629–43.

13. Brake, xii; Beetham, 116.

14. Arnold, "Easter," 199.

15. See Matthew Arnold, "On the Study of Celtic Literature," in *Works,* 3:291–386.

16. Chaudhry, 9–11; Frank Shovlin, *The Irish Literary Periodical, 1923–1958* (Oxford: Oxford Univ. Press, 2003), 2–5.

17. See Beetham, "Introduction"; Brian E. Maidment, "Victorian Periodicals and Academic Discourse," in Laurel Brake, Aled Jones, and Lionel Madden, eds., *Investigating Victorian Journalism* (London: Macmillan, 1990), 151.

18. Beetham, 13.

19. John Whelan, "Literature and Nationality," *Shan Van Vocht,* Jan. 1897, 10.

20. Howes, 45.

21. Sally Ledger and Scott McCracken, eds., *Cultural Politics at the* Fin de Siècle (Cambridge: Cambridge Univ. Press, 1995), 1.

22. William Butler Yeats, *Autobiographies: First Draft and Journal,* ed. Denis Donoghue (London: Macmillan, 1972), 554.

23. R. F. Foster, *Modern Ireland* (Harmondsworth, U.K.: Penguin, 1989), 454.

24. For a sampling of some of the most prominent feminist challenges to nationalism, see Eavan Boland, "A Kind of Scar: The Woman Poet in a National Tradition," in *A Dozen Lips,* ed. Ailbhe Smyth (Dublin: Attic Press, 1994), 72–92; Edna Longley, "From Cathleen

to Anorexia," in Smyth, *Lips,* 162–87; Ailbhe Smyth, "Paying our Disrespects to the Bloody States We're In: Women, Violence, Culture and the State," *Irish Women's Voices, Past and Present: Journal of Women's History* 6/7 (1995), no. 4/1: 190–216.

25. Terence Brown, "Cultural Nationalism," in *Field Day Anthology of Irish Writing,* ed. Seamus Deane (Derry, U.K.: Field Day, 1991), 518.

26. Patricia Marks, *Bicycles, Bangs, and Bloomers: The New Woman in the Popular Press* (Lexington: Univ. Press of Kentucky, 1990), 2.

27. Andrew Parker, Mary Russo, Doris Sommer, and Patricia Yaeger, eds., *Nationalisms and Sexualities* (New York: Routledge, 1992), 2.

28. Howes, 16–43.

29. Ibid., 7.

30. See Seamus Deane, *Celtic Revivals* (Winston-Salem, N.C.: Wake Forest Univ. Press, 1985), 63–74; and R. F. Foster, *W. B. Yeats, A Life,* vol. 1: *Apprentice Mage* (New York: Oxford Univ. Press, 1997), 89–111.

31. Parker et al., 6.

32. See Margaret MacCurtain, "The Historical Image," in *Irish Women: Image and Achievement,* ed. Eiléan Ní Chuilleanáin (Dublin: Arlen Press, 1985), 47.

33.See Joanna Bourke, *Husbandry to Housewifery: Women, Economic Change, and Housework in Ireland, 1890–1914* (Oxford: Clarendon Press, 1993), 1.

34. See John MacPherson, " 'Ireland Begins in the Home': Women, Irish National Identity, and the Domestic Sphere in the *Irish Homestead,* 1896–1912," *Éire/Ireland* 36, nos. 3–4 (2000–2001): 131–52.

35. See Margaret MacCurtain, "Women, The Vote, and Revolution," *Women in Irish Society: The Historical Dimension,* ed. Margaret MacCurtain and Donncha Ó Corráin (Dublin: Arlen Press, 1989), 46–50; Rosemary Cullen Owens, *Smashing Times: A History of the Irish Women's Suffrage Movement* (Dublin: Attic Press, 1984), 35–39; Cliona Murphy, *The Women's Suffrage Movement and Irish Society in the Early Twentieth Century* (New York: Harvester Wheatsheaf, 1989), 41–44; Margaret Ward, *Hanna Sheehy Skeffington: A Life* (Dublin: Attic Press, 1997), 74–75.

36. Mary Jones, *Those Obstreperous Lassies: A History of the Irish Women Workers' Union* (Dublin: Gill and Macmillan, 1988), 3–5.

37. See Maud Gonne, *A Servant of the Queen,* ed. A. Norman Jeffares and Anna MacBride White (Gerrards Cross, U.K.: Colin Smythe, 1994), 92–97, for Gonne's account of the exclusion, including her famous remark to Timothy Harrington, president of the National League: "Surely Ireland needs all her children."

38. Eric Hobsbawm, *Nations and Nationalism since 1780: Programme, Myth, Reality,* 2d ed. (Cambridge: Cambridge Univ. Press, 1990), 10.

39. See Robert Munter, *The History of the Irish Newspaper, 1685–1760* (London: Cambridge Univ. Press, 1967), 67–90.

40. Ibid., 111.

41. Niall Ó Ciosáin, *Print and Popular Culture in Ireland, 1750–1850* (London: St. Martin's Press, 1997), 154.

42. Legg, 13.

43. John Pope-Hennessy, "What Do the Irish Read," *Nineteenth Century* 15 (June 1884): 920.

44. Legg, 121.

45. Ibid., 175.

46. The Anglo-Irish Treaty (signed in 1921, ratified in 1922) established dominion status for Ireland; its failure to deliver a republic prompted the Irish Civil War. See Virginia Glandon, "Index of Irish Newspapers, 1900–1922," *Éire/Ireland* 11 (1976): 85, and "The Irish Press and Revolutionary Irish Nationalism," *Éire/Ireland* 16 (1981): 23; Glandon, *Griffith*, 1, for these numbers.

47. Glandon, *Griffith*, 1.

48. See, for example, ibid.; Liz Curtis, *The Cause of Ireland* (Belfast: Beyond the Pale Press, 1994), 168–71; Ward, *Unmanageable*, 45–47; Innes, *Woman*, 134–37; Crossman, 128–31; and Foster, *Yeats*, 1:212–13.

49. Glandon, *Griffith*, 1.

50. Novick, 15, 37–38.

51. G. B. Shaw, "Preface for Politicians," *John Bull's Other Island*, in *Bodley Head Bernard Shaw: Collected Plays with Their Prefaces* (Toronto: Bodley Head, 1971), 2:842.

52. Luke Gibbons, "Constructing the Canon: Versions of National Identity," in Deane, *Field Day*, 951.

53. See, for example, Angela Bourke et al., eds., *Field Day Anthology of Irish Writing*, vols. 4–5 (Cork: Cork Univ. Press, 2002); Elis Ni Duibhe, ed., *Voices on the Wind: Women Writers of the Celtic Twilight* (Dublin: New Island, 1995); Katie Donovan, A. Norman Jeffares, and Brendan Kennelly, eds., *Ireland's Women: Writings Past and Present* (New York: Norton, 1994); A. A. Kelly, ed., *Pillars of the House: An Anthology of Irish Verse by Women from 1690 to the Present* (Dublin: Wolfhound, 1997); Ward, *In Their Own*.

54. The Abbey Theatre, founded in 1904, took shape from and was influenced by the Irish Literary Theatre and the Irish National Dramatic Company. Named after the street in Dublin where the theater company is located, the Abbey Theatre remains today committed to developing and producing a distinctly Irish dramatic repertoire. Taking its name from the ancestral mansions owned by Anglo-Irish landlords, Big House fiction focuses on the ambivalent relationship between the colonial masters and the Irish native people and land.

55. See Glandon, *Griffith*, 9–12; Harp, "*Shan*," 79–80; Crossman, 128–31; Karen Steele, "Editing Out Factionalism: The Political and Literary Consequences in Ireland's *Shan Van Vocht*," *Victorian Periodicals Review* 35, no. 2 (Summer 2002): 113–16; and

Catherine Morris, "Becoming Irish? Alice Milligan and the Revival," *Irish University Review* 33, no. 1 (2003): 80–81.

56. Gregory Castle, *Modernism and the Celtic Revival* (Cambridge: Cambridge Univ. Press, 2001), 6.

57. Constance Markievicz, "The Future of Irishwomen," *Irish Citizen*, Oct. 23, 1915, 114.

58. Sidney Gifford Czira, *The Years Flew By*, ed. Alan Hayes (1974; reprint, Galway, Ire: Arlen Press, 2000), 42.

59. By focusing on these journals and writers, I do not mean to suggest they are exceptional in the sense of "proving the rule." Quite the contrary, they represent a different rule altogether. For an illuminating feminist reading of the idea of "the exceptional woman," see Mary D. Sheriff, *The Exceptional Woman: Elisabeth Vigée-Lebrun and the Cultural Politics of Art* (Chicago: Univ. of Chicago Press, 1996).

60. See Carol Coulter, *The Hidden Tradition: Feminism, Women, and Nationalism* (Dublin: Attic Press, 1993), 3.

1. Acts of Union: Political Desire, Protestant Nationalism, and the *Shan Van Vocht*

1. Glandon, *Griffith*, 9–10; Harp, "*Shan*," 42–43; Innes, *Woman*, 135; Racine, 49; Crossman, 128–29.

2. See Innes, *Woman*, 136; Crossman, 138; Harp, "*Shan*," 44.

3. William Butler Yeats, "To Ireland in the Coming Times," in *W. B. Yeats: The Poems*, ed. Richard Finneran (London: Macmillan, 1983), 50.

4. Alice Milligan, "Notes for the Gaelic Athletes," *Shan Van Vocht*, Mar. 1896, 44.

5. See Innes, *Woman*, 134.

6. William Butler Yeats, "The Man and the Echo," in *Poems*, 345.

7. Alice Milligan, "Guard Ireland's Honour," *Shan Van Vocht*, Oct. 1896, 181.

8. See Howes, 29.

9. Alice Milligan, "Appeal to the Women of Ireland," *Shan Van Vocht*, June 1897, 104.

10. Seumas MacManus, as quoted in Curtis, 169.

11. Gonne, *Servant*, 176.

12. Bulmer Hobson, as quoted in Leon Ó Broin, *Revolutionary Underground: The Story of the Irish Republican Brotherhood 1858–1924* (Dublin, n.p., 1976), 141.

13. See Innes, *Woman*, 135; Crossman; Harp, "*Shan*," 51; and Glandon, *Griffith*, 25.

14. James Connolly, "Can Irish Republicans Be Politicians?" *Shan Van Vocht*, Nov. 1896, 210, and "Nationalism and Socialism," *Shan Van Vocht*, Jan. 1897, 7; Maud Gonne, "Those Who Are Suffering for Ireland," *Northern Patriot*, Nov. 28, 1896, 3; J. P. Coughlan,

"Our Political Prisoners," *Shan Van Vocht,* Sept. 1896, 165–66; Thomas J. O'Brien, "How to Celebrate the Centenary of '98," *Shan Van Vocht,* May 1897, 94.

15. For an account of the role of the press in defining and reframing early debates about the New Woman, see Michelle Elizabeth Tusan, "Inventing the New Woman: Print Culture and Identity Politics During the Fin-de-Siècle," *Victorian Periodicals Review* 31, no. 2 (1998): 169–82.

16. For more on the Ladies Land League, see Ward, *Unmanageable,* 4–39.

17. John O'Leary, as quoted in Ward, *Unmanageable,* 43.

18. See Ward, *Unmanageable,* 2.

19. See Curtis, 168.

20. Morris, "Irish?" 95 n. 5.

21. Milligan, "Appeal," 104.

22. Alice Milligan, "To the Irish in America," *Shan Van Vocht,* July 1897, 122.

23. Alice Milligan, "Must Ireland Be English? A Plea for Union and Reorganisation in the Gaelic League," *Shan Van Vocht,* Feb. 1899, 30.

24. See Innes, *Woman,* 135.

25. Milligan, "Notes," 44.

26. Ibid., 45.

27. Alice Milligan, "Gaelic Athletes and the National Movement," *Shan Van Vocht,* May 1896, 89.

28. Alice Milligan, "Decoration Day, Sunday, June 21st, 1896," *Shan Van Vocht,* June 1896, 116.

29. See Innes, *Woman,* 135; Ward, *Unmanageable,* 45; Nelson Ó Ceallaigh Ritschel, "James Connolly's *Under Which Flag,* 1916," *New Hibernia Review/Irish Éireannach Nua* 2, no. 4 (Winter 1998): 55.

30. See Curtis, 169.

31. Connolly, "Can Irish?" 210, and "Nationalism," 7; James Connolly, "Other People's Opinions," *Shan Van Vocht,* Oct. 1897, 188, and "Patriotism and Nationalism," *Shan Van Vocht,* Aug. 1897, 138.

32. See "Other People's Opinions," *Shan Van Vocht,* Dec. 1896, 234–35.

33. T. J. O'Brien, "Celebrate," 94–95; Thomas Concannon, "The Irish in Mexico," *Shan Van Vocht,* June 1897, 101–2.

34. Connolly, "Patriotism and Nationalism," 139.

35. Connolly, "Nationalism," 7.

36. Alice Milligan, *Shan Van Vocht,* Oct. 1897, 188.

37. Crossman, 132.

38. See Curtis, 197.

39. Ibid.

40. See Kevin Whelan, "The United Irishmen, the Enlightenment and Popular Cul-

ture," in *The United Irishmen: Republicanism, Radicalism, and Rebellion,* ed. David Dickson, Dáire Keogh, and Kevin Whelan (Dublin: Irish Academic Press, 1993), 269–96.

41. Doris Sommer, *Foundational Fictions: The National Romances of Latin America* (Berkeley: Univ. of California Press, 1991), 5.

42. Joe Cleary, *Literature, Partition and the Nation State: Culture and Conflict in Ireland, Israel and Palestine* (Cambridge: Cambridge Univ. Press, 2002), 115.

43. Ibid., 98.

44. Sheila Turner Johnston, *Alice: A Life of Milligan* (Omagh, U.K.: Colourpoint Press, 1994), 71.

45. Boland, 91.

46. Milligan's pairing of romance and politics may have been encouraged by the publication of Young Irelander Michael Doheny's *The Felon's Track* (1875), a thrilling account of his escape after the 1848 rebellion, which was published alongside romances such as *The Turkish Slave* and *The White Queen and the Mohawk Chief.* I am indebted to Terry Eagleton, *Heathcliff and the Great Hunger* (London: Verso, 1995), 182, for this information.

47. Alice Milligan, "The Little Green Slippers: A Belfast Story of Christmas, 1798," *Shan Van Vocht,* Dec. 6, 1897, 213–18.

48. See Morris, "Irish?" 89–90.

49. Alice Milligan, "The Outlaw's Bride," *Shan Van Vocht,* Dec. 4, 1896, 231–32.

50. See Eagleton, *Heathcliff,* 181, 150.

51. For more on the Big House tradition, see Vera Kreilkamp, *The Anglo-Irish Novel and the Big House* (Syracuse, N.Y.: Syracuse Univ. Press, 1998). For several instrumental, and often differing, responses to the meaning of the controversial term "Ascendancy," see W. J. McCormack, *Ascendancy and Tradition in Irish Literary History, 1793–1839* (Oxford: Clarendon Press, 1985); Jacqueline Hill, "The Meaning and Significance of 'Protestant Ascendancy,' 1787–1840," in *Ireland after the Union: Proceedings of the Second Joint Meeting of the Royal Irish Academy and the British Academy,* ed. Lord Blake (Oxford: Oxford Univ. Press, 1989), 1–22; R. F. Foster, "The Ascendancy Mind," in *Ireland;* and Eagleton, "Ascendancy and Hegemony," in *Heathcliff.*

52. Thomas MacDonagh, "The Best Living Irish Poet," *Irish Review* 4 (Sept.–Nov. 1914): 287.

53. Susan Mitchell, as quoted in Morris, "Becoming Irish," 79.

54.See Robert Hogan, *Dictionary of Irish Literature* (Westport, Conn.: Greenwood Press, 1996), 842.

55. See Morris, "Margins."

56. See Richard Harp, "No Other Place But Ireland: Alice Milligan's Diary and Letters," *New Hibernia Review/Irish Éireannach Nua* 4, no. 1 (Spring 2000): 80.

57. Ibid., 79.

58. Harp, "*Shan,*" 44.

59. William Butler Yeats, "Municipal Gallery Revisited," in *Poems*, 321.

60. Alice Milligan, "Ode for 6 October," in *Poems*, ed. Henry Mangan (Dublin: M. H. Gill and Sons, 1954), 6, 10.

61. Howes, 65.

62. See Mary Jean Corbett, *Allegories of Union in Irish and English Writing, 1790–1870* (Cambridge: Cambridge Univ. Press, 2000), 40.

63. See Marilyn Butler, "Introduction," in *Castle Rackrent and Ennui* (Harmondsworth, U.K.: Penguin, 1992), 5–6; Johnston, 20.

64. Corbett, 40.

65. See Mary Helen Thuente, *The Harp Re-strung: The United Irishmen and the Rise of Irish Literary Nationalism* (Syracuse, N.Y.: Syracuse Univ. Press, 1994), 174–78; Nancy Curtin, *The United Irishmen: Popular Politics in Ulster and Dublin, 1791–1799* (New York: Oxford Univ. Press, 1994), 3–4.

66. Henry Joy McCracken, "The Social Thistle and the Shamrock," as quoted in Thuente, appendix B, 243.

67. Wolfe Tone, "Ierne United," as quoted in Thuente, appendix B, 237–38.

68. Alice Milligan, letter, in *United Ireland*, Dec. 16, 1893.

69. "Paddy Evermore," as quoted in Thuente, appendix B, 243–44.

70. "Why Must We Strive for Freedom," *Shan Van Vocht*, Aug. 1896, 151.

71. Alice Milligan, *Shan Van Vocht*, July 1896, 129.

72. For more extensive discussion of the influence of 1798 on the *Shan Van Vocht*, see Crossman, 129.

73. See ibid., 131.

74. "The Shan Van Vocht," as quoted in *Shan Van Vocht*, Jan. 1896, 1.

75. Alice Milligan, "When I Was a Little Girl," in *Poems*, 2–4.

76. Johnston, 189.

77. Louise Ryan, " 'Furies' and 'Die-hards': Women and Irish Republicanism in the Early Twentieth Century," *Gender and History* 11 (1999): 259.

78. See "In the North Country: 2. Betty Fryers," *Shan Van Vocht*, Apr. 1896, 61–65; "The Story of Betsy Gray," *Shan Van Vocht*, May 1896, 97–98.

79. Alice Milligan, "Speranza," *Shan Van Vocht*, Mar. 1896, 48–49.

80. Crossman, 128.

81. Alice Milligan, "The Harp That Once—! A Story of Connaught after Humbert," *Shan Van Vocht*, Mar. 1898, 37–39; "The Captain's Daughter," *Shan Van Vocht*, Feb. 1896, 17–23; Mar. 1896, 52–55; Apr. 1896, 71–73.

82. Milligan, "Harp," 38.

83. Ibid., 39.

84. Milligan, "Guard," 181.

85. Edmund Burke, *Thoughts on the Cause of the Present Discontents,* in *Writings and Speeches of Edmund Burke,* vol. 2, ed. Paul Langford (Oxford: Oxford Univ. Press, 1980), 252.

86. See Morris, "Irish?" 96 n. 25.

87. Milligan, "Captain's Daughter," Feb. 1896, 18.

88. Ibid., 21–22.

89. Milligan, "Captain's Daughter," Apr. 1896, 54.

90. See Innes, *Woman,* 135; Crossman, 136; and Glandon, *Griffith,* 12.

2. Voices for Erin: Maud Gonne, Inghinidhe na hÉireann, and the *United Irishman*

1. Maria Luddy, "Women and Politics, 1860–1918," in Bourke et al., *Field Day,* 5:70.

2. Padraic Colum, *Ourselves Alone! The Story of Arthur Griffith and the Origin of the Irish Free State* (New York: Crown Press, 1959), 45; Glandon, *Griffith,* 13.

3. R. M. Henry, *The Evolution of Sinn Féin* (New York: Huebsch, 1920), 60.

4. See Brian Maye, *Arthur Griffith* (Dublin: Griffith College Publications, 1997), 56.

5. George A. Lyons, *Some Recollections of Griffith and His Times* (Dublin: Talbot Press, 1923), 58.

6. James Stephens, *Arthur Griffith: Journalist and Statesman* (Dublin: Wilson, Hartness, 1922), 18.

7. Augustine Birrell, as quoted in Maye, 63.

8. F. S. L. Lyons, *Ireland Since the Famine* (1971; reprint, London: Fontana Press, 1985), 248.

9. Novick, 32.

10. See William Butler Yeats, *The Collected Letters of W. B. Yeats,* ed. Warwick Gould, John Kelly, and Deirdre Toomey (Oxford: Clarendon Press, 1997), 2:695–707; Curtis, 175–77; Crossman, 128–39.

11. *United Irishman,* Mar. 4, 1899, 2.

12. Henry, 63.

13. The *United Irishman* often combined anti-Semitism with Irish-Ireland nationalism. See "Jew Press Against Transvaal," *United Irishman,* Oct. 16, 1899, 5; and "Gold of the Jew against the Irish Brigade," *United Irishman,* Feb. 4, 1900, 4. Virginia E. Glandon observes that "Griffith rationalized the anti-Semitic bias in his early newspapers in terms of Irish nationalist resentment against members of another race, who, in his words, 'came to Ireland penniless' and were able to secure loans through the Bank of Ireland for the purchase of land and business property, while Irishmen were denied this opportunity." Glandon, *Griffith,* 43.

14. *United Irishman,* Mar. 15, 1899, 2.

15. Gonne, *Servant*, 317.

16. For information about Griffith's evolution from journalist to statesmen, see Glandon, *Griffith;* and Maye.

17. Arthur Griffith, *The Resurrection of Hungary: A Parallel for Ireland.* 1904 (Dublin: University College Press, 2003).

18. Glandon, *Griffith*, 40.

19. See Seán Ó Lúing, "Arthur Griffith and Sinn Féin," in *Leaders and Men of the Easter Rising: Dublin 1916*, ed. F. X. Martin (Ithaca, N.Y.: Cornell Univ. Press, 1967), 68.

20. Francis Jones, *History of the Sinn Féin Movement and the Irish Rebellion of 1916* (New York: Kenedy and Sons, 1917), 179.

21. See Glandon, *Griffith*, 13.

22. Literary women who wrote or were discussed in the pages of the *United Irishman* include Alice Milligan, Charlotte Grace O'Brien, Olive Schreiner, Augusta Holmes, Ethna Carbery, Katharine Tynan, Nora Harper, Kathleen O'Meara, Mrs. Patrick Campbell, Elizabeth Robins, Helen Sheridan, Sarah Bernhardt, Grace Rhys, Rose Kavanagh, Ella Young, Elis Ni Chraoibhin, and Jane Barlow. Some political and historical women discussed include Margaret of Ely, Enghean Dubh (mother of Red Hugh O'Donnell), Anna Parnell, Anne Devlin, and Ellen O'Leary.

23. For a sampling of some of the most prominent feminist challenges to nationalism, see Boland; Longley; Smyth, "Paying."

24. Mary E. L. Butler, "Womanhood and Nationhood," *United Irishman*, Jan. 3, 1903, 6–7; Jan. 10, 1903, 6; Jan. 17, 1903, 6–7; Jan. 24, 1903, 6.

25. See Mary E. L. Butler, *Irishwomen and the Home Language* in Bourke et al., *Field Day*, 5:84–86. First published in Dublin as undated pamphlet by Gaelic League, ca. 1900.

26. Mary E. L. Butler, "Irishwomen's Work," *United Irishman*, Mar. 25, 1899, 3.

27. Maud Gonne, "National Education of the Children," in *Maud Gonne's Irish Nationalist Writings*, ed. Karen Steele (Dublin: Irish Academic Press, 2004), 140. First published in *United Irishman*, Aug. 23, 1902, 6–9.

28. Maud Gonne, "Ireland and Her Children," *United Irishman*, June 7, 1902, 3.

29. See "The Famine and Young Ireland," in Deane, *Field Day*, 115–208. See also Bourke et al., *Field Day*, both of whose volumes exuberantly redress the occlusion of women writers in Ireland.

30. See May Curran, "Irishwomen and the Home Industries," *United Irishman*, Nov. 19, 1904, 6; Blake O'Connor, "Industrial Women," *United Irishman*, Nov. 26, 1904, 3.

31. D. E. S. Maxwell, "Irish Drama 1899–1929: The Abbey Theatre," in Deane, *Field Day*, 562.

32. Gonne, *Servant*, 119.

33. See MacCurtain, "Women"; Beth McKillen, "Irish Feminism and Nationalist

Separatism, 1914–23," *Éire/Ireland* 17, nos. 3–4 (1982): 52–67, 72–90; Rosemary Cullen Owens, " 'Votes for Ladies, Votes for Women': Organised Labour and the Suffrage Movement, 1876–1922," *Saothar* 9 (1983): 34–47; Mary Cullen, "How Radical was Irish Feminism Between 1860 and 1920?" in *Radicals, Rebels, and Establishments,* ed. Patrick J. Corish, 185–201 (Belfast: Appletree Press, 1985); Anna Parnell, *The Tale of a Great Sham,* ed. Dana Hearne (Dublin: Arlen House, 1986); Owens, *Smashing;* Murphy; Louise Ryan, "Women Without Votes: The Political Strategies of the Irish Suffrage Movement," *Irish Political Studies* 9 (1994): 119–39, and "A Question of Loyalty: War, Nation, and Feminism in Early Twentieth-Century Ireland," *Women's Studies International Forum* 20, no. 1 (1997): 21–32; Ward, *Hanna.*

34. Murphy, 14.

35. See Ward, *Unmanageable,* 40–87.

36. Arthur Griffith, *United Irishman,* Jan. 26, 1901, 6; see also Glandon, *Griffith,* 135.

37. See Colum, 50.

38. See ibid., 50–51, 74; Glandon, *Griffith,* 177.

39. See Margaret Ward, *Maud Gonne: Ireland's Joan of Arc* (London: Pandora, 1990), 60; Antoinette Quinn, "Cathleen ni Houlihan Writes Back: Maud Gonne and Irish National Theater," in *Gender and Sexuality in Modern Ireland,* ed. Anthony Bradley and Maryann Gialanella Valiulis (Amherst: Univ. of Massachusetts Press, 1997), 57.

40. In 1900, when Inghinidhe na hÉireann was founded, the *United Irishman* published twenty-four articles by or about women, in addition to twenty by or about Gonne; the following year, the numbers of articles climbed to thirty-five and thirty, respectively.

41. Gonne, *Servant,* 178.

42. Colum, 74.

43. See "A Paper for Irishwomen," *United Irishman,* Apr. 8, 1905, 6–7.

44. Helena Molony, as quoted in R. M. Fox, *Rebel Irishwomen* (Dublin: Talbot Press, 1935), 121.

45. See Karen Steele, "Reading Maud Gonne: The Poetics of the Advanced Nationalist Press," *Prose Studies* 25, no. 2 (Aug. 2003): 102–21.

46. See Elizabeth Butler Cullingford, "Thinking of Her as Ireland," in *Gender and History in Yeats's Love Poetry* (Cambridge: Cambridge Univ. Press, 1993). Examination of the preface to her 1938 autobiography reveals Gonne's own ambivalence about her relationship to Mother Ireland. Although she claims to be "one of the little stones" that "the Queen" might use on her path to freedom, Gonne's physical description of a tall, auburn-haired Mother Ireland sounds suspiciously like Gonne herself.

47. Elsewhere I have interpreted Gonne's instances of self-aggrandizement as symptoms of her personal and gendered struggles working in a strongly patriarchal culture and political climate. See Karen Steele, "Biography as a Promotional Discourse: The Case of

Maud Gonne," *Cultural Studies* 15, no. 1 (Jan. 2001): 138–60, and "Raising Her Voice for Justice: Maud Gonne and the Irish Nationalist Press," *New Hibernia Review/Irish Éireannach Nua* 3, no. 2 (Summer 1999): 85–104.

48. See Jack Stillinger, *Multiple Authorship and the Myth of Solitary Genius* (New York: Oxford Univ. Press, 1991), 11–16; Wayne Koestenbaum, *Double Talk: The Erotics of Male Literary Collaboration* (New York: Routledge, 1989), 2–7.

49. Gonne, *Servant,* 176.

50. Holly A. Laird, *Women Coauthors* (Urbana: Univ. of Illinois Press, 2000), 5.

51. See Ward, *Unmanageable,* 47–48.

52. See appendix to Gonne, *Irish Nationalist,* 283–97, for the monthly reports and the minutes for the first meeting of Inghinidhe.

53. Maud Gonne, "The Goddess Brigid," in *Irish Nationalist,* 189–92. First published in *United Irishman,* Nov. 3, 1900, 3.

54. Gonne, "Goddess," 190.

55. See C. L. Innes, "Orientalism and Celticism" in *Irish and Post-Colonial Writing,* ed. Glen Hooper and Colin Graham (Basingstoke: Palgrave, 2002), 142–56. For extensive discussion of the interactions of Orientalism and Celticism from the eighteenth to the twentieth century, see Joseph Lennon, "Irish Orientalism: An Overview," in *Ireland and Postcolonial Theory,* ed. Clare Carroll and Patricia King (South Bend, Ind.: Notre Dame Press, 2003), 129–57, and *Irish Orientalism: A Literary and Intellectual History* (Syracuse, N.Y.: Syracuse Univ. Press, 2004).

56. Innes, "Orientalism," 154.

57. Declan Kiberd, "The Elephant of Revolutionary Forgetfulness," in *Revising the Rising,* ed. Máirín Ní Dhonnchadha and Theo Dorgan (Derry, U.K.: Field Day, 1991), 14.

58. *Nation,* Oct. 31, 1846, as quoted in Quinn, 5:899.

59. Alice Milligan, *The Last Feast of the Fianna* (Chicago: DePaul Univ. Press, 1967), 10. Milligan's play was initially serialized in the *Daily Express,* Sept. 23, 1899, and Sept. 1899, as quoted in Morris, "Irish?" 97.

60. Augusta Gregory, *A Book of Saints,* in *Lady Gregory: Selected Writings,* ed. Lucy McDiarmid and Maureen Waters (Harmondsworth, U.K.: Penguin, 1995), 145.

61. Gonne, "Goddess," 191.

62. Alexander Carmichael, *Carmina Gadelica: Hymns and Incantations; with Illustrative Notes on Words, Rites, and Customs, Dying and Obsolete: Orally Collected in the Highlands and Islands of Scotland and Translated into English,* 6 vols. (Edinburgh, Scottish Academic Press: 1900–71).

63. Maud Gonne, "Eitne," 3, in *Irish Nationalist,* 193–96. First published in *United Irishman,* Apr. 12, 1902.

64. Ibid., 194.

65. Gonne, "National Education," 138–40.

66. Maud Gonne, "In the Event of War," in *Irish Nationalist,* 75–77. First published in *United Irishman,* Dec. 22, 1900, 7.

67. Maud Gonne, "Ireland and Irish America," in *Irish Nationalist,* 182–84. First published in *United Irishman,* June 22, 1901, 5.

68. Maud Gonne, "The Irish Press," in *Irish Nationalist,* 100. First published in *United Irishman,* Feb. 7, 1903, 6.

69. Ibid., 100.

70. Maud Gonne, "Inghinidhe na hÉireann's First Meeting," in *Irish Nationalist,* 296. First published in *United Irishman,* Oct. 13, 1900, 8.

71. Declan Kiberd, "White Skins, Black Masks: Celticism and *Négritude,*" *Éire/Ireland* 31, nos. 1–2 (1996): 168.

72. Gonne, "Irish Press," 100. The phrasing "great money or vested interest" was common anti-Semitic code for Jews. In the early 1890s in France, Gonne joined her lover Lucien Millevoye in supporting General George Boulanger (1837–91), a fiercely nationalist, anti-German politician with fascist and anti-Semitic leanings. Although Gonne's ideology moved to the left as she aged, she never overcame her strong distrust of Jews.

73. Edward S. Herman and Noel Chomsky, *Manufacturing Consent: The Political Economy of the Mass Media* (New York: Pantheon, 1988).

74. Maud Gonne, "Letter to the Editor," *United Irishman,* May 16, 1903, 5.

75. Gonne, *Servant,* 252–53.

76. Maud Gonne, "Famine Queen," in *Irish Nationalist,* 54–56. First published in *United Irishman,* Apr. 7, 1900, 5.

77. See, for example, Alfred, Lord Tennyson, "To the Queen" (1889) and Mark Twain, "Queen Victoria's Jubilee" (1897), in Barbara Harlow and Mia Carter, eds., *Imperialism and Orientalism: A Documentary Sourcebook* (Malden, Mass.: Blackwell, 1999).

78. Maud Gonne, "The Boer Women," in *Irish Nationalist,* 164–66. First published in *United Irishman,* Mar. 17, 1900, supplement 4.

79. Byron Farwell, *The Great Anglo-Boer War* (New York: Norton, 1976), 17.

80. Christopher Saunders and Iain R. Smith, "Southern Africa, 1795–1910," in *The Oxford History of the British Empire,* vol. 3, ed. Andrew Porter (Oxford: Oxford Univ. Press, 1999), 617.

81. See press excerpts of Maud Gonne's lecture series in *United Irishman,* Oct. 1899–Apr. 1900; see also Elleke Boehmer, *Empire, the National, and the Postcolonial, 1890–1920* (Oxford: Oxford Univ. Press, 2002).

82. Gonne, "Boer Women," 165; see also Gonne, "Inghinidhe," 296–97.

83. H. S., "The Boer Woman," *United Irishman,* Apr. 28, 1900, 2.

84. See Ward, *Unmanageable.*

85. Gonne, "Boer Women," 165.

86. Arthur Griffith, Editorial, *United Irishman,* June 17, 1899, 1, and "The English Stirring-up the Natives," *United Irishman,* Oct. 28, 1899, 1.

87. Chandra Talpade Mohanty, " 'Under Western Eyes': Feminist Scholarship and Colonial Discourse," in *Feminist Post-Colonial Theory,* ed. Reina Lewis and Sara Mills (New York: Routlege: 2003), 50–52.

88. Lorraine York, *Rethinking Women's Collaborative Writing* (Toronto: Univ. of Toronto Press, 2002), 5, 20.

89. Ibid., 60.

90. Maud Gonne, *Dawn,* in *Irish Nationalist,* 204–12; first published in *United Irishman,* Oct. 29, 1904, 4–5; also reprinted in Bourke et al., *Field Day,* 5:913–17.

91. See Steele, "Reading Maud."

92. See Gonne, "Goddess," 190; Quinn, "Cathleen," 55.

93. Jane Marcus, *Suffrage and the Pankhursts* (New York: Routledge, 1987), 1.

94. Marina Warner, "What the Virgin of Knock Means to Women," *Magill,* Sept. 1979, 39. For another perspective on the language-silence dichotomy, see Luke Gibbons, "The Politics of Silence: *Anne Devlin,* Women and Irish Cinema," in *Transformations in Irish Culture* (Cork: Cork Univ. Press, 1996).

95. Marcus, 9 (emphasis original).

96. See Francis MacManus, "The Delicate High Head: A Portrait of a Great Lady," *Capuchin Annual* 1960:129–31.

97. Mary Trotter, *Ireland's National Theatres: Political Performance and the Origins of the Irish Dramatic Movement* (Syracuse: Syracuse Univ. Press, 2001), 92.

98. Antoinette Quinn and Mary Trotter have highlighted how the song, oration, and *tableaux vivants* of the Inghinidhe's ceilidhe influenced the later styles and subjects popularized in the Irish National Theatre. See Quinn; Trotter, 73–99.

99. Gonne, *Dawn,* 206.

100. Ibid., 207.

101. See "Milligan, Alice," in Hogan, 447.

102. See note 58.

103. Milligan, *Last Feast,* 13.

104. Ibid., 10, 17.

105. Quinn, 51.

106. *United Irishman,* Oct. 24, 1903, 3.

107. Gonne, *Dawn,* 205.

108. Ibid., 204.

109. See, for example, Gonne, "India," 167–71. First published in *United Irishman,* May 12, 1900, 5.

110. Gonne, *Dawn,* 207–8.

111. Ibid., 210.

112. Ibid.

113. See Crossman, 130.

114. Gonne, *Dawn*, 212.

115. Quinn, 54–55.

116. Laird, 5.

117. Gonne, *Servant*, 117.

3. Allegory as Resistance: Constance Markievicz, *Bean na hÉireann*, and the *Irish Citizen*

1. See William Butler Yeats, "Easter 1916" and "On a Political Prisoner," in *Poems*, 180–82, 183–84, respectively; Sean O'Casey, *Drums under the Window* (New York: Macmillan, 1950), 315.

2. D. J. Smith, "The Countess and the Poets: Constance Gore-Booth Markievicz in the Work of Irish Writers," *Journal of Irish Literature* 12, no. 1 (1983): 15, 23.

3. Sean O'Faolain, *Constance Markievicz or the Average Revolutionary* (London: Jonathan Cape, 1934), 105.

4. Arthur Mitchell, *Labour in Irish Politics 1890–1930* (New York: Harper and Row, 1974), 72.

5. Elizabeth Coxhead, *Daughters of Erin: Five Women of the Irish Renascence* (London: Secker and Warburg, 1965), 81.

6. For a complete list of Markievicz's journalistic works, see Jacqueline Van Voris, *Constance de Markievicz in the Cause of Ireland* (Boston: Univ. of Massachusetts Press, 1967), 361–63.

7. O'Faolain, 9. For an extended commentary on Markievicz's journalism after 1920, see Karen Steele, "Constance Markievicz and the Politics of Memory," in *Irish Women and Nationalism: Soldiers, New Women, and Wicked Hags*, ed. Louise Ryan and Margaret Ward (Dublin: Irish Academic Press, 2004), 62–79.

8. Kiberd, *Inventing*, 1.

9. See MacCurtain, "Women"; Owens, *Smashing*, 35–39; C. Murphy, 41–44; Ward, *Unmanageable*, 83–85; Margaret Ward, "Conflicting Interests: The British and Irish Suffrage Movements," *Feminist Review* 50:128–31.

10. See McKillen; Maryann Gialanella Valiulis, " 'Free Women in a Free Nation': Nationalist Feminist Expectations for Independence," in *The Creation of the Dáil*, ed. Brian Farrell, (Dublin: Blackwater, 1994), 75–90; Aideen Sheehan, "Cumann na mBan: Policies and Activities," in *Revolution? Ireland 1917–23*, ed. David Fitzpatrick (Dublin: Trinity History Workshop, 1990), 88–97.

11. See Smith, 7.

12. Statement of Miss Helena Molony, Bureau of Military History, 1913–21, document no. W.S. 391, file no. S.164, Military Archives, Cathal Brugha Barracks. Quoted with kind permission of the Military Archives.

13. Helena Molony, as quoted in Fox, 121.

14. See M. Jones, 14.

15. See Ward, *Unmanageable*, 68.

16. Ibid., 70.

17. Constance Markievicz, "To Miss Nora Cassidy and the Young Girls of Ireland," *Bean na hÉireann* 8 (June 1909): 14.

18. See Glandon, *Griffith*, 129.

19. See Eileen O'Halloran, "From Boucicault to Beckett: Irish Modernism and the Myth of Mother Ireland" (Ph.D. diss., Univ. of Wisconsin, 2004).

20. Hanna Sheehy Skeffington, "Sinn Féin and Irishwomen," *Bean na hÉireann* 20, no. 13 (Nov. 1909): 5–6.

21. Markievicz, "Miss Nora," 14.

22. James Connolly, "Woman," in *James Connolly: Selected Writings*, ed. Peter Beresford Ellis (London: Pluto Press, 1997), 191. First published as chapter 6 of *The Re-Conquest of Ireland* (1915; reprint, Dublin: New Books, 1972).

23. Kiberd, *Inventing*, 399.

24. Markievicz, *Women*, 24. For highlights of Markievicz's lecture, see Ward, *In Their Own*, 30–32. An editorial in the April 1909 issue of *Bean na hÉireann* alerted readers to the talk but lamented that space did not permit publishing it in its entirety. In July 1909, another editorial informed readers that the talk had been published and quoted Markievicz's concluding remarks; on pages 10–11 of the same issue, two advertisements read: "Woman, Ideals, and the Nation. We are pleased to see Constance Markievicz's lecture in pamphlet form. It marks an epoch in the Women's Movement when we see a pamphlet devoted entirely to women and their place in the Nation."

25. See O'Casey, 314–16; Smith, 15; Ward, *Unmanageable*, 115; Anne Haverty, *Constance Markievicz: An Independent Life* (London: Pandora, 1988).

26. Markievicz, *Women*, 1.

27. Ibid., 4.

28. Ibid., 12.

29. Ibid., 4.

30. Ibid., 8, 11.

31. Constance Markievicz, "Free Women in a Free Nation," *Bean na hÉireann* 5 (Mar. 1909): 8–9.

32. Ibid., 9.

33. Ibid.

34. Constance Markievicz, "Woman with a Garden," *Bean na hÉireann* 4 (Feb. 1909)–17 (Mar. 1910).

35. Haverty, 78.

36. Curtis, 193.

37. Kiberd, *Inventing*, 399.

38. Innes, *Woman*, 142–43.

39. Markievicz, "Woman," 7 (May 1909): 9–10; 15 (Jan. 1910): 7.

40. Ibid., 9 (July 1909): 12.

41. Ibid., 12 (Oct. 1909): 12.

42. Ibid., 6 (Apr. 1909): 3; 7 (May 1909): 9–10; 8 (June 1909): 10–11; 10 (Aug. 1909): 6–7.

43. Ibid., 4 (Feb. 1909): 12.

44. Barbara Harlow, *Resistance Literature* (New York: Methuen, 1987), 54.

45. Gibbons, *Transformations*, 142.

46. Ibid.

47. Corbett, 182.

48. John Mitchel, as quoted in Jan Cannavan, "Romantic Revolutionary Irishwomen: Women, Young Ireland and 1848," in *Gender Perspectives in Nineteenth Century Ireland: Public and Private Spheres*, ed. Margaret Kelleher and James Murphy (Dublin: Irish Academic Press, 1997), 217.

49. Markievicz, "Woman," 4 (Feb. 1909): 6.

50. See, for example, ibid., 6 (Apr. 1909): 3; 13 (Nov. 1909): 7.

51. Ibid., 10 (Aug. 1909): 6–7.

52. Ibid., 11 (Sept. 1909): 5.

53. Ibid., 17 (Mar. 1910): 13–14.

54. Ibid., 7 (May 1909): 9–10.

55. Ibid., 10 (Jan. 1910): 7.

56. Pádraig Pearse, "O'Donovan Rossa Graveside Panegyric," in *Political Writings and Speeches* (Dublin: Talbot Press, 1958), 136.

57. "Physical Force," *Bean na hÉireann* 11 (Sept. 1909): 3–5; 12 (Oct. 1909): 3–4.

58. Helena Molony, *Bean na hÉireann* 13 (Nov. 1909): 3.

59. Amy Benton, "Woman Disarmed: The Militarization of Politics in Ireland 1913–1923," *Feminist Review* 50 (Summer 1995): 155.

60. Markievicz, "Woman," 12 (Oct. 1909): 12.

61. Ibid., 8 (June 1909): 10–11.

62. Pádraig Pearse, *Plays, Stories, Poems* (Dublin, n.p., 1924), 44.

63. Markievicz, "Woman," 9 (July 1909): 12.

64. Pádraig Pearse, "The Coming Revolution," in Deane, *Field Day*, 558. First published in *An Claidheamh Soluis*, Nov. 1913.

65. Benton, 161.

66. Markievicz, "Woman," 8 (June 1909): 11.

67. Constance Markiewicz, as quoted in Van Voris, 309.

68. Louise Ryan, "The *Irish Citizen*, 1912–1920," *Saothar* 17 (1992): 107.

69. Ibid.

70. See Ward, *Unmanageable*, 95.

71. Markievicz, "Future," 114.

72. Although both Mabel O'Kennedy and Maud Gonne made frequent reference to women warriors at Inghinidhe's ceilidhe, they emphasized the women's "strength and . . . beauty," rather than their militant qualities. See Mabel O'Kennedy, "Macha," *United Irishman*, Jan. 5, 1901, 3; Maud Gonne, "Maedb," *United Irishman*, Oct. 5, 1901, 3. Markievicz's sister, Eva Gore-Booth, a poet and feminist activist, addressed the obliteration of women's history in many of her lyric poems, such as "Lament of the Daughters of Ireland" and "To Maeve." See Eva Gore-Booth, *Collected Poems* (London: Longmans Green, 1929), 112–13, 60–63.

73. John O'Leary, as quoted in Gonne, *Servant*, 95.

74. Markievicz, "Future."

75. Ibid.

76. See Boland, who laments the frequent and, for women, alienating poetic motif of "passive, decorative, . . .emblematic" female figures, "a fusion of the national and the feminine which seemed to simplify both," 76.

77. Markievicz, "Future," 114.

78. See Steele, "Constance."

79. Agnes O'Farrelly, as quoted in Ward, *Unmanageable*, 93.

80. Markievicz, "Future," 114.

81. Ibid.

82. Constance Markievicz, "The Women of '98," *Irish Citizen*, Nov. 6, 1915–Dec. 4, 1915.

83. Benton, 155.

84. Walter Benjamin, "Theses on the Philosophy of History," in *Illuminations: Essays and Reflections* (New York: Schocken Books, 1968), 255.

85. Markievicz, "Women of '98," Nov. 6, 1915, 177.

86. Ibid., 177.

87. Adrienne Rich, "Diving into the Wreck," in *Diving into the Wreck: Poems 1971–1972* (New York: Norton, 1973), 24.

88. Markievicz, "Women of '98," Nov. 13, 1915.

89. Ibid., Dec. 4, 1915.

90. Ibid., Nov. 6, 1915.

91. Ibid., Nov. 13, 1915.

92. See Gibbons, *Transformations*, 141.

93. Constance Markievicz, *Broken Dreams*, NLI Manuscript 24, 185. For further discussion of Markievicz's development of the linkage of clothes and politics in *Broken Dreams*, see Steele, "Constance."

94. O'Faolain, 198.

95. Smith, 9.

96. Bernadette Devlin overtly acknowledged her link with Markievicz in her maiden speech in Parliament, delivered on April 22, 1969, where she declared, "I stand here as the youngest woman in Parliament, in the same tradition as the first woman ever to be elected to this Parliament, Constance Markievicz, who was elected on behalf of the Irish people." See *Parliamentary Debates (Hansard)*, 5th series, vol. 782 (London: Her Majesty's Stationery Office, 1969), 281.

4. The Art of Contention: Delia Larkin, Augusta Gregory, and the Workers of Ireland

1. Joseph O'Brien, *Dear, Dirty Dublin: A City in Distress, 1899–1916* (Berkeley: Univ. of California Press, 1982), 222–23.

2. See "A Woman's Way," *Irish Worker*, May 2, 1914, 2; "Lady Gregory and an Injury to the Workers," *Irish Worker*, May 23, 1914, 2.

3. Lucy McDiarmid and Maureen Waters, in Gregory, *Selected Writings*, 281.

4. Augusta Gregory, *The Workhouse Ward*, in *Selected Writings*, 374.

5. When Jim Larkin formed the Irish Transport and General Workers' Union in 1911, "thousands of families had to exist on less than 15s. a week and there were many cases of families' total earnings being as low as 10s. and less. The highest wage cited for a labourer was 20s. and the minimum hours worked were twelve a day. The highest paid labourers were the dockers who earned 24s. for a seventy-four hour week. Conditions were terrible." Peter Berresford Ellis, *A History of the Irish Working Class* (1972; reprint, London: Pluto Press, 1996), 184. See also Foster, *Ireland*, 437.

6. Ellis, *History*, 184.

7. See, for example, the Irish Citizen Army vote, in May 1914, over Markievicz's membership in both the Irish Citizen Army and the Irish Volunteers, in Anne Marreco, *The Rebel Countess* (London: Phoenix Press, 2000), 181.

8. See Foster, *Yeats*, 1:326–28, 478–83, 493–98.

9. Ibid., 1:449–50.

10. See Theresa Moriarty, "Delia Larkin: Relative Obscurity," in *James Larkin: Lion of the Fold*, ed. Donal Nevin (Dublin: Gill and Macmillan, 1998), 428–38; Maria Luddy,

"The Labour Movement in Ireland, 1800–2000," in Bourke et al., *Field Day,* ed. Bourke, 5:548–551; Alison Buckley, " 'Let the Girls Come Forth': The Early Feminist Ideology of the Irish Women Workers' Union," in *Irish Women's History,* ed. Alan Hayes and Diane Urquhart (Dublin: Irish Academic Press, 2004), 103–114.

11. Moriarty, "Delia Larkin," 429–31; Curtis, 206.

12. Samuel Levenson, *James Connolly, A Biography* (London: Martin Brian and O'-Keeffe, 1973), 219.

13. For more information about the "kiddie transport" debacle, see Lucy McDiarmid, "Hunger and Hysteria," in *The Irish Art of Contention* (Ithaca, N.Y.: Cornell Univ. Press, 2005), 123–66; O'Brien, 235; and Moriarty, "Delia Larkin," 433–34.

14. M. Jones, 9.

15. See C. Desmond Greaves, *The Irish Transport and General Workers' Union: The Formative Years 1909–1923* (Dublin: Gill and Macmillan, 1982), 122.

16. Augusta Gregory, as quoted in *Irish Worker,* May 23, 1914, 3.

17. Ritschel, 60.

18. To express her opposition to the ITGWU leadership, however, Delia Larkin edited and wrote for a new trade union journal, the *Red Hand,* from July to September 1918. See Moriarty, "Delia Larkin," 436.

19. M. Jones, 3. See also Patricia McCaffrey, "Jacob's Women Workers During the 1913 Lock-Out," *Saothar* 16 (1991): 118–29; Theresa Moriarty, "Larkin and the Women's Movement," in Nevin, *Larkin,* 93–101.

20. Delia Larkin, "Women Workers' Column," *Irish Worker,* Aug. 3, 1912, 2. After a four-day conference, held in December 1913, members of the Irish Women's Reform League reported to *Irish Citizen* readers that the average wage for working women in Ireland was four to five shillings a week (approximately $1.20), compared with seven and a half-shillings a week (approximately $1.60) for women in England. See *Irish Citizen,* Dec. 6, 1913.

21. Ellis, *History,* 184. In his column "Patriotism and Labour" in *Shan Van Vocht,* Aug. 2, 1897, 138–39, James Connolly cited figures from the Board of Trade that reported 78 percent of Irish wage earners received less than 1 pound per week; by comparison, only 40 percent of English workers and 50 percent of Scottish workers received such paltry incomes. Reprinted in Connolly, *Writings,* 129.

22. M. Jones, 279.

23. Ibid., 3.

24. See Mary Daly, "Women, Work, and Trade Unionism," in *Women and Irish Society,* ed. Margaret MacCurtain and Donncha Ó Corráin (Westport, Conn.: Greenwood Press, 1979)71–80, and "Women and Trade Unions," in *Trade Union Century,* ed. Donal Nevin (Dublin: Mercier Press, 1994), 106–16.

25. Donal Nevin posits that the readership would have been much larger if the presses

used by the *Irish Worker* could have printed more copies per week. See Donal Nevin, "The Irish Worker, 1911–1914," in Nevin, *Larkin*, 155; see also Ellis, *History*, 187.

26. Constance Markievicz, as quoted in M. Jones, 1.

27. Seamus Cody, John O'Dowd, and Peter Rigney, *The Parliament of Labour: 100 Years of the Dublin Council of Trade Unions* (Dublin: Dublin Council of Trade Unions, 1986), 187.

28. See Buckley, 106.

29. Larkin, Aug. 12, 1911, 2.

30. See June Hannam, "New Histories of the Labour Movement," in *Re-Presenting the Past: Women and History*, ed. Ann-Marie Gallagher, Cathy Lubelska, and Louise Ryan (London: Longman, 2001), 173.

31. See *Irish Worker*, Dec. 1911, 3; Dec. (Christmas issue) 1912, iv–v.

32. Larkin, Mar. 8, 1913, 2.

33. Connolly, "Woman," 194.

34. Friedrich Engels, *The Origin of Family, Private Property, and the State*, in *Karl Marx, Friedrich Engels: Collected Works* (New York: International, 1990), 26:262.

35. See Mary Clancy, "Aspects of Women's Contributions to the Oireachtas Debate in the Irish Free State, 1922–1937," in *Women Surviving*, ed. Maria Luddy and Cliona Murphy, 206–32 (Dublin: Poolbeg, 1990).

36. Larkin, Nov. 25, 1911, 2.

37. Ibid., Sept. 9, 1911, 2.

38. Connolly, "Woman," 189.

39. Larkin, Dec. 7, 1912, 2.

40. Ibid., Feb. 8, 1913, 2.

41. Ibid., Oct. 7, 1911, 2.

42. Ibid., Apr. 27, 1912, 2.

43. Ibid., May 31, 1913, 2.

44. Ibid., Nov. 23, 1912, 2; May 24, 1912, 2; Dec. 14, 1912, 2; Dec. 14, 1912, 2.

45. Robin Miller Jacoby, *The British and American Women's Trade Union Leagues, 1890–1925: A Case Study of Feminism and Class* (Brooklyn: Carlson Press, 1994), 3.

46. See Moriarty, "Delia Larkin," 432.

47. Ibid., 430.

48. Ibid., 431.

49. Ibid., 432.

50. Daniel Corkery, as quoted in Nevin, *Larkin*, 257, said it best: "I never heard him speak to the class for which he stood that he did not half offend them by dwelling on the failings which kept them powerless and timid."

51. Keir Hardie, as quoted in Nevin, *Larkin*, 266.

52. See Nevin, *Larkin*, 153.

53. Dermot Keogh, *The Rise of the Irish Working Class: The Dublin Trade Union Movement and Labour Leadership, 1890–1914* (Belfast, Appletree Press, 1982), 242; M. Jones, 12–13.

54. Gregory, *Workhouse Ward,* 380.

55. Lucy McDiarmid and Maureen Waters, "Introduction," in Gregory, *Selected Writings,* xii.

56. See Elizabeth Coxhead, *Lady Gregory: A Literary Portrait* (New York: Harcourt, Brace and World, 1961); Ann Saddlemyer, *In Defence of Lady Gregory, Playwright* (Dublin: Dolmen Press, 1966); James Pethica, "A Dialogue of Self and Service: Lady Gregory's Emergence as an Irish Writer and Partnership with W. B. Yeats" (Ph.D. diss., Oxford Univ., 1987); Innes, *Woman and Nation;* McDiarmid and Waters; Kiberd, *Inventing;* Anne Fogarty, " 'A Woman of the House': Gender and Nationalism in the Writings of Augusta Gregory," in *Border Crossings: Irish Women Writers and National Identities,* ed. Kathryn Kirkpatrick (Tuscaloosa: Univ. of Alabama Press, 2000), 100–122.

57. McDiarmid and Waters, xx.

58. Christopher Murray, *Twentieth Century Irish Drama: Mirror Up to Nation* (Manchester: Manchester Univ. Press, 1997), 40.

59. James Pethica, "Introduction," in Augusta Gregory, *Lady Gregory's Diaries, 1892–1902,* ed. James Pethica (New York: Oxford Univ. Press, 1996), xiii.

60. Kiberd, *Inventing,* 69.

61. Augusta Gregory, as quoted in Colin Smythe, "Afterword," in *Lady Gregory's Journals,* vol. 1, books 1–29, Oct. 10, 1916–Feb. 24, 1925, ed. Daniel J. Murphy (New York: Oxford Univ. Press, 1978), 641.

62. Augusta Gregory, *Lady Gregory's Journals, 1916–1930,* ed. Lennox Robinson (New York: Macmillan, 1947), 340.

63.[Augusta Gregory], "A Week in Ireland," *Nation,* Oct. 16, 1920, 63–64; "Another Week in Ireland," *Nation,* Oct. 23, 1920, 123–124; "Murder by the Throat," *Nation,* Nov. 13, 1920, 215–16; "A Third Week in Ireland," *Nation,* Dec. 4, 1920, 333; "A Fourth Week in Ireland," *Nation,* Dec. 18, 1920, 413–14.

64. [Gregory], "A Week," 63.

65. I am indebted to McDiarmid and Waters, xli, for this phrase.

66. See Novick, 72–102.

67. [Gregory], "Murder by the Throat," 216.

68. See Foster, *Yeats,* 1:171; Fogarty, 101.

69. Sean O'Casey, as quoted in Gregory, *Journals* (Murphy), 105.

70. Gregory, *Journals* (Robinson), 239.

71. Ibid., 329.

72. George Bernard Shaw, as quoted in *Shaw, Lady Gregory and the Abbey,* ed. Dan H. Laurence and Nicholas Grene (Gerrards Cross, U.K.: Colin Smythe, 1993), xxv.

73. Gregory, *Journals* (Murphy), 621.

74. Ronald Ayling, "Lady Gregory and Sean O'Casey: An Unlikely Friendship Revisited," in *Lady Gregory Fifty Years After*, ed. Ann Saddlemyer and Colin Smythe (Gerrards Cross, U.K.: Colin Smythe, 1987), 168.

75. See Foster, *Yeats*, 1:493.

76. Augusta Gregory, *Seventy Years: Being the Autobiography of Lady Gregory*, ed. Colin Smythe (Gerrards Cross, U.K.: Colin Smythe, 1974), 411.

77. Ibid., 467–68, 326.

78. Ibid., 326.

79. Saddlemyer, 31.

80. Gregory, *Workhouse Ward*, 374.

81. Ibid., 373.

82. Augusta Gregory, *Kincora*, in *Collected Plays*, ed. Ann Saddlemyer (Gerrards Cross, U.K.: Colin Smyth, 1970), 2:6.

83. Gregory, *Workhouse Ward*, 376.

84. Ibid.

85. Oscar Wilde, "The Decay of Lying," in *The Writings of Oscar Wilde*, ed. Isobel Murray (Oxford: Oxford Univ. Press, 1989), 221.

86. Ibid., 230.

87. Terry Eagleton, *The Truth about the Irish* (New York: St. Martin's Press, 1999), 26.

88. McDiarmid and Waters, xxxiii.

89. See Cathy Leehy, "New Woman in a New Ireland? *Grania* after Naturalism," *Irish University Review* 34 (2004): 158.

90. James Pethica, "Lady Gregory's Abbey Theatre Drama: Ireland Real and Unreal," in *The Cambridge Companion to Twentieth-Century Irish Drama*, ed. Shaun Richards (Cambridge: Cambridge Univ. Press, 2004), 62.

91. Gregory, *Workhouse Ward*, 377.

92. Murray, 56.

93. Gregory, *Seventy Years*, 412.

94. Fogarty, 118.

95. Gregory, *Workhouse Ward*, 379.

96. Ibid., 380.

97. Augusta Gregory, as quoted in McDiarmid and Waters, xxxiv.

98. Michael MacLiammoir, as quoted in Saddlemyer, 118.

99. Kiberd, *Inventing*, 201.

100. Augusta Gregory, as quoted in *Irish Worker*, May 23, 1914, 3.

5. Suffrage on the Barricades: Motherhood and Militancy in the *Irish Citizen*

1. Adrienne Rich, *Of Woman Born* (London: Virago, 1977), 51.

2. See David Lloyd, "Nationalisms Against the State," in *Politics and Culture in the Age of Capital*, ed. Lisa Lowe and David Lloyd (Durham: Duke Univ. Press, 1997), 173–75.

3. See Clair Wills, "Women, Domesticity and the Family: Recent Feminist Work in Irish Cultural Studies," *Cultural Studies* 15, no. 1 (Jan. 2001): 40–45.

4. MacCurtain and Ó Corráin, 52.

5. Ian Christopher Fletcher, " 'Women of the Nations, Unite!': Transnational Suffragism in the United Kingdom, 1912–14," in *Women's Suffrage in the British Empire: Citizenship, Nation, and Race*, ed. Ian Fletcher, Laura E. Nym Mayhall, and Philippa Levine (London: Routledge, 2000), 103.

6. Ward, "Conflicting," 127–47.

7. Ibid., 130.

8. Ibid.

9. Ibid.

10. Fletcher, 105; Ward, *Hanna*, 104; Murphy, 165–200.

11. Ward, *Hanna*, 104.

12. Francis Sheehy Skeffington, as quoted in James H. and Margaret E. Cousins, *We Two Together* (Madras: Ganesh, 1950), 203; see also Ward, *Hanna*, 80. For an excellent overview of the major social issues of Irish suffrage, and for substantive excerpts from the *Irish Citizen* throughout the eight years it was in print, see Louise Ryan, *Irish Feminism and the Vote: An Anthology of the Irish Citizen Newspaper, 1912–1920* (Dublin: Folens, 1996).

13. Ryan, *Irish Feminism*; Dana Hearne, "The *Irish Citizen* 1914–1916: Nationalism, Feminism, and Militarism," *Canadian Journal of Irish Studies* 18, no. 1 (1992), 12; Ward, *Hanna*, 142; Rosemary Cullen Owens, *Louie Bennett* (Cork: Cork Univ. Press, 2001), 22–27.

14. *Irish Citizen*, May 25, 1912, 1.

15. See "Our Brilliant Press," *Irish Citizen*, Sept. 13, 1913, 133; "The Press Still at It," *Irish Citizen*, Sept. 20, 1913, 141; "The Belfast Press," *Irish Citizen*, Sept. 27, 1913, 149; and "The Need for a Free Press," *Irish Citizen*, Oct. 25, 1913, 181.

16. Francis Sheehy Skeffington to Mrs. Bernard Shaw, Dec. 14, 1914, National Library of Ireland, Francis Sheehy Skeffington Papers, MS 22259. Quoted with permission of the National Library of Ireland.

17. For more on anonymity in the advanced nationalist press, see Novick, 35.

18. See *Irish Citizen*, June 22, 1912, 35.

19. *Irish Citizen*, Dec. 21, 1912, 244.

20. Rosamund Jacob, "Letter to the Editor," *Irish Citizen*, July 12, 1913, 61.

21. *Irish Citizen,* May 3, 1913, 393.

22. Rosamund Jacob, "Letter to Editor," *Irish Citizen,* May 30, 1914, 10.

23. Glandon, *Griffith,* 147.

24. "Grave Crisis," *Irish Citizen,* Jan. 8, 1916, 208.

25. "Women and Education," *Irish Citizen,* Feb. 7, 1914, 300; L. A. M. Priestley, *Irish Citizen,* Mar. 14, 1914, 340.

26. Mairie Johnson [*sic*], "Correspondence," *Irish Citizen,* Sept. 5, 1914, 123.

27. Ryan, *Irish Feminism,* 53.

28. [Marion Duggan], "Votes for All Women," *Irish Citizen,* Aug. 8, 1914, 99.

29. Marion Duggan, "Two Roads to Liberty," *Irish Citizen,* Dec. 12, 1914, 235.

30. Lillian Suffern, "Militancy and Motherhood," *Irish Citizen,* Dec. 19, 1914, 243.

31. Ibid., Dec. 26, 1914, 250.

32. Marion Duggan, "Motherhood v. Militancy," *Irish Citizen,* Jan. 9, 1915, 259.

33. Louie Bennett, "Peace, Women and Internationalism," *Irish Citizen,* Apr. 10, 1915, 276.

34. Louie Bennett, "Concerning the Protest Meeting," *Irish Citizen,* May 22, 1915, 293.

35. Meg Connery, *Irish Citizen,* Nov. 6, 1912, 202.

36. Hanna Sheehy Skeffington, "Why We Throw Stones at Government Glass Houses," *Irish Citizen,* June 22, 1912, 37.

37. Hanna Sheehy Skeffington, "Jail, a University," *Irish Citizen,* Aug. 10, 1912, 95.

38. "Prisoners for Liberty: Members of Irish Women's Franchise League on Trial for Breaking Government Windows," *Irish Citizen,* June 22, 1912, 33.

39. See, for example, the front-page lead story, "Women Feared by Government: Three of the Irish Delegates to the Hague Congress to Whom [Home Secretary] Mr. McKenna Refused Permits," *Irish Citizen,* May 8, 1915, 395; and "The Voice of Irish Womanhood: A Demand and a Warning. Points from Historic Speeches," *Irish Citizen,* June 8, 1912, 22.

40. Francis Sheehy Skeffington, *The Prodigal Daughter,* in *Irish Citizen,* Nov. 7, 1914, 196–98.

41. Ward, *Hanna,* 127.

42. Ibid.

43. F. Sheehy Skeffington, *Prodigal Daughter,* 198.

44. Ibid.

45. Ibid.

46. Ibid.

47. My thanks to Kathryn Conrad for this observation.

48. Elizabeth Robins, *Votes for Women!* (London: Mills and Boon, 1909), 115.

49. *Irish Citizen,* Apr. 14, 1914, 365.

50. See Novick, 145.

51. See Murphy, 41.

52. See Novick, 51–53; Ward, *Hanna*, 135.

53. See Sophia A. Van Wingerden, *The Women's Suffrage Movement in Britain, 1866–1928* (London: Macmillan, 1999), 157; and Johanna Alberti, *Beyond Suffrage: Feminists in War and Peace, 1914–28* (London: Macmillan, 1989), 46–50. See also Nina Boyle's commentary in the *Irish Citizen*, Nov. 7, 1914, 195: "Not for one week did our usual work and meetings flag; and feeling a strong desire to help to mitigate the many miseries induced by the war, we started a Women's Suffrage National Aid Corps in addition to, and not in lieu of, our legitimate work. Many of our members hold conflicting views on the subject of whether the war was or was not necessary, whether or not Britain should have joined in, and what were the real reasons that induced the Government to act."

54. Van Wingerden, 157.

55. Ryan, *Irish Feminism*, 75–84.

56. Rich, *Woman*, 33.

57. See, for example, A. Adams, "Maternal Bonds: Recent Literature on Mothering," *Signs* 20, no. 2 (1995): 414–27; Donna Bassin, Margaret Honey, and Meryle Mahrer Kaplan, eds., *Representations of Motherhood* (New Haven: Yale Univ. Press, 1994); Toni Bowers, *The Politics of Motherhood: British Writing and Culture, 1680–1760* (New York: Cambridge Univ. Press, 1996); Ann Daly, *Inventing Motherhood: The Consequences of an Ideal* (London: Burnett Books, 1982); Patrice DiQuinzio, *The Impossibility of Motherhood: Feminism, Individualism and the Problem of Mothering* (New York: Routledge, 1999); Alexis Jetter, Annelise Orleck, and Diana Taylor, eds., *The Politics of Motherhood: Activist Voices from Left to Right* (Hanover, N.H.: Univ. Press of New England, 1997); E. Ross, "New Thoughts on 'The Oldest Vocation': Mothers and Motherhood in Recent Feminist Scholarship," *Signs* 20, no. 2 (1995): 397–413; Sara Ruddick, *Maternal Thinking: Towards a Politics of Peace* (Boston: Beacon Press, 1989).

58. Anne Morey, "Sexuality, Maternity, and Femininity in Films Exhibited in Britain, 1914–1919," in *Maternal Instincts: Visions of Motherhood and Sexuality in Britain, 1875–1925*, ed. Claudia Nelson and Ann Sumner Holmes (London: Macmillan, 1997), 144.

59. Coventry Patmore, *The Angel in the House* (London: J. W. Parker and Sons, 1854–56); Nora Tynan O'Mahony, "The Mother," *Irish Monthly* 41 (Oct. 1913): 529–32.

60. O'Mahony, 529.

61. Ibid.

62. See MacPherson, 145.

63. See ibid., 150. See also Caitriona Clear, *Women of the House: Women's Household Work in Ireland, 1922–1961* (Dublin: Irish Academic Press, 2000); and Bourke.

64. See E. A. Browning, "Concerning Christabel," *Irish Citizen*, Oct. 10, 1914, 166.

65. Louie Bennett to Hanna Sheehy Skeffington, Oct. 1, 1914, National Library of Ireland, Sheehy Skeffington Papers, MS 22667(ii). Quoted with kind permission of the National Library of Ireland.

66. See Lloyd, "Nationalisms," 174.

67. Bassin, Honey, and Kaplan, 17.

68. Morey, 142.

69. See Susan R. Grayzel, " 'The Mothers of Our Soldiers' Children': Motherhood, Immorality and the War Baby Scandal, 1914–1918," in Nelson and Holmes, 122; Laura E. Nym Mayhall, Phillipa Levine, and Ian Christopher Fletcher, "Introduction," in Fletcher, Mayhall, and Levine, xvi; Morley, 141.

70. David Lloyd, *Ireland after History* (South Bend, Ind.: Univ. of Notre Dame Press, 1999), 26.

71. Margaret Ward, "Nationalism, Pacifism, Internationalism: Louie Bennett, Hanna Sheehy Skeffington, and the Problems of 'Defining Feminism," in Bradley and Valiulis, 61.

72. Mayhall, Levine, and Fletcher, xv.

73. Hearne, 2.

74. Lillian Suffern, "The War: A Reply," *Irish Citizen,* Sept. 5, 1914, 125.

75. Lillian Suffern, "Suffrage and Sacrifice," *Irish Citizen,* Nov. 28, 1914, 231.

76. Violet Crichton, "IWFL and the War: An Open Letter to Mrs. Sheehy Skeffington," *Irish Citizen,* July 24, 1915, 62.

77. Margaret Cousins, "Sparks from the Anvil of War," *Irish Citizen,* Sept. 12, 1914, 132.

78. "Votes for Giving Life," *Irish Citizen,* Feb. 27, 1915, 313.

79. Ruddick, 92 (emphasis original).

80. Bennett, "Peace," 363.

81. Ryan, *Irish Feminism,* 78.

82. Margaret McCoubrey, "The Chivalry of War," *Irish Citizen,* Feb. 27, 1915, 313.

83. Meg Connery, "Women and Militants," *Irish Citizen,* Jan. 9, 1915, 262.

84. Ibid.

85. Francis Sheehy Skeffington, "War and Feminism," *Irish Citizen,* Sept. 12, 1914, 133.

86. Ibid.

87. Hanna Sheehy Skeffington, "The Duty of Suffragists," *Irish Citizen,* Aug. 15, 1914, 100–101.

88. Ibid., 100.

89. Ibid.

90. See, for example, "Prisoners for Liberty," 33.

91. Hanna Sheehy Skeffington, "The Women's Movement—Ireland" *Irish Review* 2, no. 17 (July 1912): 225–27.

92. Marcus, 2.

93. Meg Connery, "Women and Militants II," *Irish Citizen*, Jan. 16, 1915, 268.

94. H. Sheehy Skeffington, "Women's Movement," 225.

95. A. Daly, 92.

96. Breda Gray and Louise Ryan, "The Politics of Irish Identity and the Interconnections Between Feminism, Nationhood, and Colonialism," in *Nation, Empire, Colony: Historicizing Gender and Race*, ed. Ruth Roach Pierson and Nupur Chaudhuri (Bloomington: Indiana Univ. Press, 1998), 122.

97. See Jean Bethke Elshtain, "The Mothers of the Disappeared: Passion and Protest in Maternal Action," in Bassin, Honey, and Kaplan, 75–91.

98. See Steele, "Constance."

Coda

1. Brian Moore, "Invisible Women," as quoted in Ruth Taillon, *When History Was Made: The Women of 1916* (Belfast: Beyond the Pale Press, 1996), vii.

2. See Lil Conlon, *Cumann na mBan and the Women of Ireland, 1913–1925* (Kilkenny, Ire.: Kilkenny People, 1969), 8–12; Ward, *Unmanageable*, chaps. 3–4; Ward, *In Their Own*, 46–51; Maria Luddy, *Women in Ireland, 1800–1918: A Documentary History* (Cork: Cork Univ. Press, 1995), 309–15; Taillon, chap 3; Sineád McCoole, *Guns and Chiffon: Women Revolutionaries and Kilmainham Gaol, 1916–1923* (Dublin: Stationery Office, Government of Ireland, 1997), chap. 2, and *No Ordinary Women: Irish Female Activists in the Revolutionary Years 1900–1923* (Madison: Univ. of Wisconsin Press, 2003), chap. 2.

3. Taillon, 49; McCoole, *Guns and Chiffon*, 15.

4. Helena Molony, as quoted in McCoole, *Guns and Chiffon*, 15.

5. Lisa Weihman, "*Doing My Bit for Ireland:* Transgressing Gender in the Easter Rising," *Éire/Ireland* 39, nos. 3–4 (Fall–Winter 2004), 228.

6. Hanna Sheehy Skeffington, "Constance Markievicz: What She Stood For," *An Phoblacht*, July 16, 1932, 7–8.

7. Margaret Ward, *The Missing Sex* (Dublin: Attic Press, 1991), 4.

8. Cullingford, 121–29; Innex, *Woman*, 77–78.

9. William Butler Yeats, "Easter 1916," in *W. B. Yeats: The Poems*, 144.

10. See Steele, "Constance," 78–79.

11. See Statement of Mrs. Maeve Cavanagh MacDowell, *Bureau of Military History, 1913–21*, Document no. W.S. 258, File no. S.191. Military Archives, Cathal Brugha Barracks. Quoted with kind permission of the Military Archives.

12. Constance Markievicz, "Speech to America," Apr. 1922. In the Joseph McGarrity

papers, NLI manuscript 17, 463. Quoted with kind permission of the National Library of Ireland.

13. Steele, "Constance," 66–71.

14. See Valiulis; Mary Clancy, "Aspects of Women's Contribution to the Oireachtas Debates in the Irish Free State," in Maria Luddy and Cliona Murphy, eds., *Women Surviving,* 206–32 (Dublin: Poolbeg, 1990).

15. Constance Markievicz, "Women in the Fight: A Memoir by Countess de Markievicz," in *Dublin 1916,* ed. Roger McHugh (New York: Hawthorn Books, 1966), 122.

16. Gonne, *Servant,* 247.

17. See Sineád McCoole, "Foreward: Finding Women," in *No Ordinary Women* for a sampling of representative accounts by Christy Halpin, Fintan Norris, and Anna MacBride White about the taboos and silences in Irish families about women's experiences in war and prison.

18. Alice Milligan to Sineád de Valera, as quoted in Johnston, 131–32.

19. Gregory, *Seventy Years,* 536.

20. Diarmaid Ferriter, " 'In Such Deadly Earnest,' " *Dublin Review* 12 (Autumn 2003): 47.

21. I am grateful to Maria Luddy for alerting me to the opening of these archives and for supplying me with copies of interviews.

22. Ferriter, 49.

◆ ◆ ◆

Bibliography

Published Sources

Adams, A. "Maternal Bonds: Recent Literature on Mothering." *Signs* 20, no. 2 (1995): 414–27.

Alberti, Johanna. *Beyond Suffrage: Feminists in War and Peace, 1914–28.* London: Macmillan, 1989.

Arnold, Matthew. *Complete Prose Works of Matthew Arnold.* Edited by R. H. Super. 11 vols. Ann Arbor: Univ. of Michigan Press, 1960–77.

———. "On the Study of Celtic Literature." In *Complete Prose Works of Matthew Arnold,* edited by R. H. Super, 3:291–386. Ann Arbor: Univ. of Michigan Press, 1962.

———. "Up to Easter." In *Complete Prose Works of Matthew Arnold,* edited by R. H. Super, 11:190–209. Ann Arbor: Univ. of Michigan Press, 1970–77. First published in *Nineteenth Century* 21 (1887): 629–43.

Ayling, Ronald. "Lady Gregory and Sean O'Casey: An Unlikely Friendship Revisited." In *Lady Gregory Fifty Years After,* edited by Ann Saddlemyer and Colin Smythe, 163–78. Gerrards Cross, U.K.: Colin Smythe, 1987.

Bassin, Donna, Margaret Honey, and Meryle Mahrer Kaplan, eds. *Representations of Motherhood.* New Haven: Yale Univ. Press, 1994.

Beetham, Margaret. *A Magazine of Her Own? Domesticity and Desire in the Women's Magazine 1800–1914.* London: Routledge, 1996.

Benjamin, Walter. *Illuminations: Essays and Reflections.* New York: Schocken Books, 1968.

Bennett, Louie. "Concerning the Protest Meeting." *Irish Citizen,* May 22, 1915, 293.

———. "Peace, Women and Internationalism." *Irish Citizen*, Apr. 10, 1915, 276.

Benton, Sarah. "Woman Disarmed: The Militarization of Politics in Ireland 1913–1923." *Feminist Review* 50 (Summer 1995): 148–72.

Boehmer, Elleke. *Empire, the National, and the Postcolonial, 1890–1920*. Oxford: Oxford Univ. Press, 2002.

Boland, Eavan. "A Kind of Scar: The Woman Poet in a National Tradition." In *A Dozen Lips*, edited by Ailbhe Smyth, 72–92. Dublin: Attic Press, 1994.

Bourke, Angela, et al., eds. *Field Day Anthology of Irish Writing*. Vols. 4–5. Cork: Cork Univ. Press, 2002.

Bourke, Joanna. *Husbandry to Housewifery: Women, Economic Change, and Housework in Ireland, 1890–1914*. Oxford: Clarendon Press, 1993.

Bowers, Toni. *The Politics of Motherhood: British Writing and Culture, 1680–1760*. New York: Cambridge Univ. Press, 1996.

Bradley, Anthony, and Maryann Gialanella Valiulis, eds. *Gender and Sexuality in Modern Ireland*. Amherst: Univ. of Massachusetts Press, 1997.

Brake, Laurel, Aled Jones, and Lionel Madden, eds. *Investigating Victorian Journalism*. London: Macmillan, 1990.

Brake, Laurel. *Subjugated Knowledges: Journalism, Gender and Literature in the Nineteenth Century*. New York: New York Univ. Press, 1994.

Brown, Terence. "Cultural Nationalism." In *Field Day Anthology of Irish Writing*, edited by Seamus Deane, 516–20. Derry, U.K.: Field Day, 1991.

Browning, E. A. "Concerning Christabel." *Irish Citizen*, Oct. 10, 1914, 166.

Buckley, Alison. " 'Let the Girls Come Forth': The Early Feminist Ideology of the Irish Women Workers' Union." In *Irish Women's History*, edited by Alan Hayes and Diane Urquhart, 103–14. Dublin: Irish Academic Press, 2004.

Burke, Edmund. *Writings and Speeches of Edmund Burke*. Vol. 2. Edited by Paul Langford. Oxford: Oxford Univ. Press, 1980.

Butler, Marilyn. "Introduction." In Maria Edgeworth, *Castle Rackrent* and *Ennui*, edited by Maria Marilyn Butler, 1–56. Harmondsworth, U.K.: Penguin, 1992.

Butler, Mary E. L. *Irishwomen and the Home Language*. In *Field Day Anthology of Irish Writing*, edited by Angela Bourke et al., 5:84–86. Cork: Cork Univ. Press, 2002. First published in Dublin as undated pamphlet by Gaelic League, ca. 1900.

———. "Irishwomen's Work." *United Irishman*, Mar. 25, 1899, 3.

———. "Womanhood and Nationhood," *United Irishman*, Jan. 3, 1903, 6–7; Jan. 10, 1903, 6–7; Jan. 17, 1903, 6; Jan. 24, 1903, 6.

Cannavan, Jan. "Romantic Revolutionary Irishwomen: Women, Young Ireland and 1848." In *Gender Perspectives in Nineteenth Century Ireland: Public and Private Spheres*, edited by Margaret Kelleher and James Murphy, 212–20. Dublin: Irish Academic Press, 1997.

Carmichael, Alexander. *Carmina Gadelica: Hymns and Incantations; with Illustrative Notes on Words, Rites, and Customs, Dying and Obsolete: Orally Collected in the Highlands and Islands of Scotland and Translated into English*, 6 vols. Edinburgh, Scottish Academic Press: 1900–71.

Castle, Gregory. *Modernism and the Celtic Revival*. Cambridge: Cambridge Univ. Press, 2001.

Chaudhry, Yug Mohit. *Yeats, the Irish Literary Revival and the Politics of Print*. Cork: Cork Univ. Press, 2001.

Clancy, Mary. "Aspects of Women's Contributions to the Oireachtas Debate in the Irish Free State, 1922–1937." In *Women Surviving*, edited by Maria Luddy and Cliona Murphy, 206–32. Dublin: Poolbeg, 1990.

Clear, Caitriona. *Women of the House: Women's Household Work in Ireland, 1922–1961*. Dublin: Irish Academic Press, 2000.

Cleary, Joe. *Literature, Partition and the Nation State: Culture and Conflict in Ireland, Israel and Palestine*. Cambridge: Cambridge Univ. Press, 2002.

Cody, Seamus, John O'Dowd, and Peter Rigney. *The Parliament of Labour: 100 Years of the Dublin Council of Trade Unions*. Dublin: Dublin Council of Trade Unions, 1986.

Colum, Padraig. *Ourselves Alone! The Story of Arthur Griffith and the Origin of the Irish Free State*. New York: Crown Press, 1959.

Concannon, Thomas. "The Irish in Mexico." *Shan Van Vocht*, June 1897, 101–2.

Conlon, Lil. *Cumann na mBan and the Women of Ireland, 1913–1925*. Kilkenny, Ire.: Kilkenny People, 1969.

Connery, Meg. "Women and Militants." *Irish Citizen*, Jan. 9, 1915, 262.

———. "Women and Militants II." *Irish Citizen*, Jan. 16, 1915, 262.

Connolly, James. "Can Irish Republicans Be Politicians?" *Shan Van Vocht*, Nov. 1896, 210.

———. "Nationalism and Socialism." *Shan Van Vocht*, Jan. 8, 1897, 7–8.

———. "Other People's Opinions." *Shan Van Vocht*, Oct. 1897, 188.

———. "Patriotism and Labour." *Shan Van Vocht*, Aug. 2, 1897, 138–39.

———. *Selected Writings.* Edited by Peter Beresford Ellis. London: Pluto Press, 1997.

———. "Woman." In *Selected Writings,* edited by Peter Beresford Ellis, 30–33. London: Pluto Press, 1997. First published as chapter 6 of *The Re-Conquest of Ireland,* 1915. Reprint. Dublin: New Books, 1972.

Corbett, Mary Jean. *Allegories of Union in Irish and English Writing, 1790–1870.* Cambridge: Cambridge Univ. Press, 2000.

Coughlan, J. P. "Our Political Prisoners." *Shan Van Vocht,* Sept. 1896, 165–66.

Coulter, Carol. *The Hidden Tradition: Feminism, Women, and Nationalism.* Dublin: Attic Press, 1993.

Cousins, James H., and Margaret E. Cousins. *We Two Together.* Madras: Ganesh, 1950.

Cousins, Margaret. "Sparks from the Anvil of War." *Irish Citizen,* Sept. 12, 1914, 132.

Coxhead, Elizabeth. *Daughters of Erin.* London: Secker and Warburg, 1965.

———. *Lady Gregory: A Literary Portrait.* New York: Harcourt, Brace and World, 1961.

Crichton, Violet. "IWFL and the War: An Open Letter to Mrs. Sheehy Skeffington." *Irish Citizen,* July 24, 1915, 62.

Crossman, Virginia. "The *Shan Van Vocht:* Women, Republicanism, and the Commemoration of the 1798 Rebellion." *Eighteenth Century Life: Ireland, 1798–1998: From Revolution to Revisionism and Beyond* 22, no. 3 (1998): 128–39. Edited by Robert P. Maccubbin.

Cullen, Mary. "How Radical was Irish Feminism between 1860 and 1920?" In *Radicals, Rebels, and Establishments,* edited by Patrick J. Corish, 185–201. Belfast: Appletree Press, 1985.

Cullingford, Elizabeth Butler. *Gender and History in Yeats's Love Poetry.* Cambridge: Cambridge Univ. Press, 1993.

Curtin, Nancy. *The United Irishmen: Popular Politics in Ulster and Dublin, 1791–1799.* New York: Oxford Univ. Press, 1994.

Curtis, Liz. *The Cause of Ireland.* Belfast: Beyond the Pale Press, 1994.

Daly, Ann. *Inventing Motherhood: The Consequences of an Ideal.* London: Burnett Books, 1982.

Daly, Mary. "Women and Trade Unions." In *Trade Union Century,* edited by Donal Nevin, 106–16. Dublin: Mercier Press, 1994.

———. "Women, Work, and Trade Unionism." In *Women and Irish Society,* edited by Margaret MacCurtain and Donncha Ó Corráin, 71–80. Westport, Conn.: Greenwood Press, 1979.

Deane, Seamus. *Celtic Revivals.* Winston-Salem, N.C.: Wake Forest Univ. Press, 1985.

——, ed. *Field Day Anthology of Irish Writing.* Vol. 2. Derry, U.K.: Field Day, 1991.

DiBattista, Maria, and Lucy McDiarmid, eds. *High and Low Moderns: Literature and Culture, 1889–1939.* New York: Oxford Univ. Press, 1996.

Dickson, David, Dáire Keogh, and Kevin Whelan, eds. *United Irishman: Republicanism, Radicalism, and Rebellion.* Dublin: Lilliput, 1993.

DiQuinzio, Patrice. *The Impossibility of Motherhood: Feminism, Individualism and the Problem of Mothering.* New York: Routledge, 1999.

Donovan, Katie, A. Norman Jeffares, and Brendan Kennelly, eds. *Ireland's Women: Writings Past and Present.* New York: Norton, 1994.

Duggan, Marion. "Motherhood v. Militancy." *Irish Citizen,* Jan. 9, 1915, 259.

[——]. "Votes for All Women." *Irish Citizen,* Aug. 8, 1914, 99.

Duggan, Marion. "Two Roads to Liberty." *Irish Citizen,* Dec. 12, 1914, 235.

Eagleton, Terry. *Heathcliff and the Great Hunger.* New York: Verso, 1995.

——. *The Truth about the Irish.* New York: St. Martin's Press, 1999.

Engels, Friedrich. *The Origin of Family, Private Property, and the State.* In *Karl Marx, Friedrich Engels: Collected Works,* 26:129–276. New York: International, 1990.

Ellis, Peter Beresford. *A History of the Irish Working Class.* 1972. Reprint. London: Pluto Press, 1996.

Elshtain, Jean Bethke. "The Mothers of the Disappeared: Passion and Protest in Maternal Action." In *Representations of Motherhood,* edited by Donna Bassin, Margaret Honey, and Meryle Mahrer Kaplan, 75–91. New Haven: Yale Univ. Press, 1994.

Farwell, Byron. *The Great Anglo-Boer War.* New York: Norton, 1976.

Ferriter, Diarmaid. " 'In Such Deadly Earnest.' " *Dublin Review* 12 (Autumn 2003): 36–64.

Fletcher, Ian Christopher. " 'Women of the Nations, Unite!' Transnational Suffragism in the United Kingdom, 1912–14." In *Women's Suffrage in the British Empire: Citizenship, Nation, and Race,* edited by Ian Christopher Fletcher, Laura E. Nym Mayhall, and Philippa Levine, 103–20. London: Routledge, 2000.

Fletcher, Ian Christopher, Laura E. Nym Mayhall, and Philippa Levine, eds. *Women's Suffrage in the British Empire: Citizenship, Nation, and Race*. London: Routledge, 2000.

Fogarty, Anne. " 'A Woman of the House': Gender and Nationalism in the Writings of Augusta Gregory." In *Border Crossings: Irish Women Writers and National Identities*, edited by Kathryn Kirkpatrick, 100–22. Tuscaloosa: Univ. of Alabama Press, 2000.

Foster, R. F. *Modern Ireland*. Harmondsworth, U.K.: Penguin, 1989.

———. *W. B. Yeats, A Life*. Vol. 1: *Apprentice Mage*. New York: Oxford Univ. Press, 1997.

———. *W. B. Yeats, A Life*. Vol. 2: *The Arch-Poet*. New York: Oxford Univ. Press, 2003.

Fox, R. M. *Rebel Irishwomen*. Dublin: Talbot Press, 1935.

Fyfe, Anne-Marie. "Women and Mother Ireland." In *Image and Power: Women in Fiction in the Twentieth Century*, edited by Sarah Sceats and Gail Cunningham, 184–94. London: Longman, 1996.

Gibbons, Luke. "Constructing the Canon: Versions of National Identity." In *Field Day Anthology of Irish Writing*, edited by Seamus Deane, 950–55. Derry, U.K.: Field Day, 1991.

———. *Transformations in Irish Culture*. Cork: Cork Univ. Press, 1996.

Gifford Czira, Sidney. *The Years Flew By*. Edited by Alan Hayes. 1974. Reprint. Galway, Ire.: Arlen Press, 2000.

Glandon, Virginia E. *Arthur Griffith and the Advanced-Nationalist Press Ireland, 1900–1922*. New York: Peter Lang, 1985.

———. "Index of Irish Newspapers, 1900–1922." *Éire-Ireland* 11 (1976): 84–121.

———. "The Irish Press and Revolutionary Irish Nationalism." *Éire-Ireland* 16 (1981): 21–33.

Gonne, Maud. "The Boer Women." In *Maud Gonne's Irish Nationalist Writings*, edited by Karen Steele, 164–66. Dublin: Irish Academic Press, 2004. First published in *United Irishman*, Mar. 17, 1900, supplement 4.

———. *Dawn*. In *Maud Gonne's Irish Nationalist Writings*, edited by Karen Steele, 204–12. Dublin: Irish Academic Press, 2004. First published in *United Irishman*, Oct, 29, 1904, 4–5. Reprinted also in Angela Bourke et al., eds. *Field Day Anthology of Irish Writing*, 5:913–17. Cork: Cork Univ. Press, 2002.

———. "Eitne." In *Maud Gonne's Irish Nationalist Writings*, edited by Karen

Steele, 193–96. Dublin: Irish Academic Press, 2004. First published in *United Irishman*, Apr. 12, 1902, 3.

———. "Famine Queen." In *Maud Gonne's Irish Nationalist Writings*, edited by Karen Steele, 54–56. Dublin: Irish Academic Press, 2004. First published in *United Irishman*, Apr. 7, 1900, 5.

———. "The Goddess Brigid." In *Maud Gonne's Irish Nationalist Writings*, edited by Karen Steele, 189–91. Dublin: Irish Academic Press, 2004. First published in *United Irishman*, Nov. 3, 1900, 3.

———. "India." In *Maud Gonne's Irish Nationalist Writings*, edited by Karen Steele, 167–71. Dublin: Irish Academic Press, 2004. First published in *United Irishman*, May 12, 1900, 5.

———. "Inghinidhe na hÉireann's First Meeting." In *Maud Gonne's Irish Nationalist Writings*, edited by Karen Steele, 296–97. Dublin: Irish Academic Press, 2004. First published in *United Irishman*, Oct. 13, 1900, 5.

———. "In the Event of War." In *Maud Gonne's Irish Nationalist Writings*, edited by Karen Steele, 140. Dublin: Irish Academic Press, 2004. First published in *United Irishman*, Dec. 22, 1900, 4.

———. "Ireland and Her Children." *United Irishman*, June 7, 1902, 3.

———. "Ireland and Irish America." In *Maud Gonne's Irish Nationalist Writings*, edited by Karen Steele, 182–84. Dublin: Irish Academic Press, 2004. First published in *United Irishman*, June 22, 1901, 5.

———. "The Irish Press." In *Maud Gonne's Irish Nationalist Writings*, edited by Karen Steele, 100. Dublin: Irish Academic Press, 2004. First published in *United Irishman*, Feb. 7, 1903, 6.

———. "Maedb." *United Irishman*, Oct. 5, 1901, 3.

———. *Maud Gonne's Irish Nationalist Writings, 1895–1946*. Edited by Karen Steele. Dublin: Irish Academic Press, 2004.

———. "National Education of the Children." In *Maud Gonne's Irish Nationalist Writings*, edited by Karen Steele, 140. Dublin: Irish Academic Press, 2004. First published in *United Irishman*, Aug. 23, 1902, 6.

———. *A Servant of the Queen*. Edited by A. Norman Jeffares and Anna MacBride White. London: Victor Gollanz, 1938. Reprint. Gerrards Cross, U.K.: Colin Smythe, 1994.

———. "Those Who Are Suffering for Ireland." *Northern Patriot*, Nov. 23, 1896, 28.

Gore-Booth, Eva. *Collected Poems*. London: Longmans Green, 1929.

Gray, Breda, and Louise Ryan. "The Politics of Irish Identity and the Interconnections Between Feminism, Nationhood, and Colonialism." In *Nation, Empire, Colony: Historicizing Gender and Race,* edited by Ruth Roach Pierson and Nupur Chaudhuri, 121–38. Bloomington: Indiana Univ. Press, 1998.

Grayzel, Susan. " 'The Mothers of Our Soldiers' Children': Motherhood, Immorality and the War Baby Scandal, 1914–1918." In *Maternal Instincts: Visions of Motherhood and Sexuality in Britain, 1875–1925,* edited by Claudia Nelson and Ann Sumner Holmes, 122–40. London: Macmillan, 1997.

Greaves, C. Desmond. *The Irish Transport and General Workers' Union: The Formative Years 1909–1923.* Dublin: Gill and Macmillan, 1982.

[Gregory, Augusta]. "Another Week in Ireland." *Nation,* Oct. 23, 1920, 123–24.

Gregory, Augusta. *Collected Plays.* Edited by Ann Saddlemyer. Gerrards Cross, U.K.: Colin Smythe, 1970.

[——]. "A Fourth Week in Ireland." *Nation,* Dec. 18, 1920, 413–14.

Gregory, Augusta. *Lady Gregory's Diaries, 1892–1902.* Edited by James Pethica. New York: Oxford Univ. Press, 1996.

——. *Lady Gregory's Journals.* Vol. 1. Books 1–29. Oct. 10, 1916–Feb. 24, 1925. Edited by Daniel J. Murphy. New York: Oxford Univ. Press, 1978.

——. *Lady Gregory's Journals, 1916–1930.* Edited by Lennox Robinson. New York: Macmillan, 1947.

——. *Lady Gregory: Selected Writings.* Edited by Lucy McDiarmid and Maureen Waters. Harmondsworth, U.K.: Penguin, 1995.

[——]. "Murder by the Throat." *Nation,* Nov. 13, 1920, 215–16.

Gregory, Augusta. *Seventy Years: Being the Autobiography of Lady Gregory.* Edited by Colin Smythe. Gerrards Cross, U.K.: Colin Smythe, 1974.

[——]. "A Third Week in Ireland." *Nation,* Dec. 4, 1920, 333.

[——]. "A Week in Ireland." *Nation,* Oct. 16, 1920, 63–64.

Gregory, Augusta. *The Workhouse Ward.* In *Lady Gregory: Selected Writings,* edited by Lucy McDiarmid and Maureen Waters, 373–82. Harmondsworth, U.K.: Penguin, 1995.

Hannam, June. "New Histories of the Labour Movement." In *Re-Presenting the Past: Women and History,* edited by Ann-Marie Gallagher, Cathy Lubelska, and Louise Ryan, 162–78. London: Longman, 2001.

Harlow, Barbara. *Resistance Literature*. New York: Methuen, 1987.

Harlow, Barbara, and Mia Carter, eds. *Imperialism and Orientalism: A Documentary Sourcebook*. Malden, Mass.: Blackwell, 1999.

Harp, Richard. "No Other Place But Ireland: Alice Milligan's Diary and Letters." *New Hibernia Review* 4, no. 1 (Spring 2000): 79–87.

———. "The *Shan Van Vocht* (Belfast, 1896–1899) and Irish Nationalism." *Éire-Ireland* 24 (1989): 42–52.

Haverty, Anne. *Constance Markievicz: An Independent Life*. London: Pandora, 1988.

Hearne, Dana. "The *Irish Citizen* 1914–1916: Nationalism, Feminism, and Militarism." *Canadian Journal of Irish Studies* 18, no. 1 (1992): 1–14.

Henry, R. M. *The Evolution of Sinn Féin*. New York: Huebsch, 1920.

Herman, Edward S. and Noel Chomsky. *Manufacturing Consent: The Political Economy of the Mass Media*. New York: Pantheon, 1988.

Hill, Jacqueline. "The Meaning and Significance of 'Protestant Ascendancy,' 1787–1840." In *Ireland after the Union: Proceedings of the Second Joint Meeting of the Royal Irish Academy and the British Academy*, edited by Lord Blake, 1–22. Oxford: Oxford Univ. Press, 1989.

Hobsbawn, Eric. *Nations and Nationalism since 1780: Programme, Myth, Reality*. 2d ed. Cambridge: Cambridge Univ. Press, 1990.

Hogan, Robert. *Dictionary of Irish Literature*. Westport, Conn.: Greenwood Press, 1996.

Howes, Marjorie. *Yeats's Nations: Gender, Class and Irishness*. Cambridge: Cambridge Univ. Press, 1996.

Innes, C. L. "Orientalism and Celticism." In *Irish and Post-Colonial Writing*, edited by Glen Hooper and Colin Graham, 142–156. Basingstoke: Palgrave, 2002.

———. *Woman and Nation in Irish Literature and Society, 1880–1935*. New York: Harvester, 1993.

Jacoby, Robin Miller. *The British and American Women's Trade Union Leagues, 1890–1925: A Case Study of Feminism and Class*. Brooklyn: Carlson Press, 1994.

Jetter, Alexis, Annelise Orleck, and Diana Taylor, eds. *The Politics of Motherhood: Activist Voices from Left to Right*. Hanover, N.H.: Univ. Press of New England, 1997.

Johnston, Sheila Turner. *Alice: A Life of Alice Milligan.* Omagh, U.K.: Colourpoint Press, 1994.

Jones, Francis. *History of the Sinn Féin Movement and the Irish Rebellion of 1916.* New York: Kenedy and Sons, 1917.

Jones, Mary. *Those Obstreperous Lassies: A History of the Irish Women Workers' Union.* Dublin: Gill and Macmillan, 1988.

Kelly, A. A., ed. *Pillars of the House: An Anthology of Irish Verse by Women from 1690 to the Present.* Dublin: Wolfhound, 1997.

Kiberd, Declan. "The Elephant of Revolutionary Forgetfulness." In *Revising the Rising,* edited by Máirín Ní Dhonnchadha and Theo Dorgan, 1–20. Derry, U.K.: Field Day, 1991.

———. *Inventing Ireland.* Cambridge, Mass.: Harvard Univ. Press, 1995.

———. "White Skins, Black Masks: Celticism and *Négritude.*" *Éire/Ireland* 31, nos. 1–2 (1996): 163–175.

Koestenbaum, Wayne. *Double Talk: The Erotics of Male Literary Collaboration.* New York: Routledge, 1989.

Kreilkamp, Vera. *The Anglo-Irish Novel and the Big House.* Syracuse, N.Y.: Syracuse Univ. Press, 1998.

Laird, Holly A. *Women Coauthors.* Urbana: Univ. of Illinois Press, 2000.

Larkin, Delia. "Women Worker's Column." *Irish Worker,* Aug. 12, 1911–Nov. 8, 1913.

Laurence, Dan H., and Nicholas Grene, eds. *Shaw, Lady Gregory and the Abbey.* Gerrards Cross, U.K.: Colin Smythe, 1993.

Ledger, Sally, and Scott McCracken, eds. *Cultural Politics at the Fin de Siècle.* Cambridge: Cambridge Univ. Press, 1995.

Leehy, Cathy. "New Woman in a New Ireland? *Grania* after Naturalism." *Irish University Review* 34 (2004): 157–71.

Legg, Marie-Louise. *Newspapers and Nationalism: The Irish Provincial Press, 1850–1892.* Four Courts Press, 1999.

Lennon, Joseph. *Irish Orientalism: A Literary and Intellectual History.* Syracuse, N.Y.: Syracuse Univ. Press, 2004.

———. "Irish Orientalism: An Overview." In *Ireland and Postcolonial Theory,* edited by Clare Carroll and Patricia King, 129–57. South Bend, Ind.: Notre Dame Press, 2003.

Levenson, Samuel. *James Connolly, A Biography.* London: Martin Brian and O'Keeffe, 1973.

Levin, Donal, ed. *James Larkin: Lion of the Fold.* Dublin: Gill and Macmillan, 1998.

Lloyd, David. *Ireland after History.* South Bend, Ind.: Univ. of Notre Dame Press, 1999.

———. "Nationalisms Against the State." In *The Politics of Culture in the Age of Capital,* edited by Lisa Lowe and David Lloyd, 173–97. Durham, N.C.: Duke Univ. Press, 1997.

Longley, Edna. "From Cathleen to Anorexia." In *A Dozen Lips,* edited by Ailbhe Smyth, 162–87. Dublin: Attic Press, 1994.

Luddy, Maria. "Women and Politics, 1860–1918." In *Field Day Anthology of Irish Writing,* edited by Angela Bourke, et al., 5:69–74. Cork: Cork Univ. Press, 2002.

———. *Women in Ireland, 1800–1918: A Documentary History.* Cork: Cork Univ. Press, 1995.

Lyons, F. S. L. *Ireland since the Famine.* 1971. Reprint. London: Fontana Press, 1985.

Lyons, George A. *Some Recollections of Griffith and His Times.* Dublin: Talbot Press, 1923.

MacCurtain, Margaret. "The Historical Image." In *Irish Women: Image and Achievement,* edited by Eiléan Ní Chuilleanáin, 37–50. Dublin: Arlen Press, 1985.

———. "Women, the Vote, and Revolution." In *Women in Irish Society: The Historical Dimension,* edited by Margaret MacCurtain and Donncha Ó Corráin, 46–57. Dublin: Arlen Press, 1989.

MacCurtain, Margaret, and Donncha Ó Corráin, eds. *Women in Irish Society: The Historical Dimension.* Dublin: Arlen Press, 1989.

MacDonagh, Thomas. "The Best Living Irish Poet." *Irish Review* 4 (Sept.–Nov. 1914): 287.

MacManus, Francis. "The Delicate High Head: A Portrait of a Great Lady." *Capuchin Annual* (1960): 129–31.

MacPherson, John. " 'Ireland Begins in the Home': Women, Irish National Identity, and the Domestic Sphere in the *Irish Homestead,* 1896–1912." *Éire-Ireland* 36, nos. 3–4 (2000–2001): 131–52.

Maidment, Brian E. "Victorian Periodicals and Academic Discourse." In *Investigating Victorian Journalism,* edited by Laurel Brake, Aled Jones, and Lionel Madden, 143–154. London: Macmillan, 1990.

Marcus, Jane. *Suffrage and the Pankhursts.* London: Routledge, 1987.

Markievicz, Constance. "Free Women in a Free Nation." *Bean na hÉireann* 5 (Mar. 1909): 8–9

———. "The Future of Irishwomen." *Irish Citizen,* Oct. 23, 1915, 114.

———. "To Miss Nora Cassidy and the Young Girls of Ireland." *Bean na hÉireann* 8 (June 1909): 14.

———. "Woman with a Garden." *Bean na hÉireann* 4 (Feb. 1909)–17 (Mar. 1910).

———. *Women, Ideals and the Nation.* Dublin: Inghinidhe na hÉireann, 1909.

———. "Women in the Fight: A Memoir by Countess de Markievicz." In *Dublin 1916,* edited by Roger McHugh, 122–25. New York: Hawthorn Books, 1966.

———. "The Women of '98." *Irish Citizen,* Nov. 6, 1915–Dec. 4, 1915.

Marks, Patricia. *Bicycles, Bangs, and Bloomers: The New Woman in the Popular Press.* Lexington: Univ. Press of Kentucky, 1990.

Marreco, Anne. *The Rebel Countess.* London: Phoenix Press, 2000.

Maxwell, D. E. S. "Irish Drama 1899–1929: The Abbey Theatre." In *Field Day Anthology of Irish Writing,* edited by Seamus Deane, 562–68. Derry, U.K.: Field Day, 1991.

Maye, Bryan. *Arthur Griffith.* Dublin: Griffith College Publications, 1997.

Mayhall, Laura E. Nym, Phillipa Levine, and Ian Christopher Fletcher. "Introduction." In *Women's Suffrage in the British Empire: Citizenship, Nation, and Race,* edited by Ian Christopher Fletcher, Laura E. Nym Mayhall, and Phillipa Levine, xviii–xxii. London: Routledge, 2000.

McCaffrey, Patricia. "Jacob's Women Workers During the 1913 Lock-Out." *Saothar* 16 (1991): 118–29.

McCoole, Sinéad. *Guns and Chiffon: Women Revolutionaries and Kilmainham Gaol, 1916–1923.* Dublin: Stationery Office, Government of Ireland, 1997.

———. *No Ordinary Women: Irish Female Activists in the Revolutionary Years 1900–1923.* Madison: Univ. of Wisconsin Press, 2003.

McCormack, W. J. *Ascendancy and Tradition in Irish Literary History, 1793–1839.* Oxford: Clarendon Press, 1985.

McCoubrey, Margaret. "The Chivalry of War." *Irish Citizen,* Feb. 27, 1915, 313.

McDiarmid, Lucy. *The Irish Art of Contention.* Ithaca, N.Y.: Cornell Univ. Press, 2005.

McDiarmid, Lucy, and Maureen Waters. "Introduction." In *Lady Gregory: Se-*

lected Writings, edited by Lucy McDiarmid and Maureen Waters, xi–xiiv. Harmondsworth, U.K.: Penguin, 1995.

McKillen, Beth. "Irish Feminism and Nationalist Separatism, 1914–23." *Éire/Ireland* 17, nos. 3–4 (1982): 52–67; 72–90.

Mellor, Anne K. *Mothers of the Nation: Women's Political Writing in England.* Bloomington: Indiana Univ. Press, 2000.

Milligan, Alice. "Appeal to the Women of Ireland." *Shan Van Vocht*, June 1897, 104.

———. "The Captain's Daughter." *Shan Van Vocht*, Feb. 7, 1896, 17–23; Mar. 6, 1896, 52–58; Apr. 3, 1896, 71–73.

———. "Decoration Day, Sunday, June 21st, 1896." *Shan Van Vocht*, June 1896, 116.

———. "Gaelic Athletes and the National Movement." *Shan Van Vocht*, May 1896, 89.

———. "Guard Ireland's Honour." *Shan Van Vocht*, Oct. 1896, 181.

———. "The Harp That Once—! A Story of Connaught after Humbert." *Shan Van Vocht*, Mar. 1898, 37–39.

———. *The Last Feast of the Fianna.* Chicago: DePaul Univ. Press, 1967.

———. "The Little Green Slippers: A Belfast Story of Christmas, 1798." *Shan Van Vocht*, Dec. 6, 1897, 213–18.

———. "Must Ireland Be English? A Plea for Union and Reorganisation in the Gaelic League." *Shan Van Vocht*, Feb. 1899, 30.

———. "Notes for the Gaelic Athletes." *Shan Van Vocht*, Mar. 1896, 44.

———. "The Outlaw's Bride." *Shan Van Vocht*, Dec. 4, 1896, 231–32.

———. *Poems.* Edited by Henry Mangan. Dublin: Gill and Son, 1954.

———. "Speranza." *Shan Van Vocht*, Mar. 1896, 48–49.

———. "To the Irish in America." *Shan Van Vocht*, July 1897, 122.

Mitchell, Arthur. *Labour in Irish Politics 1890–1930.* New York: Harper and Row, 1974.

Mohanty, Chandra Talpade. " 'Under Western Eyes': Feminist Scholarship and Colonial Discourse." In *Feminist Post-Colonial Theory*, edited by Reina Lewis and Sara Mills, 49–74. New York: Routlege: 2003.

Morey, Anne. "Sexuality, Maternity, and Femininity in Films Exhibited in Britain, 1914–1919." In *Maternal Instincts: Visions of Motherhood and Sexuality in Britain, 1875–1925*, edited by Claudia Nelson and Ann Sumner Holmes, 141–165. London: Macmillan, 1997.

Moriarty, Theresa. "Delia Larkin: Relative Obscurity." In *James Larkin: Lion of the Fold*, edited by Donal Nevin, 428–38. Dublin: Gill and Macmillan, 1998.

———. "Larkin and the Women's Movement." In *James Larkin: Lion of the Fold*, edited by Donal Nevin, 93–101. Dublin: Gill and Macmillan, 1998.

Morris, Catherine. "Becoming Irish? Alice Milligan and the Revival." *Irish University Review* 33, no. 1 (2003): 79–98.

———. "From the Margins: Alice Milligan and the Irish Cultural Revival, 1888–1905." Ph.D. diss., Univ. of Aberdeen, 1999.

Munter, Robert. *The History of the Irish Newspaper, 1685–1760*. London: Cambridge Univ. Press, 1967.

Murphy, Cliona. *The Women's Suffrage Movement and Irish Society in the Early Twentieth Century*. New York: Harvester Wheatsheaf, 1989.

Murray, Christopher. *Twentieth Century Irish Drama: Mirror Up to Nation*. Manchester: Manchester Univ. Press, 1997.

Nelson, Claudia, and Ann Sumner Holmes, eds. *Maternal Instincts: Visions of Motherhood and Sexuality in Britain, 1875–1925*. London: Macmillan, 1997.

Nevin, Donal, ed. *James Larkin: Lion of the Fold*. Dublin: Gill and Macmillan, 1998.

——, ed. *Trade Union Century*. Dublin: Mercier Press, 1994.

Ni Duibhe, Elis, ed. *Voices on the Wind: Women Writers of the Celtic Twilight*. Dublin: New Island, 1995.

Novick, Ben. *Conceiving Revolution: Irish Nationalist Propaganda during the First World War*. Dublin: Four Courts Press, 2001.

O'Brien, Joseph. *Dear, Dirty Dublin: A City in Distress, 1899–1916*. Berkeley: Univ. of California Press, 1982.

O'Brien, Thomas J. "How to Celebrate the Centenary of '98." *Shan Van Vocht*, May 1897, 94.

Ó Broin, Leon. *Revolutionary Underground: The Story of the Irish Republican Brotherhood 1858–1924*. Dublin, n.p., 1976.

O'Casey, Sean. *Drums under the Window*. New York: Macmillan, 1950.

Ó Ciosáin, Niall. *Print and Popular Culture in Ireland, 1750–1850*. St. Martin's Press, 1997.

O'Faolain, Sean. *Constance Markievicz or the Average Revolutionary*. London: Jonathan Cape, 1934.

O'Halloran, Eileen. "From Boucicault to Beckett: Irish Modernism and the Myth of Mother Ireland." Ph.D. diss., Univ. of Wisconsin, 2004.

Ó Lúing, Seán. "Arthur Griffith and Sinn Fein." In *Leaders and Men of the Easter Rising: Dublin 1916*, edited by F. X. Martin, 55–66. Ithaca, N.Y.: Cornell Univ. Press, 1967.

O'Mahony, Nora Tynan. "The Mother." *Irish Monthly* 41 (Oct. 1913): 529–32.

Owens, Rosemary Cullen. *Louie Bennett.* Cork: Cork Univ. Press, 2001.

———. *Smashing Times: A History of the Irish Women's Suffrage Movement.* Dublin: Attic Press, 1984.

———. " 'Votes for Ladies, Votes for Women': Organised Labour and the Suffrage Movement, 1876–1922." *Saothar* 9 (1983): 34–47.

Parker, Andrew, Mary Russo, Doris Sommer, and Patricia Yaeger, eds. *Nationalisms and Sexualities.* New York: Routledge, 1992.

Parliamentary Debates (Hansard). 5th series. Vol. 782. London: Her Majesty's Stationery Office, 1969.

Parnell, Anna. *The Tale of a Great Sham.* Edited by Dana Hearne. Dublin: Arlen House, 1986.

Patmore, Coventry. *The Angel in the House.* London: J. W. Parker and Sons, 1854–56.

Pearse, Pádraig. "The Coming Revolution." In *Field Day Anthology of Irish Writing*, edited by Seamus Deane, 556–58. Derry, U.K.: Field Day, 1991. First published in *An Claidheamh Soluis*, Nov. 1913.

———. *Plays, Stories, Poems.* Dublin, n.p., 1924.

———. *Political Writings and Speeches.* Dublin: Talbot Press, 1958.

Pethica, James. "A Dialogue of Self and Service: Lady Gregory's Emergence as an Irish Writer and Partnership with W. B. Yeats." Ph.D. diss., Oxford Univ., 1987.

———. "Introduction." In *Lady Gregory's Diaries, 1892–1902*, edited by James Pethica, xi–xxxvi. New York: Oxford Univ. Press, 1996.

———. "Lady Gregory's Abbey Theatre Drama: Ireland Real and Unreal." In *The Cambridge Companion to Twentieth-Century Irish Drama*, edited by Shaun Richards, 62–78. Cambridge: Cambridge Univ. Press, 2004.

Pope-Hennessy, John. "What Do the Irish Read." *Nineteenth Century* 15 (June 1884): 920.

"Prisoners for Liberty: Members of Irish Women's Franchise League on Trial for Breaking Government Windows." *Irish Citizen*, June 22, 1912, 33.

Quinn, Antoinette. "Cathleen ni Houlihan Writes Back: Maud Gonne and Irish National Theater." In *Gender and Sexuality in Modern Ireland,* edited by Anthony Bradley and Maryann Gialanella Valiulis, 73–99. Amherst: Univ. of Massachusetts Press, 1997.

Racine, Carl. "Alice Milligan and Irish Nationalism." *Harvard Library Bulletin* 3, no. 1 (1992): 47–52.

Rich, Adrienne. *Diving into the Wreck: Poems, 1971–1972.* New York: Norton, 1973.

———. *Of Woman Born.* London: Virago, 1977.

Ritschel, Nelson Ó Ceallaigh. "James Connolly's *Under Which Flag,* 1916." *New Hibernia Review/Irish Éireannach Nua* 2, no. 4 (Winter 1998): 54–68.

Robins, Elizabeth. *Votes for Women!* London: Mills and Boon, 1909.

Ross, E. "New Thoughts on 'The Oldest Vocation': Mothers and Motherhood in Recent Feminist Scholarship." *Signs* 20, no. 2 (1995): 397–413.

Ruddick, Sara. *Maternal Thinking: Towards a Politics of Peace.* Boston: Beacon Press, 1989.

Ryan, Louise. " 'Furies' and 'Die-hards': Women and Irish Republicanism in the Early Twentieth Century." *Gender and History* 11 (1999): 256–75.

———. "The *Irish Citizen,* 1912–1920." *Saothar* 17 (1992): 105–11.

———. *Irish Feminism and the Vote: An Anthology of the Irish Citizen Newspaper, 1912–1920.* Dublin: Folens, 1996.

———. "A Question of Loyalty: War, Nation, and Feminism in Early Twentieth-Century Ireland." *Women's Studies International Forum* 20, no. 1 (1997): 21–32.

———. "Women Without Votes: The Political Strategies of the Irish Suffrage Movement." *Irish Political Studies* 9 (1994): 119–39.

Saddlemyer, Ann. *In Defence of Lady Gregory, Playwright.* Dublin: Dolmen Press, 1966.

Saunders, Christopher and Iain R. Smith. "Southern Africa, 1795–1910." In *The Oxford History of the British Empire.* Vol. 3, edited by Andrew Porter, 597–623. Oxford: Oxford Univ. Press, 1999.

Shaw, G. B. "Preface for Politicians." *John Bull's Other Island.* In *Bodley Head Bernard Shaw: Collected Plays with their Prefaces,* 2:842–60. Toronto: Bodley Head, 1971.

Sheehan, Aideen. "Cumann na mBan: Policies and Activities." In *Revolution? Ireland 1917–23*, edited by David Fitzpatrick, 88–97. Dublin: Trinity History Workshop, 1990.

Sheehy Skeffington, Francis. *The Prodigal Daughter*, in *Irish Citizen*, Nov. 7, 1914, 196–98.

———. "War and Feminism." *Irish Citizen*, Sept. 12, 1914, 133.

Sheehy Skeffington, Hanna. "Constance Markievicz: What She Stood For." *An Phoblacht*, July 16, 1932, 7–8.

———. "The Duty of Suffragists." *Irish Citizen*, Aug. 15, 1914, 100–101.

———. "Jail, a University." *Irish Citizen*, Aug. 10, 1912, 95.

———. "Sinn Féin and Irishwomen." *Bean na hÉireann* 20, no. 13 (Nov. 1909): 5–6.

———. "Why We Throw Stones at Government Glass Houses." *Irish Citizen*, June 22, 1912, 37.

———. "The Women's Movement—Ireland." *Irish Review* 2, no. 17 (July 1912): 225.

Sheriff, Mary D. *The Exceptional Woman: Elisabeth Vigée-Lebrun and the Cultural Politics of Art*. Chicago: Chicago Univ. Press, 1996.

Shovlin, Frank. *The Irish Literary Periodical, 1923–1958*. Oxford: Oxford Univ. Press, 2003.

Smith, D. J. "The Countess and the Poets: Constance Gore-Booth Markievicz in the Work of Irish Writers." *Journal of Irish Literature* 12, no. 1 (1983): 3–63.

Smyth, Ailbhe, ed. *A Dozen Lips*. Dublin: Attic Press, 1994.

———. "Paying Our Disrespects to the Bloody States We're In: Women, Violence, Culture and the State." *Irish Women's Voices, Past and Present: Journal of Women's History* 6/7 (1995), no. 4/1: 190–216. Edited by J. Hoff and M. Coulter.

Smythe, Colin. "Afterword." In *Lady Gregory's Journals*. Vol. 1. Books 1–29. Oct. 10, 1916–Feb. 24, 1925. Edited by Daniel J. Murphy, 641. New York: Oxford Univ. Press, 1978.

Sommer, Doris. *Foundational Fictions: The National Romances of Latin America*. Berkeley: Univ. of California Press, 1991.

Steele, Karen. "Biography as a Promotional Discourse: The Case of Maud Gonne." *Cultural Studies* 15, no. 1 (Jan. 2001): 138–60.

———. "Constance Markievicz and the Politics of Memory." In *Irish Women and*

Nationalism: Soldiers, New Women, and Wicked Hags, edited by Louise Ryan and Margaret Ward, 62–79. Dublin: Irish Academic Press, 2004.

———. "Editing Out Factionalism: The Political and Literary Consequences in Ireland's *Shan Van Vocht.*" *Victorian Periodicals Review* 35, no. 2 (Summer 2002): 113–32.

———. "Raising Her Voice for Justice: Maud Gonne and the Irish Nationalist Press." *New Hibernia Review/Iris Éireannach Nua* 3, no. 2 (Summer 1999): 85–104.

———. "Reading Maud Gonne: Gendered Poetics in the Advanced Nationalist Press." *Prose Studies* 25, no. 2 (Aug. 2003): 102–21.

Stephens, James. *Arthur Griffith: Journalist and Statesman.* Dublin: Wilson, Hartness, 1922.

Stillinger, Jack. *Multiple Authorship and the Myth of Solitary Genius.* New York: Oxford Univ. Press, 1991.

Suffern, Lillian. "Militancy and Motherhood." *Irish Citizen*, Dec. 12, 1914, 235; Dec. 19, 1914, 243.

———. "Suffrage and Sacrifice." *Irish Citizen*, Nov. 28, 1914, 231.

———. "The War: A Reply." *Irish Citizen*, Sept. 5, 1914, 125.

Taillon, Ruth. *When History Was Made: The Women of 1916.* Belfast: Beyond the Pale Press, 1996.

Thuente, Mary Helen. *The Harp Re-strung: The United Irishmen and the Rise of Irish Literary Nationalism.* Syracuse, N.Y.: Syracuse Univ. Press, 1994.

Trotter, Mary. *Ireland's National Theatres: Political Performance and the Origins of the Irish Dramatic Movement.* Syracuse, N.Y.: Syracuse Univ. Press, 2001.

Tusan, Michelle Elizabeth. "Inventing the New Woman: Print Culture and Identity Politics During the Fin-de-Siècle." *Victorian Periodicals Review* 31, no. 2 (1998): 169–82.

Valiulis, Maryann Gialanella. " 'Free Women in a Free Nation': Nationalist Feminist Expectations for Independence." In *The Creation of the Dáil*, edited by Brian Farrell, 75–90. Dublin: Blackwater, 1994.

Van Voris, Jacqueline. *Constance de Markievicz in the Cause of Ireland.* Boston: Univ. of Massachusetts Press, 1967.

Van Wingerden, Sophia A. *The Women's Suffrage Movement in Britain, 1866–1928.* London: Macmillan, 1999.

Ward, Margaret. "Conflicting Interests: The British and Irish Suffrage Movements." *Feminist Review* 50:127–47.

———. *Hanna Sheehy Skeffington: A Life*. Dublin: Attic Press, 1997.

———. *In Their Own Voice: Woman and Irish Nationalism*. Dublin: Attic Press, 1995.

———. *Maud Gonne: Ireland's Joan of Arc*. London: Pandora, 1990.

———. *The Missing Sex*. Dublin: Attic Press, 1991.

———. "Nationalism, Pacifism, Internationalism: Louie Bennett, Hanna Sheehy Skeffington, and the Problems of 'Defining Feminism.' " In *Gender and Sexuality in Modern Ireland*, edited by Anthony Bradley and Maryann Gialanella Valiulis, 60–84. Amherst: Univ. of Massachusetts Press, 1997.

———. " 'Suffrage First—Above All Else!' An Account of the Irish Suffrage Movement." In *Irish Women's Studies Reader*, edited by Ailbhe Smyth, 20–44. Dublin: Attic Press, 1993.

———. *Unmanageable Revolutionaries: Women and Irish Nationalism*. 1983. Reprint. London: Pluto Press, 1989.

Warner, Marina. "What the Virgin of Knock Means to Women." *Magill* Sept. 1979:39.

Weihman, Lisa. "*Doing My Bit for Ireland*: Transgressing Gender in the Easter Rising." *Éire-Ireland* 39, nos. 3–4 (Fall–Winter 2004): 228–49.

Whelan, John. "Literature and Nationality." *Shan Van Vocht*, Jan. 1897, 10.

Whelan, Kevin. *The Tree of Liberty: Radicalism, Catholicism and the Construction of Irish Identity*. Cork: Cork Univ. Press, 1996.

———. "The United Irishmen, the Enlightenment and Popular Culture." In *The United Irishmen: Republicanism, Radicalism, and Rebellion*, edited by David Dickson, Dáire Keogh, and Kevin Whelan, 269–96. Dublin: Irish Academic Press, 1993.

Wilde, Oscar. "The Decay of Lying." In *The Writings of Oscar Wilde*, edited by Isobel Murray, 215–39. Oxford: Oxford Univ. Press, 1989.

Wills, Clair. "Women, Domesticity and the Family: Recent Feminist Work in Irish Cultural Studies." *Cultural Studies* 15, no. 1 (Jan. 2001): 33–57.

Yeats, William Butler. *Autobiographies: First Draft and Journal*. Edited by Denis Donoghue. London: Macmillan, 1972.

———. *The Collected Letters of W. B. Yeats*. Edited by Warwick Gould, John Kelly, and Deirdre Toomey. Vol. 2. Oxford: Clarendon Press, 1997.

———. *W. B. Yeats: The Poems*. Edited by Richard Finneran. London: Macmillan, 1983.

York, Lorraine. *Rethinking Women's Collaborative Writing*. Toronto: Univ. of Toronto Press, 2002.

Periodicals

An Phoblacht
Bean na hÉireann
Daily Express
Irish Citizen
Irish Independent
Irish Monthly
Irish Review
Irish Times
Irish Worker
Nation
Northern Patriot
Shan Van Vocht
Spark
United Ireland
United Irishman

Index

Italic page number denotes illustration.